The Social Thought of
Rousseau and Burke

The Social Thought of Rousseau and Burke

A Comparative Study

David Cameron

University of Toronto Press

© 1973 David Cameron

First published 1973
in Canada and the United States
by University of Toronto Press
Toronto and Buffalo

ISBN 0 = 8020 = 1992 = 7

Printed in Great Britain

Contents

Editions and Abbreviations used

Edmund Burke

Works   *The Works of Edmund Burke.* George Bell and Sons
                 (Bohn's Standard Library) (London 1900),
                 8 vols.

Corr.   *The Works and Correspondence of the Right Honourable
                 Edmund Burke.* Francis and John Rivington
                 (London 1852),8 vols. (First two volumes contain
                 correspondence of Burke 1744–97, edited by
                 Earl Fitzwilliam and Sir Richard Bourke.)

Jean-Jacques Rousseau

Oeuvres   *Oeuvres complètes de Jean-Jacques Rousseau.* Edited by
                 Bernard Gagnebin and Marcel Raymond.
                 Gallimard (Bibliothèque de la Pléiade)
                 (Dijon 1959–67), 4 vols so far.

Corr.   *Correspondance générale de J. J. Rousseau.*
                 Edited by T. Dufour. Librairie Armand Colin
                 (Paris 1924–34), 20 vols.

Émile   *Émile ou de l'éducation.* Edited by François et
                 Pierre Richard. Garnier Frères (Paris 1964).

Lettre à   Lettre à Mr d'Alembert sur les spectacles.
d'Alembert*   Edited by M. Fuchs. Librairie Giard
                 (Lille 1948).

Dialogues   *Rousseau juge de Jean Jacques: dialogues.* Edited by
                 Michel Foucault. Librairie Armand Colin
                 (Bibliothèque de Cluny) (Paris 1962).

Rêveries   *Les Rêveries du promeneur solitaire.*
                 Edited by Henri Roddier. Garnier
                 Frères (Paris 1960).

Unless otherwise indicated, all citations are from these editions. Where appropriate, the volume or book number is cited by upper-case Roman numerals, and in all cases the page number is cited by arabic numerals. Apparent errors in French spelling and accentuation in quotations from the Pléiade *Oeuvres complètes* are attributable to the eighteenth-century writing style reproduced in that text.

Acknowledgements

I am indebted to many people and to a number of institutions for assistance in the writing and publication of this work.

It began as a University of London doctoral thesis, undertaken with the financial support of Canada Council and I.O.D.E. fellowships. Arrangements for its appearance in book form were made by the Publications Committee of the London School of Economics, and I am indebted to its members and to the School's Publications Officer, Mr P. D. C. Davis, for their assistance. In particular, I am most grateful to Professor Maurice Cranston for his unfailing encouragement and advice, and for his help in guiding the study through the various stages of publication. A part of Chapter 2, Section IV appeared originally in *Political Studies*, XX, 2 (June 1972) under the title of 'Rousseau, Professor Derathé and Natural Law', and I thank the Clarendon Press for permission to republish that material here.

A number of my colleagues at Trent University – F. A. Hagar, David Kettler, J. I. MacAdam and W. F. W. Neville – were kind enough to read the manuscript at various stages in its drafting, and I am most appreciative of their comments and advice. Professor J. H. Burns of University College London read the manuscript as well and offered many thoughtful suggestions from which I was able to benefit.

I am particularly happy to have this opportunity to express my deep appreciation to William Pickles, my supervisor at the L.S.E. I learned a great deal from him – much about political thought and the eighteenth century, and much about the proper role of the research supervisor. He knew when to press hard and ask awkward questions, and when to give a slowly forming idea time to mature; and most of all he recognized and respected the autonomy of

A*

academic work. Happily, he and his wife, Dorothy, recognized the pleasures of association as well, and their friendship was an unanticipated delight.

Rousseau, in an excess of rhetorical enthusiasm, advised readers of his *Discours sur l'inégalité* that Nature was responsible for what was true in the treatise, he for the errors: 'Tout ce qui sera d'elle, sera vrai. Il n'y aura de faux que ce que j'y aurai mêlé du mien sans le vouloir.' Unlike Rousseau, I cannot say that this study was torn from the grasp of Nature, but I can certainly echo him in saying that the errors and imperfections are mine alone.

DAVID CAMERON
Keene, Ontario
July, 1973

Introduction

1 The Critical Orthodoxy

'Poor Burke', wrote Edward Gibbon in his celebrated *Autobiography*, is 'the most eloquent and rational madman that I ever knew.' At first glance, it is startling to discover that this witty and rather malicious paradox could with equal justice be applied to Rousseau. Yet such is the case. In fact Gibbon's sentiment is echoed by d'Alembert in a comment he makes about Rousseau : 'Jean-Jacques est un malade de beaucoup d'esprit et qui n'a d'esprit que quand il a la fièvre. Il ne faut ni le guérir ni l'outrager.'[1] Indeed it is surprisingly often true that an aphorism describing one of the two men catches the other as well.

However, when the names of Jean-Jacques Rousseau and Edmund Burke are mentioned together, it is usually to illustrate the opposite extremes of opinion which men of the time had with respect to a particular social question. It sometimes seems to be the case that the discovery of Burke on one side of an argument is taken to be virtually conclusive proof that Rousseau will be found on the other. Burke has written that 'to know what the received notions are upon any subject, is to know with certainty what those of Rousseau are not';[2] a postulate of eighteenth-century criticism during the subsequent two centuries appears to have been that to know what Burke's notions are upon any subject is to know with certainty what those of Rousseau are not. The two men are seen in terms of contrast, dissimilarity, opposition, and they are brought together only to reveal divergences of thought and to disclose differences of intellectual habit.

Very often Rousseau is said to have fathered a style of social and political thinking which it was the purpose of Edmund Burke, especially in his later years, to attack at every opportunity. It is clear that Burke was arguing *against* something at least as strenuously as he was arguing in favour of something else, and it is also undeniable that he judged Rousseau to be his particular *bête noire*. But it is doubtful if Burke identified his real antagonist as accurately as he might have done, and it is important for the comparative purpose of this study to show that in so far as his argument was directed at Rousseau it was not really properly deployed at all.

The prevalent critical disposition to *contrast* rather than compare Rousseau and Burke provides the context for this enquiry. It is obvious that there would be little point in a comparative enterprise of the sort we are undertaking if orthodox criticism tacitly or explicitly accepted the proposition of intellectual proximity, and if this proximity had been thoroughly examined. This, however, is not the case, and as a consequence the understanding to be gained from this study derives in a particularly obvious way from the proposition adopted and defended; in fact, from the 'thesis'. Carl Becker's position *vis-à-vis* conventional scholarship was similar in this respect when in 1932 he wrote an essay on the Enlightenment which went against the critical grain; he suggested that 'we are accustomed to think of the eighteenth century as essentially modern in its temper', and outlined his task as an attempt 'to show that the "Philosophes" demolished the Heavenly City of St Augustine only to rebuild it with more up-to-date materials'.[3] The book was worth writing primarily because in it the author challenged a customary manner of thinking; he was not flogging a dead horse.

Becker noted that there was a tendency among students of the eighteenth century to take the *philosophes* at their word in their assertions of modernity, or rather in their denial that any medieval tincture lingered on in their thought. A similar ready acceptance seems evident among students of Burke and Rousseau. Edmund Burke's antipathy to Jean-Jacques Rousseau and his ideas, an antipathy which with the advent of the French Revolution mounted to hatred, is notorious; and his belief that Rousseau stood at the head of a school of thinkers whose doctrine he abhorred and whose influence he attempted to combat, has encouraged subsequent writers to place the two men at opposite poles of social and political thought.[4]

Of course, Edmund Burke's attitude to Rousseau is a part of the general problem of Rousseauist interpretation. Prior to and during

2

the French Revolution, Rousseau was taken as an authority by many of the political figures whom Burke was concerned with attacking,[5] and if they claimed the Genevan as their intellectual progenitor, then it is not surprising that Burke adopted the more obvious of the two polemical courses open to him, that of assaulting their predominant authority. It is clear, I think, given Burke's temperament, that the other course would have been uncongenial to him; that is to say, if he had been sympathetic to Rousseau and his writings, Burke might have attempted to knock down the intellectual support of his antagonists by showing that what they claimed to find in Rousseau's work could not properly be found there. However, his sentiments predisposed him and his interests encouraged him, to take the alternative (and, I think, tactically more powerful) line of assault. If Rousseau's followers misunderstood his doctrines, that was no concern of Burke; what *was* his concern was the discrediting of a theory whose practical influence he deemed to be pernicious.

It is worth pointing out that, although Burke at no time in his career approved of what he took to be the style of thinking and the doctrines of the Rousseauist school (one of his first publications was a satire on Bolingbroke), it was not until the turmoil in France towards the end of the century that Burke's disaffection grew into active abhorrence.[6] The reviews of Rousseau's publications in the *Annual Register* during Burke's editorship are not unsympathetic, although they do contain critical comment. In the Preface to the first volume of the *Register* (1758), the spirit in which books are to be selected for review is described : 'We have observed upon none that we could not praise; not that we pretend to have observed on all that are praise-worthy. Those that do not deserve to be well spoken of, do not deserve to be spoken of at all.' A passage from the review of *Émile* is characteristic of this period :

In this System of Education there are some very considerable parts that are impracticable, others that are chimerical; and not a few highly blameable, and dangerous both to piety and morals. It is easy to discern how it has happened, that this book should be censured as well at Geneva as in Paris. However, with those faults in the design, with the whimsies into which his paradoxical genius continually hurries him, there are a thousand noble hints relative to his subject, grounded on a profound knowledge of the human mind, and the order of its operations. There are many others which, though they have little relation to the subject, are admirable on their own account; and even in his wildest sallies, we now and then discover strokes of the most solid sense and instructions of the most useful nature.[7]

With the advent of the French Revolution the British Parliamentarian's dislike of Rousseau became intense and passionate. What had changed was not Rousseau's ideas (he had been dead for more than a decade), but the political situation in Europe. Burke's increasingly acute aversion to Rousseau's reputation was just a small part of his general detestation of a powerful French movement of ideas. We need not, then, be overly concerned by Burke's opinion of Rousseau; its general tenor and the warmth with which it was held varied over the years, and there is no reason to accept uncritically Burke's conception of his famous contemporary, particularly when it was entangled with occurrences about which he felt so passionately.

Writers who have touched upon the differences between Jean-Jacques Rousseau and Edmund Burke may be said to fall into two general categories : first, those who come upon the subject in the course of a large-scale study of some aspect of the historical period, whether of the French Revolution, English or French political thought, the rise of Romanticism, or of the eighteenth century itself; and second, those who allude to Rousseau in a study specifically on Burke. It is relatively unusual for a student of Rousseau (particularly one writing in French) to attempt to illuminate his subject by showing the distinctions which may be drawn between the works and style of the two men; the impulse which in other circumstances might lead such a person to Burke is perhaps satisfied by the more readily available figure of Montesquieu. (Writers who have compared rather than contrasted Burke and Rousseau will be discussed in the fourth section of this chapter.)

The dichotomy noted by the critics is not as a rule elaborately developed, although allusions to it may recur in an attenuated form throughout a given study. The usual pattern may be suggested in the sketch below; when fully delineated, most of the following points are made. Edmund Burke, though Irish by birth, had got into his bones the English way of practising politics, and it was ultimately to be Burke who provided the most brilliant and persuasive account of the English way of life in the face of the French revolutionary challenge. He was excited into political theory by the outbreak of disorder,[8] and driven by the events of 1789 to set down

4

in matchless language the principles which had guided his behaviour throughout his life. Among the salient features of his doctrine were : that the political and social worlds of man formed but a part of a divinely created universal order, and that therefore political issues were inevitably moral issues as well (this is sometimes replaced or supplemented by the view that Burke is a type of conservative utilitarian); that the understanding of political life was radically defective if the temporal dimension was ignored, and that in fact the primary duty of the student of politics was to gather the sense of ancient institutions and customary manners of behaviour before ever presuming to attempt to identify the nonsense in such things, let alone to effect its actual removal; and that, as the rational faculty of man is weak, so should the human tolerance of national and individual diversity and the reverence for the unique character of a given situation be strong.

Negatively, Burke was seen to exhibit a mistrust of argumentation (particularly political argumentation) appealing solely to reason, an intense dislike of abstract speculation, and a hatred of all rapid and ill-considered social reform (and, for him, all rapid reform was ill-considered). The French Revolution, then, was an event which challenged not only the old European order, but the entire body of Burke's social thought.

Frequently, Rousseau is considered by such critics to be the simple antithesis of Burke, and, when this is not the case, the significant issues are thought to be those on which they oppose one another. Burke is empirical, seeking his answers in a study of the historical process and the details of the particular occasion; Rousseau is speculative, deductive, *a priori*, and his authorities are Reason and Nature. Burke has a reverence for the past; Rousseau has a revolutionary's hatred of the present. Burke has a disposition to conserve; Rousseau, a rage to renovate or overturn. Burke's appeal is to experience; Rousseau's, to natural rights. Unlike Burke, Rousseau, if he believes in God at all, removes Him from his transcendental dwelling place and situates Him in the heart of each feeling man. Edmund Burke, the defender of the British aristocracy even against itself, sees in politics a world of infinite complexity, and, both by sentiment and design, restricts his speculation to the practically feasible; Rousseau, the rigid egalitarian and herald of modern democracy, has the courage (or foolhardiness) to draw radical conclusions from speculation unadorned by qualification and uncluttered by empirical observation. Rousseau, in a word, is considered to be the intellectual father of the French Revolution, and Edmund Burke its most outstanding opponent.

Elements of this description can be found in the writings of many critics. Sir Leslie Stephen is a particularly good example, for in his *History of English Thought in the Eighteenth Century* he has given us one of the most elaborate pictures of Rousseau, the antithesis of Burke. In a section on the French influence upon English political speculation, Stephen identifies Montesquieu and Rousseau as the two most important figures of the time, and writes :

Montesquieu, like many of his countrymen in later years, is the scientific observer, struck by the strange phenomena which were so familiar to Englishmen, and endeavouring to account for them by an ingenious apparatus of philosophical theory. Rousseau represents a very different sentiment. Philosophically, he is the rigid logical observer, simply disgusted by elaborate combinations, which suggest dishonest juggling, and seem to be calculated to bewilder simple lovers of the truth in their endless labyrinths. Politically, he is the mouthpiece of that new spirit which was to find a stubborn opposition in the English embodiment of ancient prejudice.[9]

In a colourful passage he likens the experience of turning from Montesquieu to Rousseau to the experience of turning from an elegant philosopher in some Parisian salon to a 'blood-boltered Banquo', 'a man stained with the filth of the streets, his utterance choked with passion, a savage menace lurking in every phrase, and announcing himself as the herald of a furious multitude, ready to tear to pieces all the beautiful theories and formulas which may stand between them and their wants'.[10] Burke, needless to say, would be as shocked as any elegant philosopher at the sight of such an intruder :

Burke's judgments upon Montesquieu and Rousseau ... are sufficiently indicative of the speculative tendencies of his writings from first to last. His first political publication was directed against a teaching identical with that of Rousseau.[11]

What is the teaching of Rousseau? According to Stephen, it includes the following major points :

[The formulas of politics] are deducible by rigorous logic from a fundamental axiom absolutely independent of time and place. History and observation are simply irrelevant. We have an a priori system of politics. ... Society will be put together on a geometrical plan, without reference to idiosyncrasies of men and races, or to their historical development.[12]

Rousseau's theory . . . implies the sweeping away of the whole elaborate growth of beliefs, superstitions and sentiments, and the institutions in which they have been embodied, which have been developed in the course of man's life on the earth, unless they can be justified by abstract reasoning. He would annihilate history, and preaches the true gospel of revolutionary fanaticism.[13]

Edmund Burke's doctrine is quite otherwise. In the same volume Stephen enumerates a number of important principles; 'to have grasped those now familiar truths, and to have seen their bearing upon political speculation,' he says, 'is the great merit of Burke; the utter unconsciousness of their importance is characteristic of the whole revolutionary school'. The familiar truths in question are:

The complex organization of human society can be understood only by a careful study of the processes of evolution. Its most intimate structure, as well as each of its superficial peculiarities, bears the traces of forces which have been operating since the earliest dawn of thought. The most trifling customs and the most vital laws will only give up their secret when regarded in the light of history. Man, as we see him, is the product of innumerable forces; his character has been inherited from a long series of ancestors; his beliefs are, for the most part, a tradition from remote ages, modified superficially by his own activity.[14]

In Stephen's presentation, the intellectual gulf between Burke and Rousseau could hardly be more profound.[15]

It is worth noting briefly the Procrustean critical methods which such an interpretation of Rousseau and Burke makes necessary. Stephen has somehow to cope with the presence in each man's writings of passages fundamentally inconsistent with his interpretation. In Rousseau's work, the cautious empirical side of his thought (as seen, for example, in parts of Book III, *Contrat social*, in *Lettres de la montagne* and in the works on Poland and Corsica) must somehow be dealt with; in Burke's, the employment of natural-right language has to be got over. We can see Stephen chopping Rousseau to size with the phrase, 'politics with him, in spite of some cursory remarks, becomes a quasi-mathematical science'.[16] Perhaps because he is concerned specifically with English thought, Stephen finds Burke more troublesome. He admits that 'passages may be found in Burke's writings where language is used superficially resembling that of his antagonists', and he gives examples of Burkean natural-right language. However, he concludes,

These transient deviations into the [sic] quasi-metaphysical language, when

7

more closely examined, are easily intelligible. The natural equality of mankind, in Burke's mouth, is simply an expression of the axiom which must necessarily lie at the base of all utilitarian, as well as of all metaphysical systems, [that is,] that the happiness of the governed, and not the happiness of any particular class, is the legitimate end of government.[17]

We shall have occasion to examine more closely the 'cursory remarks' and 'transient deviations' which Stephen finds in Burke and Rousseau.

Yet if the actual understanding of Burke and Rousseau has been in many cases faulty and the juxtaposition of the two men misconceived, nevertheless the tendency to mark distinguishing characteristics has been neither surprising nor objectionable. It is no doubt folly to attempt to judge whether there is 'more' to contrast than to compare in the works of Rousseau and Burke, but certainly there is generous scope in which to explore the former theme. The more arresting characteristics of the two men and their writings encourage the reader to assume that a deep intellectual gulf lies between them; and, as has already been noted, Burke's late-blossoming and vigorously expressed contempt for Rousseau pushes the student in the same direction. In addition, there are, of course, many notable differences of substance and method which cannot be ignored, and we shall attempt to indicate schematically the type of differences that one can expect to find.

Let us begin with a few biographical points. Jean-Jacques Rousseau was a French-speaking continental, Burke an English-speaking Briton.[18] Burke was given an orthodox classical education in Ireland, and came to revere the steady, generally tranquil cadence of British history. Rousseau received a fragmentary and intermittent education, much of it self-acquired, and his historical imagination was kindled by images of ancient glory more than by the vision of a continuous process of change in which the past becomes the present. Burke loved chivalry; Rousseau admired Spartan asceticism and fortitude. Burke's deeply religious nature found solace in the institutions of the Anglican Church, and he was a good deal more disposed than Rousseau to discern in the social arrangements of a country the handiwork of God.[19] Rousseau, for his part, though he was alternately Calvinist, Roman Catholic, and Calvinist again, was never able to settle successfully into any established religious pattern; probably it would be most accurate to describe his genuine but very eccentric religious belief as pantheism. Burke was a family man; he was throughout his life intensely loyal to his kin, loyal at times, it seemed, to the point of moral blindness, and his country house at Beaconsfield was a stopping-place of indefinite duration for many visitants from across the Irish Sea. Nothing need be said here about Rousseau's domestic situation except that it was highly unconventional from first to last, and that not by the farthest stretch of the expression could he be called a family man. And while Burke, after a period of uncertainty, found his most congenial employment in politics and stuck to that field throughout his life, Rousseau took up an astonishing variety of activities, but settled on none, and he displayed a peculiarly ambivalent attitude towards his enormous success as a writer. If he had been asked even at the height of his fame what his occupation was, a very likely reply would have been 'music copyist'.

So much for Burke and Rousseau as men. What of the distinction to be made between them as writers? It is clear that with regard to a great many specific points of doctrine Burke and Rousseau differed drastically (for example, in their opinions about the degree of social inequality and property concentration tolerable in a legitimate state). But to explore this protean subject is neither possible nor necessary here. Instead, we shall try to provide a brief, general account of the situation by considering the purpose or purposes for which Rousseau and Burke wrote, and the method or style of argumentation which each employed in attempting to achieve those purposes. We are seeking, then, short answers to the following questions. What broad, literary goals do Burke and Rousseau have? What objectives are they seeking to advance, and what views are they attempting to combat? For whom are their arguments designed? What style or styles of discourse do they employ in their effort to convince? Let us consider the two writers with these questions in mind.

It seems clear that if one were forced to choose a single area into which the writings of Edmund Burke best fitted, it would be necessary to select the practical world of social and political affairs, the sphere of political action, rather than the dizzy heights of political philosophy.[20] His writings were most frequently drafted in response to and in the atmosphere of some pressing contemporary issue,[21] and they were undoubtedly placed before the public in the expectation that they would influence general opinion. As is well known, a good number of Burke's writings at one point or another in their formulation were given as speeches in the House of Commons, a practical political institution if ever there was one. A very strong case, then, can be made for situating much of Burke's work in the realm of political practice.

Fortunately, however, the student of political ideas need not regard Burke's writings as *either* political tracts *or* theoretical treatises. His work, like that of most prominent authors of his time, serves a variety of purposes, and the student who wants fully to understand what he has to say must follow him from one sphere of thought to another as best he can. Besides, certain of his non-political pieces are clearly not of practical intent (e.g. his *Philosophical Inquiry* in aesthetics, and his essay on English history), and this should alert us to the possibility of political writings which are of a mixed theoretical and practical character; one cannot adequately come to terms with Burke if he is regarded simply as a brilliant political polemicist writing tracts for the moment. He is something more than a conservative Tom Paine. In many instances, a particular political situation occasioned Burke's writing, and, although its practical or persuasive purpose ought never to be lost sight of, the explanatory nature of the piece often can be neglected only at the cost of serious distortion.

Jean-Jacques Rousseau is in many ways very different. To a much greater extent than Burke, his thinking was stimulated by happenings, not in the practical world of affairs, but in the world of speculation inhabited by some of his *philosophe* contemporaries and by earlier philosophers and political thinkers. The problems which he encountered and which fired his imagination flourished in a sphere of thought which was already highly theoretical, and his arguments were quite properly conceived and shaped in terms of this speculative environment.[22] For example, an early chapter in the *Contrat social* is entitled 'De l'Esclavage'; even a cursory reading of this passage would be enough to convince one that Rousseau is not arguing in the manner of a William Wilberforce against any actual contemporary institution of slavery, and that he is not proposing particular practical reforms; he is rather considering the nature of the concept of slavery with a view to eliciting what it entails in the way of other ideas. He is sharing a world of discourse with Grotius, Pufendorf, Hobbes, Aristotle and other thinkers who have addressed themselves to the concept of slavery. It is with reference to his intellectual predecessors, rather than to his practical contemporaries, that Rousseau is writing.

But while this is frequently the case with Rousseau, it is by no means always so, for he, like Burke, wrote in a variety of moods and with a variety of purposes in mind. For example, in the works on Poland and Corsica Rousseau is facing current political situations which demanded a kind of consideration issuing in policies of reform. Like the founding fathers of the American republic a few years later, he is searching, not for the 'principes du droit politique', but for the principles which will successfully guide the operation of a particular state. As with Burke, the presence within Rousseau's total literary production of many non-political compositions as well as the existence of unequivocal evidence that he subjected political questions to more than one kind of treatment must make one chary of adopting too rigid or too restricted an approach. So various were his interests, in fact, that we might mark it as one of the distinguishing features of Rousseau that he ranged much more widely than Burke beyond the field of politics.[23]

However, within the field of politics the difference between them is not so much that they inhabited distinct realms of discourse, but that, each inhabiting a variety of realms, they nevertheless did so in seriously different proportions. It can easily be demonstrated that both Rousseau and Burke addressed themselves to questions of political action; but they did so in respect of different questions and with differing degrees of frequency. One might say that Rousseau wrote philosophically 'more frequently' than Burke, and that Burke wrote practically 'more often' than Rousseau, but it would be hazardous to insist that Burke or Rousseau wrote in either fashion to the exclusion of the other. The further methodological complication should also be kept in mind, that in general the eighteenth century was a good deal less fastidious than the twentieth in separating explanation from prescription. This being so, the boundary between the two is often extremely hard to fix.[24]

As for the question of method or style or argumentation, if in Rousseau's work we restrict ourselves simply to the *Contrat social* we encounter a striking multiplicity of styles. First, there are the passages written in a philosophical vein, taking up most of the first book, much of the second, and scattered portions of the third and fourth. It is in these places that Rousseau is most obviously concerned with what is described in the sub-title of the treatise as 'principes du droit politique', and he employs as a rule current philosophical techniques for enquiring into the nature of certain important political ideas. He is trying, in a sense, to compel the reader's intellectual agreement by arguing to his conclusion in accordance with conventional canons of logic.

But this is not his only approach. By the time he came to write the *Contrat*, the writings of Montesquieu had had an opportunity of making themselves felt on Rousseau, and a considerable portion of the treatise bears the marks of what might be called early social-science techniques. Much of this part of the *Contrat* provides rough guides to social analysis, as when the proper relation between territory and population ('pour donner à l'État sa véritable grandeur') is given (Bk. II, ch. x), or when 'des signes d'un bon gouvernement' are set down (Bk. III, ch. ix). It is interesting to note that in these social-science passages, Machiavelli and Montesquieu are often quoted or referred to, while in the philosophical passages references to Locke, Hobbes and the natural-law thinkers take precedence. There is specious mathematical calculation, of which two instances will suffice. In Book II, chapter iii, there is a passage designed to elucidate the difference between the will of all and the general will which is reminiscent of Bentham's 'felicific calculus'; it runs '. . . mais ôtez de ces mêmes volontés [i.e. the sum of particular wills which composes the will of all] les plus et les moins qui s'entredétruisent, reste pour somme des différences la volonté générale.' The other instance occurs in the first chapter of Book III, in which the maxim, 'plus l'État s'aggrandit, plus la liberté diminue', is reached by a flourish of mathematical reasoning. The venerable argument by correspondence crops up from time to time as well, often supported by illustrative cases from history; Book II, chapter viii, provides examples of this : 'Les Peuples ainsi que les hommes ne sont dociles que dans leur jeunesse, ils deviennent incorrigibles en vieillissant.' And in the last book of the treatise, three chapters are devoted to an historical examination of some Roman political institutions, a subject which seems to sit particularly poorly with the rest of the work. Rousseau's most famous political text, then, the *Contrat social*, must be recognized as a multi-purpose composition, extremely varied in its content and in its styles of argumentation; and this observation is no less applicable to his other social and political writings.

To what extent does this conclusion apply to the writings of

Edmund Burke? How does he put his case? Does he employ a number of distinct styles of argument? For purposes of illustration we need consider here only Burke's most famous publication, the *Reflections on the Revolution in France*. It would seem that, not only the actual effect, but also the explicit intention of Burke in writing the *Reflections* was to appeal to the general reading public of Europe, particularly of England; paramount among the purposes of his writing appears to have been that of influencing the political affairs of Europe (and especially England) by influencing the attitudes and opinions of literate men. His argument is both critical and constructive. In the critical mood, it is Burke's task to expose the fallacies and inconsistencies of an opposing ideology, and to demolish as far as possible its practical influence in political affairs. He regards the French Revolution as a new phenomenon in the world because he sees men actually behaving – destroying, building and fighting – in terms of abstract ideas; such men are busily extending the 'new conquering empire of light and reason'[25] into all the nooks and crannies of everyday life, and Burke judges this to be a stupendous misconception of the proper function of speculative thought. When he adopts the constructive mood, Burke gives an account of the way in which he believes that men think and act politically, an account which is in keeping with his conception of political man and which is in his view a sounder representation of the character of human knowledge.

The *Reflections* opens with an attack on Dr Richard Price and the English Revolution Society, and in the prosecution of this polemic Burke reveals the habit of a lifetime. His method of proceeding is to isolate the cardinal tenets of his opponents' doctrine and then to subject them to an historico-legal examination with a view to ascertaining their validity. In this case, the controversy revolves around the proper understanding to be derived from the events of the Glorious Revolution of 1688 and their similarity or dissimilarity to those of the contemporary revolution in France. Burke appeals generally to the lessons of English constitutional history and specifically to the legislative acts of the revolutionary period concerning the rights of the English and the arrangements for the succession of the crown. This is an instance of Burke's customary approach to political affairs; for him, present habits and institutions are to be understood as the perennial harvest of past attitudes and actions, and guidance in contemporary affairs is to be

sought primarily in the past.[26] Even the unfortunate Dr Price,
though he does not appear to have known it, is seen by Burke to be
blessed with a 'precursor' in the seventeenth-century divine, the
Rev Hugh Peters. Burke's mind was saturated with the European
past, and his imagination was easily excited by the colour and
variety which he saw there; like Sir Walter Scott's Edward
Waverley, Burke loved to round out 'the cold, dry, hard outlines
which history delineates ... with the colouring of a warm and vivid
imagination, which gives light and life to the actors and speakers
in the drama of past ages'.[27] It is no wonder, then, that his opinions
about current issues were founded upon his knowledge of past
events. He knew how contemporary matters stood, and sometimes
had a notion of how they would change, because he knew what
they had been.

But it should not be thought that this, perhaps his most distinctive style of argument, was his only one. The bent of his mind was
undoubtedly historical, but this by no means excluded other modes
of discussion. Consistent with, but different from, Burke's historico-
legal approach was his habit of addressing himself to the 'differ-
entise' of a given political situation and utilizing general principles
only as they passed through the refracting medium of actual
events.[28] He considered government to be an awesomely complex
art, and one which could only be successfully carried on by the
simultaneous adjustment of a multitude of factors; a policy, to be
successful, had to approximate in detail and intricacy the problem
which gave rise to it, and little or no practical help was to be
found in resorting to abstract principles or universally applicable
ideologies. An important part of Burke's approach, then, was
dictated by his understanding of politics.

He is not, however, above the employment of certain maxims of
social analysis when these are available. Take, for example, the
following :

Among the standards upon which the effects of government on any country
are to be estimated, I must consider the state of its population as not the
least certain. No country in which population flourishes, and is in progressive improvement, can be under a *very* mischievous government.[29]

This is strikingly reminiscent of the Rousseauist proposition :

Toute chose d'ailleurs égale, le Gouvernement sous lequel, sans moyens

étrangers, sans naturalisations, sans colonies les citoyens peuplent et multi-
plient davantage, est infailliblement le meilleur.[30]

A consideration of how France stands with respect to this criterion and one other, wealth, is the topic of a lengthy passage in the
Reflections, written much in the manner of such seventeenth-
century political arithmeticians as Sir William Petty and John
Collins.[31] Finally, we must note the presence in the *Reflections* of
references to nature and its derivative conceptions, the hallmark of
speculative political thought in the eighteenth century. We need
not stop here to distinguish between Burke's conception of nature
and that of his opponents; it is enough to recognize its presence in
his writings and the distinctive style of argument in which it finds
expression.[32]

Edmund Burke, then, like Rousseau, can be seen in his most
famous work to have utilized a number of different methods of
argument. Some of them bear a certain similarity to some of
Rousseau's, while others are quite absent from the latter's writings.
In general, however, it is necessary to mark an important distinction
between the two men in the extent to which they relied upon
different styles of discourse. Edmund Burke's style was in the main
historical; Jean-Jacques Rousseau's was to a considerable degree in
the tradition of abstract speculation then fashionable in France.
Furthermore, we have seen that Burke's interests and objectives
were much more practical in character than those of Rousseau,
whose writings were very frequently directed towards the resolution of certain theoretical issues of current interest in contemporary
European intellectual circles.[33]

II The Philosophical and Political Context

It is apparent that towards the end of the eighteenth century
recognizably novel styles of thought and behaviour were beginning
to appear. Not only was there the gradual emergence of a new
mode of philosophical thinking, which is from our point of view
one of the most important occurrences, but there was also, on a wide
variety of fronts, a turning away from the old procedures and
attitudes, and a quest for what were thought to be more satisfactory
practical and intellectual arrangements. It is not necessary (and
probably not possible) to uncover any integrating principle or definite unifying links between what happened in the various areas of

life; it is enough if these changes are seen to have occurred, and to have roughly coincided.

These years can be interpreted as a period of termination in which the cardinal doctrines providing the intellectual support of the preceding age gradually dwindle and disappear. Writers have described the era as one of reaction and revolt,[34] as the age of great revolutions,[35] as the moment of death of the old order,[36] as the time of the decadence of natural law and the social-contract theory.[37] John Morley exemplifies this sort of critical sentiment in a graphic phrase when he describes the Maréchale de Luxembourg as one of the most brilliant leaders of the last aristocratic generation 'that was destined to sport on the slopes of the volcano'.[38] The image is one of impending destruction, of a natural force leaving nothing but useless rubble in its wake. On the other hand, these years can be seen as a time of birth or revival, as an era of intellectual exploration and discovery, as a period of human innovation and social progress. Writers have discovered in it the birth or rise of conservatism, of nationalism, of the romantic movement and philosophical idealism.[39] The beginnings of the liberal experiment have been traced back to this time, and it has been said to constitute the threshold of scientific history.[40] A passage from C. E. Vaughan represents the flavour of this critical disposition very well. It was, he writes,

a change from the spirit of criticism to that of creation; from wit to humour and pathos; from satire and didactic verse to the poetry of passion and impassioned reflection; above all, a change from a narrow and cramping conception of man's reason to one far wider and more adequate to his powers.[41]

It is interesting to note the frequency with which the names of Edmund Burke and Jean-Jacques Rousseau have been associated with many of the phenomena which are said to have formed a part of, or to have owed something to, the eighteenth century: conservatism and liberalism, revolution and reaction, the modern democratic and the modern totalitarian state, nationalism, the romantic movement, philosophical idealism – all these have found writers who are ready to connect them in one way or another with the names of Rousseau or Burke, and very often with both.

Where in this turmoil of intellectual change ought Rousseau and Burke to be situated? Our understanding of their position may be expressed most economically by brief reference to the history of philosophy. Not only is political thought a field which has traditionally been closely allied to (and which, indeed, sometimes *is*) philosophy, but also it is in philosophical thinking that one finds the concepts with which men construct their view of the world most generally and most systematically delineated, and therefore most amenable to inspection.

We shall therefore set out, firstly a sketch of the history of philosophy which, while it may not enjoy universal assent, is not without influential authority, and secondly a survey of the political 'reflection' of this philosophical state of affairs as it appears in the seventeenth and eighteenth centuries. Taken together, the two will constitute what might be called an explanatory model, designed to suggest and to open up avenues of study. It should be viewed, not as an historical account of political or philosophical thinking in the eighteenth century, but as a framework for examining and comparing the writings of Rousseau and Burke.

One might identify two traditions of philosophical speculation in European thought which have perpetuated themselves since the time of the Greeks. Each of them is characterized by a distinctive theory of philosophy itself and by a distinctive theory of the world; they involve, in fact, both epistemology and metaphysics. On the one hand, there is the intellectual tradition associated with the name of Plato which holds that reality is found in a world of Being which exists above and beyond the sway of sensations and the transitory appearances of everyday life. The level of awareness at which most people pass their lives is, for philosophers of this tradition, a life of relative unreality in which the universal, the unchanging, the eternal – the *real* has no place. Most men spend all of their time in this region of continuous becoming where they live by the flickering shadows of Plato's cave, believing many things, but knowing little or nothing, not even that there is something more to know. The realm of Being, the contemplation of which constitutes true knowledge, is approached according to Plato in the course of satisfying the strenuous demands of philosophical reflection. Bare acquaintance with this realm is the reward of arduous intellectual enterprise; intimate familiarity, if possible at all, is matter for a lifetime.

On the other hand, there is a competing tradition of thought which denies the existence of a transcendental world of reality, and discerns in ordinary human sensation and experience, not a pattern of fleeting shadows, but the pattern of reality itself. Ordinary human experience is the stuff of life; the Platonic realm of Being, if it exists at all, is quite beyond the reach of human intellect, and so not a part (and still less the *whole*) of any conceivable human reality. Philosophical reflection is in this view occupied with the empirical world we have about us, with what the Platonist might call the realm of 'mere sensation'. It is easy to see that this view would provide a climate of opinion in which modern science would flourish, elevating as it does scientific discovery to the pinnacle of human knowledge.

These two traditions have a lineage extending the full length of our civilization, and throughout the centuries they have shown their mettle in an astonishing capacity to change with the changing preoccupations of the ages without losing their identity, and 'to tolerate and unite an internal variety, not insisting upon conformity to a single character'.[42] But a third tradition of philosophical specu-lation, a way of thinking which apparently cannot be properly understood as an extension of either of the two traditions sketched above, has recently come upon the scene, first appearing in the eighteenth century and very rapidly reaching its fullest expression so far in the early nineteenth century.[43] The occasion of its emerg-ence can be seen to have been a dissatisfaction with the explanatory capabilities of both existing traditions, but it has gone far beyond mere discontent and reaction, and its followers have fashioned for themselves a substantial world of positive belief. Philosophers of this tradition appear to have shared the opinion that each of the old dispositions of thought displays an impressive competence in providing satisfactory explanations of certain fragments of experience, but that they are both seriously defective in giving an adequate account of experience as a whole; each succeeds in its respective area at the expense of other areas and therefore of the whole as well. In general, then, this younger tradition constitutes an attempt, by consolidating the truths and avoiding the errors of its predecessors, to provide a philosophical account of the world which is more satisfactory because it refuses to do justice to one fragment of life by doing violence to another. Whether or not it succeeds in this is another matter, not at issue here.[44]

This is not, I think, a particularly unorthodox synopsis of the course which philosophical speculation has taken in the West. Some such view is at times made explicit by students of philosophy, although more frequently it can be discerned as a pattern of presuppositions lying behind specific pieces of writing. Three instances in which such a view is made explicit may be mentioned here. Arthur Lovejoy's book, *The Great Chain of Being*, is in part an attempt to sketch some of the extra-philosophical ramifications of the two ancient traditions of speculation which we outlined above. It is quite clear that he conceives these in terms very similar to those we have put forward here.[45] He calls the two traditions respectively 'otherworldliness' and 'thisworldliness', and describes the first in the following language : it involves

. . . the belief that both the genuinely 'real' and the truly good are radically antithetic in their essential characteristics to anything to be found in man's natural life, in the ordinary course of human experience, however normal, however intelligent, and however fortunate . . . the human will, as conceived by the otherworldly philosophers, not only seeks but is capable of finding some final, fixed, immutable, intrinsic, perfectly satisfying good, as the human reason seeks, and can find, some stable, definitive, coherent, self-contained, and self-explanatory object or objects of contemplation.[46]

He describes what the 'otherworldly' mind' thinks of the sphere of the contrary 'thisworldly' disposition :

The world we now and here know — various, mutable, a perpetual flux of states and relations of things, or an ever-shifting phantasmagoria of thoughts and sensations, each of them lapsing into nonentity in the very moment of its birth – seems to the otherworldly mind to have no substance in it; the objects of sense and even of empirical scientific knowledge are unstable, contingent, forever breaking down logically into mere relations to other things which when scrutinized prove equally relative and elusive.[47]

Lovejoy's story of the chain of being comes to an end with the close of the eighteenth century, so he is not primarily concerned to specify what paths philosophy took after that. Nevertheless, he does say enough, especially in the last chapter, to indicate that our sketch would not be generally unacceptable to him. Besides, it seems clear that the termination of the fortunes of the complex conception of the world which is the subject of his story forms a part of the general revolution of ideas which took place at about the turn of the eighteenth century; that is, its decline is contemporaneous with the rise of the new philosophical approach.

Michael Oakeshott's reference to the three traditions within the field of political philosophy is unmistakable. In the Introduction to his edition of Hobbes's *Leviathan* he identifies 'three main patterns which philosophical reflection about politics has impressed upon the intellectual history of Europe'.[48] He does this in terms of the 'master-conceptions' of each tradition, the first being distinguished by the conceptions of Reason and Nature, the second by those of Will and Artifice, and the third by the consolidated notion of the Rational Will. And just as Plato's *Republic* may be taken as the greatest representative of the first tradition of political philosophy, and the *Leviathan* as representative of the second, so Hegel's *Philosophie des Rechts* may be seen as the most outstanding example of the third mode of political speculation, a mode which Oakeshott says does not emerge until the eighteenth century. His identification of certain cardinal ideas within each tradition provides a set of guidelines which will be helpful in this enquiry.

Our third example is W. H. Greenleaf who, in an essay on Oakeshott,[49] devotes a number of pages to examining these three traditions, naming them transcendental realism, empirical nominalism, and philosophical idealism respectively. In two parallel passages which clearly owe a good deal to Oakeshott, Greenleaf outlines the apparently dialectical relationship which exists between the three traditions in the sphere of philosophy, and then in a similar manner details 'the political counterpart of this general philosophical situation'.[50]

Greenleaf's double-barrelled terminology implies a definite connection in these traditions between metaphysics and epistemology. There are clearly good historical reasons for asserting that such a link exists, but it is evident upon inspection that the relationship between the two is contingent rather than necessary. It can be seen that a thinker who asserts the objective existence of universals will find a rationalist theory of knowledge congenial, just as one who denies the objective existence of universals will be likely to adopt an empiricist position in epistemology. But this is not necessarily so, as can be seen, for example, in the case of Bishop Berkeley who was an empiricist but not a nominalist.

A few examples from the realm of social theory might help to clarify this point. A natural-law thinker (such as Aquinas or Hooker) will argue that there are a set of moral principles which are intrinsically right and universally applicable, and which derive their validity, not from the needs and wants of human beings, but from some transcendent source. From this position, he will go on to argue that men are by nature invested with the rational capacities necessary to know or recognize these principles, and in this way make the transition from a realist position in metaphysics to a rationalist position in epistemology. Just as there are natural duties and rights, so there is natural reason which makes the recognition of and voluntary obedience to natural law possible.

Thomas Hobbes, and more generally the seventeenth- and eighteenth-century sensationalist school, provide on the other side examples of the link between empiricism and nominalism. In the first part of the *Leviathan*, Hobbes establishes a clear empiricist position, arguing that the source of all knowledge is sensation, and in Chapter Four on speech denies the objective existence of universals: 'there being nothing in the world universal but names; for the things named are every one of them individual and singular.' Having built up his picture of man and established the springs of human action, he proceeds to consider the relations between men. It is at this point that he expounds what he calls the laws of nature, but it is evident that there is a profound gulf lying between his natural-law theory and that of such members of the old school as Aquinas and Hooker. Hobbes's natural laws possess no transcendental status; they are rather a set of rational precepts derived from the needs, wishes and desires of men. Hobbes emphasizes their suitability to the nature of men, not (as in traditional natural-law thought) their presumed status as the expression of objective values.

At one point in the *Leviathan* Hobbes states that nothing is simply or absolutely good or evil in itself, and adds: 'Whatsoever is the object of any man's appetite or desire, that is it which he for his part calleth *good*; and the object of his hate or aversion, *evil*. . . .'[51]

A comparison of this view with Plato's contention in the *Republic* that the Good is the supreme Form or Idea and the highest object of knowledge suggests the lines of similarity which exist between Platonic realism and natural-law theory, and at the same time, indicates the extent of the distance of Hobbes's nominalism from both.

It is possible to discern in the social literature of the seventeenth and eighteenth centuries intellectual dispositions which bear some resemblance to the three general philosophical traditions we have described, or to find, in Greenleaf's words, 'the political counterpart of this general philosophical situation'. In this study we shall employ the terms 'rationalism', 'empiricism' and 'idealism' respectively to describe the three traditions. The appropriateness of the third term to suggest the intellectual currents which began to swirl across Europe in the latter half of the eighteenth century will, I expect, be widely granted. As for the first two, we have chosen 'rationalism' and 'empiricism', rather than the more elaborate terminology of Greenleaf, for two reasons. Firstly, it is important to avoid giving the impression that we are describing coherent and highly theoretical patterns of thought, and the two terms we have chosen, both of them in ordinary use and both of them part of the vocabulary of eighteenth-century intellectual historians, are unlikely to raise false hopes. Secondly, the seventeenth and eighteenth centuries were on the whole more concerned with the problem of knowledge than with metaphysical issues and the problem of universals. The pervasive humanist and individualist assumptions of the period encouraged self-consciousness and self-analysis; both Descartes, the rationalist, and Hobbes, the empiricist, start with epistemological concerns, and their influence on later thinkers was profound. Hobbes's discussion of the phrase, *nosce teipsum*, in his introduction to *Leviathan*, brings out very clearly the themes of individualism and self-analysis which were so characteristic of the age.

In the specifically political discourse of the seventeenth and eighteenth centuries the prominent school of natural rights most fully represents the rationalist disposition. The badge of membership of this school is to be found, of course, in the belief in a universal moral law appealing to human reason and endowing a man *qua* man with certain inalienable rights, and enjoining him to perform certain actions and to abstain from performing certain other actions.

The political empiricists, seeing in ordinary human experience the source of all knowledge, tended to restrict themselves to the world of 'hard facts'. They denied the existence (or else the political relevance) of a transcendental moral order, taking as their point of departure what they regarded as empirically ascertainable principles of human behaviour. Holbach, in the Preface to his *Système de la nature*, attacked the barren speculations which had for too long drawn mankind aside from the paths of true knowledge; man, he says,

voulut pour son malheur, franchir les bornes de sa sphere; il tenta de
s'élancer au delà du monde visible, et sans cesses des chûtes cruelles et
réitérées l'ont inutilement averti de la folie de son entreprise: il voulut être
Métaphysicien, avant d'être Physicien: il méprisa les réalités, pour méditer
des chimères; il négligea l'expérience, pour se repaître de Systêmes et de
conjectures. . . .[52]

It is clear that the 'realities' of which the materialist Holbach is
speaking bear not the slightest resemblance to the transcendental
verities of the natural-right thinkers; they are rather the empirical
data and generalizations which make up the everyday world of
man.

Although the political empiricists of this period maintained the
greatest reverence for such figures as Bacon and Newton and frequently conceived their task in terms of an analogy with the natural
sciences, they were as likely to argue 'deductively' from what they
took to be irrefutable factual premises, as to engage in genuine
empirical observation of man and society. As Holbach asserts, sober
investigators of 'la nature humaine et le but de la Société' will
find that

en remontant à la nature de l'homme, on peut en déduire un Systême
Politique, un ensemble de vérités intimement liées, un enchaînement de
principes aussi sûr, que dans aucune des autres conoissances humaines. . . .[53]

However, there were writers (like Helvétius who in his statement
of objectives in *De l'Esprit* says that he intends to treat moral
philosophy like all the other experimental sciences) who abjured as
far as they could all moral evaluation (which in practice often
seemed to mean that they cloaked judgement in the idiom of
scientific explanation), and others (like Montesquieu) who, whatever their epistemological assumptions, simply followed a bent of
interest which took them away from ethical matters and towards
empirical and historical studies.[54] It is possible, then, to distinguish
in the eighteenth century between what might be called epistemological empiricism, which trod in the footsteps of Hobbes, and
methodological empiricism, which took the form of early social-
science thinking, generally on the model of the natural sciences.[55]

It would be naive to expect to find any particular writer situated
securely and exclusively within either the rationalist or the empiricist tradition. The traditions themselves are simply composed
of the predispositions, style and vocabulary of a number of indi-

B

vidual writers, and the ascription of any given writer to one or the other is a complex matter of judgement – a matter of weighing implications, and assessing intellectual debts and influence – rather than a straightforward classification. Natural-law vocabulary was 'in the air' in those two centuries, and it would have taken a man of exceptional stringency of thought entirely to forego its use, whatever his intellecutal temperament. By the same token, the experimental and theoretical advances of natural science were proving irresistibly attractive to seventeenth- and eighteenth-century men of letters, and one should not be surprised to find the most ardent rights-of-man theorist dabbling in botanical observation or expatiating upon the influence of climate in the formation of human character.

It is possible to interpret John Locke as a particularly notable example of the way in which rationalist and empiricist features can exist simultaneously in the works of one man.[56] He was of enormous importance to the eighteenth century, but his influence flowed in two contradictory directions; his work, it has been argued,[57] when taken as a whole, is flawed by a profound inconsistency. His *Essay Concerning Human Understanding* falls clearly into the empiricist tradition of thought. With its famous doctrine of the '*tabula rasa*', it formulated a theory of knowledge which was a challenge and an alternative to the natural-law manner of thinking. In his Introduction to the *Two Treatises* Peter Laslett concludes flatly : 'The *Essay* has no room for natural law.'[58] But with Locke's political theory it was quite otherwise. His *Two Treatises* falls into the natural-law style of political writing which we have associated here with the rationalist tradition, and although in that work he is nowhere very clear about the precise meaning to be ascribed to such an ambiguous expression as the 'law of nature', Locke repeatedly resorts to it as a sort of political ultimate. In Laslett's words, 'the objective existence of a body of natural law is an essential presupposition of his political theory'.[59] If the different purposes for which Locke was writing are neglected, then, his work, Janus-like, faces in two opposite directions at once, and the critic must make the best of an apparently unresolvable and disastrously fundamental inconsistency. On this reading of Locke, it can be argued that many of his continental and English followers in the next century understood his work to be a single coherent whole, not recognizing the dichotomy and so perpetuating it in their own thinking.

In the political speculation of the eighteenth century there appear to be instances of an evident dissatisfaction with the understanding of political life provided by the natural-right theorists and by the political empiricists. Both approaches, it was felt, left large (but in each case, different) patches of human life unremarked and unexplained. Hume's powerful criticisms indicate one form which the reaction to this situation took. But another more positive line was possible which, we shall argue, was adopted, however falteringly, by Rousseau and Burke. The work of both Rousseau and Burke may be interpreted from the point of view of an attempt to resolve some of the difficulties of the two major traditions of political thought, to shed light on certain unexplained areas of human life, and to move beyond the limitations of the traditional dialogue. It can readily be admitted that Burke and Rousseau owed a great deal to each of the old intellectual traditions, and that they did not perhaps travel a great distance down the new path, but the explanatory model outlined here aims at furnishing both a territory and a principle of movement in terms of which their thinking can be located; the territory being the point where the three great traditions meet, and the movement, the contingent process of change which led from the first two traditions of thought to the third. It is within this framework that systematic comparison of Burke and Rousseau can best be carried out.

III The Critical Heresy

In the first section of this chapter we looked at the practice prevalent among intellectual historians of contrasting the lives and writings of Rousseau and Burke. Yet the comparative field, if more sparsely populated than the other, has not been entirely untenanted. There are a number of writers, some of them prominent students of the eighteenth century, who have found in the writings of Edmund Burke and Jean-Jacques Rousseau matter for comparison. Some of the points of similarity are trivial or are simply the subject of a passing remark. W. E. H. Lecky for some reason, saw fit to mention their common esteem of the Spanish bullfight;[60] and G. M. Young, in a lecture to the British Academy on Burke, made the following curious remark :

Like his Americans, Burke had snuffed the tainted gale: he had felt the hot breath of Rousseau. I have often thought that if there was one man in Europe who really understood the Genevan, it was the Irishman, and the understanding reveals itself as much in their conflicts and recoils as in their approximations and inter-sections. 'The wild beast of the desert shall also meet with the wild beast of the island: and the satyr shall cry to his fellow.'[61]

But more penetrating and carefully considered comments have been made as well, and it is not without significance for us that most of them associate Burke and Rousseau with the general trans-formation of political ideas described in the previous section. C. E. Vaughan, an influential editor of Rousseau and student of the period, could be said to set the tone of much of the comparative criticism. Vaughan, of course, believed that Rousseau was a collec-tivist who flirted with individualism early on in his writing career, and the affinities he sees with Burke are along lines consistent with this interpretation. At the very beginning of his Introduction to *The Political Writings of Jean-Jacques Rousseau* (1915) Vaughan asserts :

Strike out the *Discours sur l'inégalité* with the first few pages of the *Contrat social*, and the 'individualism' of Rousseau will be seen to be nothing better than a myth. Strike out a few more chapters of the *Contrat social*, and his results, if not his methods, will be seen to be not abstract, but concrete. [62]

He discerns clear and important affinities to Burke on both counts.[63]

In his introduction to an edition of the *Contrat social* (1918), he portrays Rousseau picking up the thread of an argument that had been broken by more than a century of individualist thought. The doctrine in question came once again to be

recognized as the foundation of all truth in these matters by a long line of thinkers, at the head of whom stand Rousseau and, by a strange irony, his bitter assailant, Burke. 'He who gave our nature to be perfected by our virtue willed also the necessary means of its perfection. He willed therefore the State – without which man could not by any possibility arrive at the perfection of which his nature is capable, nor even make a remote or faint approach to it'. These are the words of Burke. And, with an added appeal to the religious sanction – an addition itself anticipated in the closing chap-ter of the *Contrat social* – what are they but an unconscious echo of what Rousseau had said before him?[64]

Five years later in *The Romantic Revolt* (1923), Vaughan says of Kant that in his moral doctrine, and in the religious belief which is closely connected with it, he offers, though with an added touch of sternness, some resemblance to Rousseau. He draws into explicit consciousness that conception of reason, as a creative faculty, which we have seen to be implicit in the ideas of Burke, and which, in fact, lay at the very heart of the romantic movement.[65]

Finally, in his *Studies in the History of Political Philosophy* (1925) Vaughan returns to his collectivist comparison :

On the continent, little as he (Burke) may have thought it, he had, no doubt, been forestalled by Rousseau. It might fairly be urged that, at least on the more speculative side of the matter, his criticism of the individualists is neither so complete, nor so deep-reaching, as that of Rousseau. Yet, even if that be the case, it must be allowed that he worked it out in entire independence of Rousseau, that his theory embodies elements of which there is no trace in Rousseau, and that the elements are of great importance.[66]

Vaughan, then, adhered consistently to his collectivist interpretation of Rousseau's political doctrine, and to a corresponding interpretation of the Burkean point of view.

One writer at least seems clearly to have got a hint from Vaughan in the comparison of Burke and Rousseau. E. H. Wright begins a footnote on the subject with, 'for when Burke indulges in an abstract idea on government he is very likely to give a perfect phrasing of the fundamental notion in the author whom he most reviles', and then proceeds to quote the very passage from the *Reflections* which Vaughan included above. Wright goes on to say that 'we need not imply with Vaughan that Burke learned this from the *Social Contract*; it is enough to say that if he believes it, his main quarrel with the *Social Contract* is imaginary....'[67] His remark about Vaughan seems a bit disingenuous, for Vaughan states specifically that Burke worked his theory out 'in entire independence of Rousseau',[68] whereas Wright himself asserts in the portion of the text to which the footnote is appended that 'possibly the only thing which ill became his (Burke's) noble mind was the rage he vented upon some of the men who may have helped to form it'.

G. H. Sabine joins Vaughan in finding in the writings of Rousseau and Burke a drawing away from the individualist theory fashionable at that time and a movement towards a doctrine which occupies itself with the creative role of the community, but he is more explicit than his predecessor in identifying the two men with the early hints of idealist thought.[69] He mentions three factors in social philosophy which the new idealist 'synthesis' involved : the depreciation of logic (or abstract reason) as compared with sentiment, or the hope that the two might be combined in a higher logic; a new estimate of the value of custom and tradition; and finally, a new sense of the meaning of history.[70] He associates Rousseau with the first of these, and Burke with the second. In a section of his *History of Political Theory* entitled 'Burke, Rousseau, and Hegel' the author, with the utmost clarity, places the two men at the beginning of the idealist tradition which in a generation or so was to play a part in transforming the intellectual face of Europe :

The pervasiveness of this change in the climate of European opinion is indicated by the astonishing similarity between the basic ideas of Burke and Rousseau. Superficially the two men had nothing in common, and Burke did not fail to record the contempt which a somewhat superficial acquaintance aroused in him for Rousseau's character. Yet Rousseau's nostalgia for the city-state and Burke's reverence for the national tradition were of a piece. Both were phases of the new cult of society which was replacing the old cult of the individual.[71]

Sabine then goes on to suggest that Burke was unable to relate his social and political ideas to the larger world of belief, and writes :

In the generation after Burke, however, it was just this broader relationship that Hegel tried to show. There is no question of direct influence; Burke seems never to have been mentioned by Hegel, though the influence of Rousseau upon him was important. But what Burke had taken for granted Hegel tried to prove: that the apparently fragmentary social tradition can be placed in a general system of social evolution.

However, Sabine could be more specific than that. In his chapter on Rousseau, he asserts that 'the obvious defect of the general will as he left it was the extreme abstractness of the conception' :

Rousseau's position as an alien in French national life, his moral incapacity to ally himself with any social cause, and the state of French politics when he wrote, all conspired to prevent him from giving the general will any concrete embodiment. This want, however, was at once supplied by Edmund Burke.[72]

Sabine goes on to specify what Burke supplied and concludes that the result was 'at once a contrast and a supplement to Rousseau'. 'In Burke the corporate life of England became a conscious reality.

The general will was released from temporary bondage to Jacobinism and made a factor in conservative nationalism.'

We need not assess just now the merits of this last suggestion. We can move directly on to a contemporary writer who takes this discovery fairly seriously.

W. H. Greenleaf remarks that Rousseau was 'notoriously unable to show how this general will might be realized in practice', that in his writings it is 'a largely abstract notion', and that 'the problem of concretizing the criterion (if the term may pass) is the major difficulty faced by idealist political thought'.[73] Having noted that both Hume and Burke had grasped the outlines of a solution, and that the latter had attempted to find a more-than-individual standard of conduct in 'prejudice' or 'the wisdom of our ancestors', Greenleaf writes : 'In this fashion (and if the suggested affinity is not too outrageous), Burke may be said to have discerned how to actualize Rousseau's general will.'

However, it is not necessary to regard Rousseau and Burke as highly abstract thinkers and to treat their major ideas as permutations of certain cardinal conceptions prevalent in speculative thought. Our last example is Alfred Cobban, who in at least two places[74] devotes some space to a consideration of a number of specific similarities which he finds in Rousseau and Burke. Although he does not neglect the philosophical significance of the two figures, he is, I think, much more inclined to understand them as political writers who were not necessarily systematic thinkers. The general category into which he places the two men is what he calls 'the political theory of romanticism', but he insists on the fluidity of this characterization :

it is not a school in the sense in which the English utilitarians, the *philosophes*, the physiocrats, or even the German idealists can be so described. We have not to deal with any fairly complete and coherent political doctrine, but rather with a tendency, and one moreover of a general and emotional character, not necessarily bound up with any definite practical proposals, and therefore capable of receiving different and even opposed interpretations.[75]

He follows this proviso in *Rousseau and the Modern State* with six pages in which he considers in some detail many of the similarities and some of the differences evident in the writings of Burke and Rousseau,[76] and in his book on Burke and the English

Romantics Cobban explores this theme in the light of a number of other topics.[77] These passages in his two books are of particular interest to us because it is apparent that the comparisons arise out of an intimate familiarity with the writings of the two men, and they are therefore drawn much more in terms of specific ideas and beliefs than of fundamental (and, hence, general) conceptions. We have seen enough instances above to realize that the more common mode of comparison is the latter.

Annie M. Osborn's *Rousseau and Burke : A Study of the Idea of Liberty in Eighteenth Century Thought*[78] is to my knowledge the only attempt to give a full-length account of the personal and intellectual affinities of the two men. However, only three of the ten chapters (slightly more than a quarter of the book) are seriously comparative, and the similarities contained therein have the appearance of being pulled out of the air; they are not shown to have issued from some fairly profound harmony of interest or approach which the two men may have shared. Indeed, J. H. Burns' evaluation of the Osborn book, which he made in an excellent review article occasioned by the appearance of a revised edition of Cobban's *Rousseau and the Modern State*, does not seem unfair :

. . . Cobban developed a point made by Vaughan – the affinity between Rousseau and Burke on certain fundamental issues. This theme was later worked out more fully, though perhaps not with any great gain in depth, by Miss A. M. Osborn.[79]

iv   Methodological Issues

We have seen in the first section of this chapter that Burke and Rousseau both wrote in a variety of political genres and with a number of different ends in view. This being so, one can obviously identify in their work certain instances of practical, philosophical and historical discourse, although the serious difficulty facing a comparative study lies in the impossibility of doing this exhaustively. It is one thing to discover isolated examples of what we mean; it is quite another to transform this perception into a method which is capable of shaping research.

Now, it is common and, I think, valid to make a radical conceptual distinction between the logic of a piece of writing designed to *recommend* or exhort, and the logic of a piece of writing designed to *explain*, between what might be called practical and theoretical or explanatory writing. In addition, it is not unusual to speak of different levels of abstraction or generality at which a piece of explanatory writing can exist. An article by J. G. A. Pocock[80] is particularly germane here, for it is addressed specifically to methodological problems in the history of political thought. Pocock argues that it is one of the major tasks of the historian of political ideas to explore the relationship between thinking and experience, to investigate the territory lying between political thought and political action, and to follow political thinking from one level of abstraction to another. A condition of success in this undertaking is clearly an ability to distinguish the various explanatory levels – from political philosophy 'at the top', as it were, down to the point where explanation merges with, and is at last replaced by recommendation.

One can fairly discern in the introductory passages of J. R. Levenson's *Confucian China* similar thoughts expressed in a different idiom, and one moreover which is helpful in specifying the approach adopted in this enquiry. Seeking a means of coming to terms with a complex change in Chinese attitudes, Levenson states that an idea

is a denial of alternatives and an answer to a question. What a man really means cannot be gathered solely from what he asserts; what he asks and what other men assert invest his ideas with meaning. In no idea does meaning simply inhere, governed only by its degree of correspondence with some unchanging objective reality, without regard to the problems of its thinker.[81]

A change, then, in the question behind an idea, like a change in the alternatives beside it, imposes change on the persisting positive content of the idea itself.[82]

More concerned with temporal change than with the changes which take place as ideas move within a single field of thought, he elucidates his point of view with the aphorism; 'An audience which appreciates that Mozart is not Wagner will never hear the eighteenth-century *Don Giovanni*.'[83] This view may be related to the notions of Pocock, for if the question which an idea or a text is designed to answer and the alternatives which it in so doing denies can both be specified, then the proper intellectual location of the idea – whether it be called the sphere of thought, the mode of discourse, or the level of abstraction – is surely discovered as well. Precisely the same words composing a question may demand a practical, an historical, or a philosophical answer, depending on the meaning placed upon them.

However, as we have already noted, Burke and Rousseau (like most social thinkers before and since) wrote with both a practical and a theoretical design, and their explanatory writings shifted between various levels of abstraction. Both men were faced with an assortment of questions, questions to which their writings could be said to constitute responses or answers on the one hand, and denials of other answers on the other : 'a thought includes what the thinker eliminates.'[84] In general Rousseau and Burke must be understood to be seeking not only to give an understanding of the world, but also to persuade men to take certain actions and to adopt certain attitudes in that world. The distinction between 'is' and 'ought' remains today a most difficult one for men to make and maintain, and it appears that the two categories were even more thoroughly fused in the eighteenth century than is common in our time. Nevertheless, Rousseau's perception of the distinction seems to have been on the whole a good deal clearer than many of his critics have allowed.[85] But both Rousseau and Burke would no doubt accept the proposition that to provide a philosophical account of the principles of political legitimacy is frequently in practice a powerful incitement to political action, and indeed it would be unwise to deny that people often do draw lessons out of philosophy, though to assert the logical validity of this is quite another matter. Pocock makes a similar point when he remarks that 'however much the conservative may deplore the fact, the human mind does pursue implications from the theoretical to the practical and from the practical to the theoretical . . .'.[86]

At any rate, a number of serious methodological problems arise at this point. First, there is the problem of disentangling within the corpus of Rousseau's and of Burke's writings the various styles of discourse, particularly the separating of the practical mood on the one hand from the various explanatory moods on the other. This would be no easy task in writings more uniform in tone and material than those of Rousseau and Burke; in the intellectual coats of many colours which these two display, however, it becomes a matter of awesome complexity. That a single work, a single passage, a single sentence in their writings is often irreducibly equivocal is enough to show that no final resolution of this problem can be hoped for. In many cases, one must select from a number of possible interpretations the one which seems to make the best sense of the passage. However, given this uncertainty, to choose one sort of understanding need not necessarily invalidate any of the others; they may all remain, and each may have a claim upon the attention of the student who wishes to make as comprehensive sense of the writing as possible.

This first problem, in fact, suggests the second : given the presence of a single style of discourse, the difficulty remains of settling which style it actually is. Even though a passage may not always speak with many voices at once, it is commonly a difficult thing to judge which particular voice one is hearing at any given time. A good ear is to be preferred to any analytical technique, but the best ear in the world cannot provide conclusive proof of accuracy. For many years, perhaps because of the 'halo effect' of the *Essay Concerning Human Understanding,* John Locke's *Second Treatise* was taken to be an instance of philosophical writing on politics, and no discomfort was experienced in removing Locke from the company of his energetic contemporaries, Shaftesbury and Somers and Algernon Sidney, and settling him in a world inhabited by Hobbes, St Augustine, Aristotle and Plato. Recently, there has been a thorough revaluation in Locke scholarship, the general tendency of which has been to disengage the *Second Treatise* from the realm of political philosophy, to reintegrate Locke the political writer into the world of his contemporaries, and to interpret his political writings, not as philosophy, but as at best an ideology and a programme of action, clothed in the trappings of highly abstract thought. Although certain characteristics of the *Second Treatise* (e.g. the unwillingness to consider fully the meaning and import of natural law) are today marshalled in an argument against placing the work on the plane of philosophy, the argument has not always been considered persuasive, and we may be forgiven for wondering whether the Lockeian revaluation owes as much to the pecularities of our own climate of opinion as it does to the discovery of new information about Locke's life and times. Whether this is true or not, it is obvious that there has not been an unchallenged and unrevised consensus among critics on the proper manner of reading Locke's *Two Treatises.* It is one of the most striking examples of the complexities which are encountered in trying to identify the proper character of political writings.

Finally, even if it were possible to deal conclusively with the first two problems, that is to say, disentangling and identifying the modes of discourse, we should still be faced with the question of comparing the works of Rousseau and Burke. Comparative study is always hazardous, because it is so difficult to ascertain whether the things to be compared are in fact comparable. The problem is particularly acute in intellectual history if one accepts the contextual conception of an idea outlined above. Although both Edmund Burke and Jean-Jacques Rousseau may speak of a 'social contract', we cannot assume prima facie that they are talking of the same thing, particularly if the former sees the contract of each state as 'but a clause in the great primaeval contract of eternal society, linking the lower with the higher natures, connecting the visible and the invisible world', and the latter describes the essence of the 'contrat social' as 'l'aliénation totale de chaque associé avec tous ses droits à toute la communauté.'[87] We must be as sure as possible that the two men are not only using a similar vocabulary or making roughly parallel positive statements, but that they are also *meaning* the same sort of thing. That is why each of the following two chapters begins by specifying their attitudes towards some of the dominant manners of thinking in the eighteenth century. If we can gather what they accepted and what they rejected in the speculative world around them, we shall be a good deal less likely to make grossly erroneous comparisons.

It must similarly be asked whether anything much can be concluded about what appears to be a matter of common concern if the passages in which Rousseau considers the matter are judged to be, for example, philosophy, and the relevant portions of Burke's thought are judged to be history. Are they simply at different levels of abstraction, and so quite inaccessible to one another? It is evident that, *if* such a judgement could be made conclusively, then this conclusion would necessarily follow, for, given the scheme presented above, we would have concluded that Burke's historical reflections by definition could not be comparable to Rousseau's philosophical speculations, since they are addressed to distinctive historical problems, and fulfil the logical canons of historical, and not philosophical discourse. The passages might look superficially like one another, but each would have its own peculiar meaning.

However, it is evident that in practice this theoretical clarity becomes obscure. If our judgements could always be as certain and as unequivocal as they are in theory, then we should have little temptation to make any such mistaken comparisons in the first place. But we have already seen that such clear-cut distinctions are not possible with Burke and Rousseau. No matter how clear the matter may seem to be, there is almost always a residual uncertainty that bedevils any given interpretation. Indeed, one tries to identify the kind of political discourse at least in part by seeing what sense can be made of it when it is viewed from different perspectives. In such an endeavour one is seeking what may be called maximum intelligibility, but discovery of this maximum (if this is possible) cannot exclude other degrees of intelligibility – indeed, it could be argued that it must *include* them. A student of political thought is, then, commonly faced with a given passage which may be interpreted in a variety of ways, and in such a case he may well have no reliable grounds for deciding between the different lines of interpretation.

So far as this enquiry is concerned, there are a number of factors which will be helpful in surmounting the difficulties outlined above. In the first place, we can so align the study that much of the light falls on the less famous portions of Jean-Jacques Rousseau's political thought; his conception of the general will is the point round which most controversy revolves, and the places in which this idea does not appear have been by comparison neglected. By attending to the writings which have not occasioned such a commotion in philosophical circles, it is possible to frame the enquiry in such a way as to make the avoidance of the above hazards easier. It is also easier to resist the temptation to which many critics of Burke have succumbed, namely, interpreting his writings at a higher level of generality than is appropriate to them.[88]

But there are also features for which we can be grateful in the lives of the two men themselves. Of considerable significance is the fact that they are contemporaries; taken together, their lives virtually span the eighteenth century. Jean-Jacques Rousseau was born in 1712 and died in 1778, Burke was born seventeen years after Rousseau and lived nineteen years after his death, dying at the age of sixty-eight in 1797. For nearly half a century they were living at the same time.[89] The importance of this should not be underrated, for as political writers they shared to a considerable extent the same universe of data and discourse. For example, the troubles in Poland and Corsica in the 1760s and 1770s occupied the pens of both Rousseau and Burke.[90]

35

Leaving the field of political events and turning to the speculative area of political discourse, the exchange of ideas between France and England is a notable phenomenon of this period, and Rousseau and Burke were as subject to this interchange as anyone else. Doctrines and opinions seem to have crossed and re-crossed the Channel, assuming the accent and habit of the adopted country, and returning to their native land to be hailed, not as long-lost countrymen, but as eccentric foreigners. Oakeshott remarks that in the French *Rights of Man* (4 August 1789) 'are disclosed, abstracted and abridged, the common law rights of Englishmen;'[91] they were to return to England in that guise in the writings of such men as Dr Price, William Godwin, and Thomas Paine. More closely related to our theme are the words of A. B. C. Cobban who points out the international influence of John Locke, noting 'a remarkable similarity between the two greatest disciples of Locke, the author of the *Contrat social* and the author of the *Reflections*'.[92] Montesquieu, too, not for nothing a devoted student of England, was to have a profound influence upon both Rousseau and his British critic. More generally, politically interested persons, whether in Britain or France, could be expected to share to a certain extent a common European heritage; not only were their problems often of a piece, but the places where they looked for enlightenment were frequently the same. All this is not meant to suggest that there was little difference between political thinking in England and France, or between the intellectual experiences of Burke and Rousseau, but rather to point out that there is a community of interest and outlook which underpins a comparative study of this kind.[93]

v The Rational Method in Burke and Rousseau

It is often said of both Burke and Rousseau that they are anti-rationalist, and it is evident that both assault what they take to be the mistaken rationalist assumptions of their contemporaries, and build their theories on rather different foundations. This can be seen in their psychological and in their political writings. Chapter ii, Part ii notes the modest part which reason plays in their conception of human nature, and Chapter iii, Part v, points out the serious limitations which they see in the power of the human intellect to order the affairs of men according to some speculative scheme. In both respects there is a substantial circumscription of reason to fields narrower than those in which it was customary to see it as functioning in the seventeenth and eighteenth centuries, but it is a question whether in either respect we could properly say that Rousseau and Burke are actively *anti*-rationalist. There is a great difference (though the two are often conjoined) between a positive assertion of the role of feeling or sentiment, and a denial of reason's place in the affairs of men.

The evidence suggests that Edmund Burke, and Jean-Jacques Rousseau as well, were attacking the apparently imperial ambitions of the rational faculty, and not reason's busy activity within what they regarded as its proper province. It is true that the kingdom of reason assumed much more modest proportions on their maps of the human constitution than it did on those of most of their contemporaries, but it is primarily in this relative sense that Burke and Rousseau can be called anti-rationalists. If the author of the *Reflections* writes of his countrymen that 'we preserve the whole of our feelings still native and entire, unsophisticated by pedantry and infidelity. We have real hearts of flesh and blood beating in our bosoms',[94] it does not follow from this that they lack minds, nor that their virtue consists in a sort of self-imposed ignorance. The native feelings of Englishmen are 'unsophisticated by pedantry', which is technical learning without practical wisdom, but there is no suggestion that they are endangered by wisdom itself. Indeed, Burke says that feelings which are not natural, which are not 'native and entire', can only 'render us unfit for rational liberty'.

But, leaving aside for the moment the conception of human nature in general, let us consider how Rousseau and Burke regarded and how they themselves employed the rational method in social analysis. Burke of course was very sceptical of the perspicacity of many social theorists, as well as of the reliability and, more important, the beneficial practical influence of rational insights. However, his scepticism did not turn him against rational speculation as such, but rather made him extremely cautious in his use of it and thoroughly suspicious of a too ready reliance upon it. The following remarks in his treatise on aesthetics seem to summarize his position on this score very well :

Men often act right from their feelings, who afterwards reason but ill on them from principle; but as it is impossible to avoid an attempt at such reasoning, and equally impossible to prevent its having some influence on our practice, surely it is worth taking some pains to have it just, and founded on the basis of sure experience.[95]

In the Preface to this work, he writes :

The characters of nature are legible, it is true; but they are not plain enough to enable those who run, to read them. We must make use of a cautious, I had almost said a timorous, method of proceeding.

On the face of it, Rousseau might be thought to provide a strong contrast to Burke. Frequently taken to be a *philosophe* and the most notorious 'abstract theorist' whom Burke selected for his attack, Jean-Jacques Rousseau seems to many critics to be a sort of Cartesian rationalist infused with passion, a thinker who would fall wholeheartedly in with the transformation of the famous Cartesian deduction to, 'je sens : donc je suis'. Here the airy, deductive method remains the same, but the content has radically changed; reason is used to attack reason itself.

Critics who consider Rousseau to be an excessively abstract thinker who weaves theories out of himself like a spider spinning a web have, I think, seriously misunderstood what he was trying to do and have also, perhaps, read Rousseau's putative influence back into his work itself, much as Burke seems to have done. For it appears that they have had a good deal less lucid conception of Rousseau's various pursuits than did Rousseau himself, who, at many times in his career, had a clear idea of the distinctiveness of his various undertakings and the consequent variety of demands which were imposed upon him. This can be seen most easily in the methodological differences between his political philosophy and his political prescription. When searching for 'quelque règle d'administration légitime et sûre', Rousseau quite understandably restricts himself in the main to the conventional methods of eighteenth-century philosophy; but when it comes to making practical recommendations, he shows very little tendency to treat the problems of particular countries as if they were abstract questions of principle, and instead suggests limited changes, and allows what he could only have regarded as unfortunate abuses (e.g. feudal institutions in Poland) to stand for fear of unwittingly making the whole situation worse by ignorant wholesale renovation. He remarks upon the practical shortcomings of speculation if it is not tied closely to personal experience. To Buttafuoco he writes : '... il me manque, enfin, l'expérience dans les affaires, qui seule éclaire plus, sur l'art de conduire les hommes, que toutes les méditations.'[96]

But he, like Burke, would maintain that to recognize the limitations of man's rational faculty is not to deny its utility; man must necessarily employ his intellect in the understanding and improvement of his affairs – the point is to use it more wisely, which in this case means to use it with greater circumspection.[97] No doubt all anti-rationalist attacks aim at a fencing in of reason, and not its complete extinction; it would be an intrepid opponent indeed who would deny the rational faculty any place at all in human affairs. But to call either Burke or Rousseau an 'anti-rationalist' seems to me misleading, because it draws attention away from their positive conceptions and focuses it on their denials, and it makes their indisputable provision of a spot for abstract speculation seem somehow perplexing and difficult to explain.

However, we must grant here that Edmund Burke's rational scepticism and his discomfiture at seeing the human mind (as he thought) misused, were a good deal more profound than Rousseau's. This might be in part accounted for by the differences in the intellectual worlds of France and England at that time; a political vocabulary of highly generalized concepts was very much in vogue on the Continent, while the idom of the common law was still embedded in the political structure and was still informing political thinking in England.[98] One might say that a certain intellectual style was implicit in the language of politics itself. But there is evidence to show that Burke himself, though he did not personally indulge much in it, had no objection to abstract speculation as such; in fact, not only did he write a philosophical treatise on a non-political subject, but within the field of politics itself, he finds a place for philosophy, arguing that 'it is the business of the speculative philosopher to mark the proper ends of government'.[99] It was the misuse of such thought, which is to say its so-called application in practical political affairs, that he attacked. In one of his speeches he asserts :

It seems to me a preposterous way of reasoning, and a perfect confusion of ideas, to take the theories which learned and speculative men have made from that government, and then, supposing it made on those theories, which were made from it, to accuse the government as not corresponding with them.[100]

It is apparent that Rousseau for his part does not fit Morley's image of him as one who wrote in what might be called the romantic abstract, as one who 'only floated languidly on a summer tide of sensation, and captured premiss and conclusion in a succession of swoons'.[101] He was not altogether unfamiliar with what Morley picturesquely describes as 'the sharpened instruments, the systematic apparatus, and the minute feelers and tentacles of the genuine thinker and solid reasoner'.[102] and Burke, on the other hand, was not always averse to theoretical speculation about politics. We shall return to this matter in subsequent chapters.

2

Notions of Human Nature in Rousseau and Burke

1   Introduction

Associated with any political theory there is some conception, either implicit or explicit, of human nature, and the more highly theoretical a writer's account of politics, the more likely it is that his conception of man will be made explicit. There are, then, two distinguishable facets to a political work. On the one hand, there is the psychological dimension containing a more or less coherent theory of man, and on the other, there is the dimension containing a particular understanding of politics. Generally, the second purports quite simply to be derived from the first, but the relationship between the two is much more subtle and ambiguous than that, and indeed there are sometimes grounds for believing that the psychological theory is worked up to satisfy the requirements of a premeditated political doctrine.

Our immediate task in this chapter is to consider the answers provided by Edmund Burke and Jean-Jacques Rousseau to a number of general questions about human nature. How are we most fully to understand the nature of man? Is he a creature with innate qualities, and, if so, what are they? What part does society play in the constitution of the human being? Is man at all times and in all places essentially the same, or do climate, geography and the passage of time work fundamental changes in his nature? What is the place of reason in his make-up? of morality? What force does the irrational have in the behaviour of mankind? In what conditions can a human being most properly be considered free? Although these questions may not have been put so explicitly by the two men, they provide the background to a great deal of the thought of

41

Rousseau and Burke, as they do indeed to a great deal of the social debate in the seventeenth and eighteenth centuries.

Actually, it would probably be more accurate to say that such questions as these have preoccupied men of thought in the western world for centuries; perhaps the distinctive thing about the seventeenth and eighteenth centuries was that there emerged a particular tradition of answers which is often generally designated as the school of natural rights or the social-contract school. This tradition was by all odds the dominant manner of social thought in the course of these two centuries. Another style of answers, less prominent and more inchoate than the natural-right school but still of great importance, perpetuated itself side by side with its better-known fellow, and so provided an alternative response (and an implicit challenge to it); this manner of thinking we have termed political empiricism.[1] Although part of an ancient tradition of political speculation, this approach was, during much of the seventeenth and eighteenth centuries, overshadowed by the rationalist school of natural rights, and it was not until towards the end of the eighteenth century that it (and, of course, idealist political thought as well) began seriously to undermine the exalted popular position of the natural-right tradition. Nevertheless, empiricist assumptions and approaches are very much in evidence throughout these two centuries.

We shall open this chapter, then, with a description of the psychological doctrines of the natural-right school followed by a brief account of the psychological doctrines of empiricist political thinking, together with an outline of the attitudes of Rousseau and Burke to both approaches. Their theories of human nature, and the affinities between these theories, can be seen most clearly, not simply in the light of what the two men positively asserted, but also in the light of what they rejected, what they refused to accept from these two major modes of thought.

II Rousseau and Burke, and the School of Natural Rights

The concept of natural rights, at least in the late seventeenth and eighteenth centuries, was a predominantly political notion.[2] That is to say, reference to the range of ideas associated with natural rights almost always occurred in the course of political discussion, and appeals to the rights of man were made, not in religious controversy, nor in psychological speculation as such, but in the course of a political argument. Natural-right doctrines would be difficult to make sense of, if their political character were missed.[3] However, though the rights of man almost always appeared in the realm of political discourse, the heart of the doctrine was to be found in a particular theory of human nature.

Here we shall attempt to do three things : first, to describe the school of natural rights and distinguish it broadly from the classical natural-law tradition; second, to outline the school's view of human nature; and third, to examine the attitudes of Rousseau and Burke to this view of human nature. Inevitably, a discussion within such a brief compass of an issue as complex as the history of natural-law thinking will involve compression and over simplification, but even a schematic picture will be helpful in allowing us to carry forward this comparative enquiry.

Although the natural-right school can be seen as constituting one chapter in the centuries-long story of the law of nature, it nevertheless, upon examination, discloses a number of important distinguishing characteristics, and it is these marks of difference which must most closely concern us. If it is not too much to attempt to identify a persisting pattern of belief in the diversified tradition of the law of nature, we might point to Cicero's famous description of natural law as exemplifying much of what is fundamental about the doctrine. He writes :

True law is right reason in agreement with Nature; it is of universal application, unchanging and everlasting; it summons to duty by its commands, and averts from wrong-doing by its prohibitions. . . . We cannot be freed from its obligations by Senate or People, and we need not look outside ourselves for an expounder or interpreter of it. And there will not be different laws at Rome and at Athens, or different laws now and in the future, but one eternal and unchangeable law will be valid for all nations and for all times, and there will be one master and one ruler, that is, God, over us all, for He is the author of this law, its promulgator, and its enforcing judge.[4]

This passage from Cicero's *Republic*, quoted on countless occasions in subsequent ages, has all the hallmarks of the classical expression of the natural law. The law of nature, like nature itself of which it is a framing principle, is an expression of divine reason. It is an eternal, fixed moral rule which imposes obligations upon man. It is in accord with 'right reason', and, as Cicero points out elsewhere,[5] its commands can be discerned by the rational faculty of man.

Now, the seventeenth and eighteenth centuries gave a distinctive twist to this conception which radically transformed the use to which it was put, and, one might say, in some measure changed the notion of natural law itself. Three distinguishing marks may be mentioned. The coming into prominence of these features constituted a profound change of emphasis, but by no means a definite break in the tradition. It entailed the drawing out and exploration of certain implications which were implicit in the old-style natural-law tradition itself. The very phrase which is used to designate the tradition in the eighteenth century, the 'school of natural *rights*', directs our attention towards the first identifying characteristic. The passage from Cicero above has the following words in it : duty, commands, prohibitions, obligations, master, ruler and enforcing judge. The image pretty clearly is one of obligation to obey the universal law laid down by God. By the eighteenth century the emphasis has shifted away from duty towards *rights*, natural rights; in this case, the predominant idea is the right given by nature to do or act in a certain manner whatever the commands of the civil authority. Duty is now assumed to attach primarily to the civil authority which must form its municipal laws in accordance with the law of nature. Basil Willey has written that

one may perhaps risk the generalization that it was the idea of a controlling *Law* of Nature which officially dominated the Middle Ages, rather than that of the liberating *Rights* of Nature; and that in passing into the seventeenth and eighteenth centuries, 'Nature' ceases to be mainly a regulating principle and becomes mainly a liberating principle.[6]

The second characteristic mark of the natural-right school is its particular view of *rationalism*. Cicero definitely sees human reason as the faculty which enables man to recognize the law of nature and its injunctions, but, so long as weight is placed upon duty rather than right, the clear implication is that men will be able to discover their obligations and fulfil their responsibilities by the exercise of their reason, rather than that they will be able to discern and demand recognition of their rights; men, says Cicero, are summoned to duty by the commands of true law, which is right reason in agreement with nature. This pattern of thought fitted in well with the medieval belief that a ruler was responsible to God for his actions, and that it was not within the province of the subject to call his ruler to account for misbehaviour. The late seventeenth- and eighteenth-century writers secularized the law of nature, and they also placed a greater reliance upon the individual's rationality. God, most such writers would agree, has fixed the nature of man, but this being so it is not to the point to study his will via biblical exegesis or theological argument; it is necessary, rather, to accept God's work as a given, and to examine the structure and principles of the human frame itself. Natural law now becomes a matter, not of human subjection to God's will, but of the individual's natural (i.e. ultimately divinely appointed) faculty of penetrating into the nature of things. Burlamaqui, who obviously accepted the ultimate sovereignty of the Creator, nevertheless wrote in 1747 :

The idea of Right, and much more that of Natural Right, are undoubtedly relative to the nature of man. 'Tis from this nature therefore, from the constitution and state of man, that we are to deduce the principles of this science.[7]

. . . we must set out with acknowledging as a fixt and uncontestable principle, that the human understanding is naturally right, and has within itself a strength sufficient to arrive at the knowledge of truth, and to distinguish it from error; especially in things wherein our respective duties are concerned, and which are requisite to form man for a virtuous, honourable, and quiet life.[8]

It has frequently been remarked that Grotius's reference to God a century before in his well-known description of natural law[9] adds nothing to the actual definition and implies no necessary religious sanction. However tentative may have been his speculations detaching natural law from God's will, those who came after him had fewer and fewer reservations : 'what Grotius had set forth as a hypothesis has become a thesis. The self-evidence of natural law has made the existence of God perfectly superfluous.'[10] It is, of course, to human reason that natural law is self-evident.

The third distinguishing characteristic of the natural-right school is its *individualism*. We have just noted the shift from duty to right, and the increasing reliance upon the rational faculty. As for the question of who possesses this rational power, and who it is that enjoys these rights of nature, the answer which the seventeenth and eighteenth centuries found most satisfactory on both counts was the 'individual'; reason was understood to reside in the individual human being, and it was he, too, who was thought to enjoy the benefits of natural law and to exercise the rights which existed under it. Now this individualist response to the two questions above was by no means the only one possible, and it is well to bear some of the alternatives in mind. It could be maintained that reason is found in one of the orders of society, in the people, in a communal past, or in the species. And rights could be thought to inhere in the virtuous, in the occupants of certain status roles (e.g. king, lord, or priest), in a nation, or in a class. None of these possible answers had much appeal for natural-right thinkers; indeed, it is doubtful that they even considered them to be possibilities. For them, the unit of analysis and the entity for whose benefit social and political life was constituted was the individual – not even the citizen, and still less the subject, but the naked, autonomous, the natural man.[11]

If one were to attempt to sum up the change which came over natural-law thinking during the course of the seventeenth and eighteenth centuries, one might say that a doctrine with liberal and, in some cases, radical or revolutionary political implications gradually supplanted a conservative body of ideas counselling orthodox behaviour and submission to constituted civil and ecclesiastical authority. Both a liberal and a conservative case may be built up on the basis of natural law; in the eighteenth century it was the liberal case that was more commonly constructed. Right took precedence over duty, secular rationalism overtook religious faith, and individual independence superseded corporate responsibility. The late seventeenth- and eighteenth-century variation of natural law was a doctrine *against* what its exponents took to be oppression by the civil authorities and *for* individual liberty; the classical version was much more a doctrine against civil disorder and for corporate cohesion and stability.

At the centre of the natural-right theory of human nature was the idea that a man possesses certain intrinsic qualities, and can therefore make certain moral claims, simply by virtue of his humanity. It was felt that these qualities (and the consequent claims) are invested in him by God (and/or by nature) prior to, or else independently of, any social or political order whatsoever. Man is not a creature of the civil order : the civil order is the immediate creation of man (though perhaps the mediate creation of God). There is not often entire accord about just what qualities are 'natural' and what 'artificial' or 'acquired', but among the natural-right thinkers there is general agreement that such a natural-artificial distinction can be made, and that it is important.

Two devices are employed in order to make the distinction; namely, the state of nature and the social contract, of which the latter provides the link between the 'natural' order and the 'artificial' order of political society (or, as some writers would have it, society itself). Thus natural man, man in the state of nature, is the concept generally utilized by the school of natural rights to elaborate its psychological theory.

Much confusion arises from this common form of seventeenth- and eighteenth-century political argument; the conventions of the extra-political state of nature with its immanent moral order, and the contract instituting political society, give one the initial impression that most of the writings in this tradition are purporting to give a description of a way of life which actually existed in the past. Many writers intended to do just this, and many more, who in moments of clarity realized that they were simply setting out hypothetical history for argument's sake, were sometimes seduced by their own construction into believing (or writing as if they believed) that they were describing an historical past. However, in both cases, the social-contract doctrines serve much the same purpose in discourse on politics; that is to say, the exposure of an author's flagrant historical inaccuracy tells little against his theory, for he is not really trying to write history. He is trying to do something else.

What, then, is he trying to do? He is generally attempting to provide an account of political life or some important part of it, or else he is seeking to prescribe a course of action in response to a current political dilemma. Most often, of course, he is doing both. So, instead of the state of nature being a description of the actual make-up of man as it existed during some hazy period in the primeval past, it is an account of the writer's theory of man; it is also, as a rule, a veiled representation of the values which the writer holds dear – the ethical premises of his argument, as it were.

Let us note briefly here other important features of the natural-right school's theory of human nature. The theory sees man in static terms.[12] Neither human nature in sum, nor any of its primary components, was considered to be subject to fundamental change.[13] John Locke's natural man is little changed by his entry into civil society, although the conditions of his life are much improved. And in the American colonies, where there was some empirical experience of building up states *ex nihilo*, this sense of a man owing little more than convenience and security to his government was understandably widespread. The June 1776 Virginian Declaration of Rights states roundly 'that all men are by nature equally free and independent, and have certain rights, of which, when they enter into a state of society, they cannot by any compact deprive or divest their posterity'. This statement has a double implication : first, that men are in some sense independent of a social order; and second, that all men are born with certain extra-legal rights of which they cannot be deprived. The socializing function of society is seen to be of little or no significance here. (In the case of the American colonies, much of the process of socialization had in fact been carried out originally by the mother country, England, a fact which the experiences of the colonists would make it easy to forget.) To argue that this natural condition of man never existed historically would be, as we have suggested, beside the point, but it would not be irrelevant to argue that the conception of man elaborated in the theory is inadequate, and we shall show below that both Rousseau and Burke took this line.

It was easy for all to see that men living in civil society had certain obligations to the ruling authority and to their fellow citizens, as well as certain rights and privileges which they could exercise without interference. These rights and obligations formed part of the system of law of the particular country. But what in the eighteenth century was also thought by many to be easy to see was that all men everywhere, in and out of society, lived under a moral order, and had by their very nature certain moral rights and, though this was not emphasized, certain moral duties.

The idea of a universal moral order, either natural or divine, had been a feature of European thought for centuries; what the natural-right school brought to the fore was an inference from this idea, that if there was such an order, then there must also be certain rights attaching to it. The correlative notion, that there must also be duties, was not generally as strenuously insisted upon. The rights which a man enjoyed in a state of nature, that is, under the exclusive jurisdiction of natural law, were (or ought to be) brought into and enjoyed in society unchanged. Liberty within civil society was qualitatively the same as liberty in the state of nature; the regulations necessary to secure this natural right might vary, but liberty itself did not. The state's primary function was to ensure the protection and to foster the full exercise of these rights. The individual before and after the social contract remained basically unaltered, with his natural rights intact and his capacity to reason, as we shall see below, little affected.

Natural-right thinkers do not simply assert that there is a moral order immanent in the universe; they also insist that it can be known or recognized by men through the use of a faculty common to all men. It is 'plain and intelligible to all rational creatures'.[14] Every human being, unless he be a child or a madman, has the power to reason, and the most common view was that it is by the employment of this rational faculty that the stipulations of nature's law can be discovered. It is not simply the heart that feels, but also the mind that knows, the justness of a just act. It must be admitted, however, that eighteenth-century 'reason' sometimes looks very much like ordinary common sense or like 'natural' sensibility.[15] In relation to the plain and intelligible law of nature, this distinctively human quality is not usually conceived as a highly abstract reasoning power (it hardly could be so conceived if it is taken to be a capacity shared by all men), but rather a faculty of moral perception, a combination, as Kingsley Martin has said, of both reasoning and intuition. Burlamaqui represents this view well with his assertion that the human understanding is naturally right and has within it the power to arrive at truth both of fact and of value, although he takes care to add cautiously that this requires the application of all possible care and attention.[16]

It tends, then, to be a persistent article of faith among natural-right theorists that a man has in some sense the capacity to *know* what is good and evil; he does not simply sense it. It follows from this that it is possible to explain evil as at least the partial effect of error or of improper social arrangements, without its being necessary to bring in the Christian doctrine of original sin. If a man knew better, or knew more, or if the community in which he lived operated upon different principles, he would not contravene the commands of natural law.

Natural man, according to most exponents of natural rights, was not wicked, and for many of them he was positively good. The origin of evil was found not in the constitution of man, but in the composition of society.[17] This shift created a number of logical and

49

doctrinal dilemmas, but nonetheless it achieved a wide measure of acceptance. John Locke's influential *Essay Concerning Human Understanding* took men to be empty vessels with respect to morals, as they were with respect to most other things as well, but it was open to believers in natural rights to maintain that some innate capacity to see and follow the good exists in mankind. Indeed, when Locke turns to a description of the state of nature in the *Second Treatise*, he moves from the *tabula rasa* doctrine to the notion of innate capacities :

> The state of nature has a law of nature to govern it, which obliges everyone; and reason, which is that law, teaches all mankind, who will but consult it, that being all equal and independent, no one ought to harm another in his life, liberty, or possessions. . . .[18]

Not only is this rational faculty universal; it is also assumed to be the same in all men. A. O. Lovejoy reckons this to be a characteristic of Enlightenment rationalism generally; he calls it its 'first and fundamental principle', and christens it with what he himself admits is the 'unlovely term', 'uniformitarianism' :

> The [sic] reason, it is assumed to be evident, is identical in all men. . . . Differences in opinion or taste are evidence of error, and universality of appeal or of acceptance tends to be taken, not merely as an effect, but as in itself a mark or criterion, of truth.[19]

It is this vital faculty which makes man unique among the animals, which enables him to comprehend the law of nature, and which makes it possible for him to live in consciously wrought civil communities.

We need for the moment to draw only one further implication out of what we have said above. With this 'uniformitarian' conception of man, there is the sense that the particularity of human beings which sets individual off from individual, class from class, and nation from nation, is of relatively minor importance; it is froth on the surface of the essential human nature lying beneath. Unlike the later romantics, the Enlightenment in general was inclined to ignore or minimize the idiosyncrasies and diversities of men, and to concentrate on what they felt was universal.[20] What Lovejoy has called 'rationalist individualism' is clearly in harmony with democratic and liberal political ideas. If men, particularly in their rational capacity, are 'basically' the same, then direction in social and religious matters from authoritarian superiors seems inappropriate;[21] judgements in politics and religion become on this reading the prerogative of each individual, unhampered by tradition or paternalistic control. The general opinion of mankind is regarded as the collective expression of this identical individual truth, despite the fact that comparative study often uncovered variations of a most serious kind in the attitudes and opinions of mankind.

These, then, are some of the important lineaments of the school's theory of human nature. Let us examine the views of Edmund Burke and Jean-Jacques Rousseau in the light of this outline of natural-right thought. The general question to be considered is, where do the two men stand with regard to the school and its psychological theory?

It must be granted straight away that both Burke and Rousseau employed the vocabulary of the natural-right school from time to time. But when they did so, did they mean the same thing as their contemporaries, or were they putting new wine in old bottles? Do their ideas concerning the nature of man rest on natural-right assumptions and buttress natural-right doctrine, or do they rest on different foundations and support a different system of ideas? We may answer these questions by examining their views with respect to the outstanding features of the school's psychological theory : its doctrine of the immutability of human nature, its individualism, its conception of rights, and its notion of reason.

Burke's hatred of 'the cannibal philosophers of France' is notorious.[22] Of himself he writes :

The author of the *Reflections* has *heard* a great deal concerning the modern lights; but he has not yet had the good fortune to *see* much of them. He has read more than he can justify to anything but the spirit of curiosity, of the works of these illuminators of the world. He has learned nothing from the far greater number of them, than a full certainty of their shallowness, levity, pride, petulance, presumption, and ignorance ... their principles are diametrically opposite to his.[23]

And yet, though this and many other passages are clear and emphatic on the point, there are in Burke's writings certain statements which suggest a fairly complete acceptance of natural-right doctrine. For example, in his *Hints for an Essay on the Drama*, Burke asserts :

I thought it would be impossible to come to any clear and definite idea on this subject [dramatic composition], without remounting to the natural passions or dispositions of men, which first gave rise to this species of writing; for from these alone its nature, its limits, and its true character, can be determined.[24]

He then goes on to write some hypothetical history ('The first species of composition ... was probably some general indefinite topic of praise or blame, expressed in a song or hymn. . . .'), for all the world like a *philosophe* in quest of natural man. Again, in the *Tracts on the Popery Laws* he states:

Everybody is satisfied, that a conservation and secure enjoyment of our natural rights is the great and ultimate purpose of civil society; and that therefore all forms whatsoever of government are only good as they are subservient to that purpose to which they are entirely subordinate.[25]

This statement, especially with its outspoken certainty of tone ('all forms whatsoever', 'entirely subordinate'), is an astonishing one to come from the pen of Edmund Burke.

This passage seems to imply that the rights of natural man are carried over unchanged into the civil community, and that they constitute the standard for judging the performance of all political authorities. One could, if one wished, take note of the many places in which Burke says that one cannot enjoy the rights of a civil and an uncivil state together, and in this light interpret the above statement as a reference to the divine natural law 'in the vocabulary of' natural rights. But this is unconvincing. The almost aggressive tenor of the passage makes such a procedure unsatisfactory. Two major distinguishing marks of the school are its emphasis on rights and its critical stance *vis-à-vis* existing governments. Both are clearly present here.

One might argue that this passage occurs in one of Burke's early writings (it was written when Burke was in his thirties) and that some provision should be made for a change of opinion or emphasis in Burke's thinking. But this approach fails when it is realized that similar statements are present in his later writings as well. For example, in an *Address to the King* concerning American affairs, drafted in the late 1770s, it is stated that at the time of the 1688 Revolution the people 'reentered into their original rights'.[26] And in a speech to the House of Commons in December 1783 Burke objects to the use to which the doctrine of natural rights is being put, and then asserts:

The rights *of men* [the phrase used by his opponents], that is to say, the natural rights of mankind, are indeed sacred things; and if any public measure is proved mischievously to affect them, the objection ought to be fatal to that measure....[27]

So another explanation of these passages must be found. It should be noted in passing that none of these passages is logically inconsistent with the classical natural-law tradition to which Burke adheres.[28] The problem therefore is one of emphasis and tone, and this can be at least partly accounted for by examining the practical context of Burke's remarks. When Burke upon occasion employs the more aggressive language of the natural-right school it is usually in connection with a group which he feels is being politically oppressed. Burleigh Wilkins, who discusses this issue with regard to the *Tracts on the Popery Laws*, makes the following point :

the primary reason why such appeals to first principles were irrelevant in the French case but not in the Irish was that, in Burke's opinion, France had enjoyed before the Revolution by and large a just civil order whereas Ireland under the rule of a harsh and hypocritical Protestant clique had not.[29]

This does not 'explain away' his use of the language of eighteenth-century radicalism, but it does place it in an intelligible context, (one, though, which is admittedly close to that of the natural-right thinkers themselves).

Generally, however, it was Burke's conviction that the rights which man was said to enjoy in the state of nature bore little or no resemblance to those civil rights which were the prerogative of the citizen :

The pretended *rights of man* . . . cannot be the rights of the people. For to be a people, and to have these rights, are things incompatible. The one supposes the presence, the other the absence, of a state of civil society.[30]

Elsewhere, Burke returns to the same point : 'Men cannot enjoy the rights of an uncivil and of a civil state together.'[31]

Although Edmund Burke accepted the law of nature in some form, it was pretty clearly not the variety adopted by the natural-right school. His principal objection to natural-right notions was not their explanatory inaccuracy, but what he regarded as their flagrant and dangerous political misuse. He detested the popular eighteenth-century habit of arguing for or against certain specific political measures on the basis of abstract rights. This appeared to him not only to reveal a thorough misunderstanding of the character of speculative thought, but also to inject into practical politics an utter irrelevancy – an irrelevancy, unfortunately, which seemed often to have revolutionary implications. It was the political consequences which were illegitimately derived from such rights to which he principally objected. For example, Burke has written :

The *extreme* of liberty (which is its abstract perfection, but its real fault) obtains nowhere, nor ought to obtain anywhere; because extremes, as we all know in every point which relates either to our duties or satisfactions in life, are destructive both to virtue and enjoyment.[32]

His remarks on the subject, therefore, were primarily aimed at disallowing natural-right discussion in current political debate. Natural-right doctrine might be true or false in theory (he in fact felt that in its contemporary form it was barren and inadequate), but in the world of practice it became a positive evil.

Burke's thought on the matter of rights might be put as follows : although there are rights secured to man by nature (but not in the form stated by contract theorists), they must suffer such radical transformation in passing from the natural to the civil state (assuming such a thing to be possible at all) that it is idle to seek in them in their original form a strict and detailed guide to actual political life.

Not only are the rights of man subject to profound modification as they are 'embodied' in the positive laws of civil society; man himself undergoes serious change, not only on the supposition that he 'enters' civil society, but also within society itself. Man is a creature of history,[33] and Burke sees little reason for assuming that he remains unchanged over the ages. Moreover he is susceptible to wide geographical variation as well, as Burke's comments on Indian affairs show clearly.[34] The ultimate moral order is universal, but, within this colossal frame, there is scope for almost infinite variation. In this respect, Burke's is the 'romantic' rather than the 'rationalist' variant of individualism. Man is *in* history; he is part of the historical process. Human nature is not an unchanging element that persists in a chaos of change. Community life has a creative role in forming the character of mankind; it is necessary for a human being's full development. As Burke says in the *Reflections*, without 'civil society man could not by any possibility arrive at the perfection of which his nature is capable, nor even make a remote and faint approach to it.[35] Man is a being of perennially unrealized possibility. He can, if he will, approach perfection, but it is not inevitable that he should do so. What is fairly certain, however, is that he will not be tomorrow just what he is today.

As a Christian, Edmund Burke believed that all this change takes place in a world where God's will or reason (it is the same thing)[36] provides an eternal moral framework, which in its political aspect is known as the law of nature. This moral order never changes, and the duties which it imposes on all rational creatures is perpetual. He is in general agreement with the school of natural rights here. However, Burke, contrary to the school of natural rights, conceives of man in dynamic terms. A human being or a human community is what it has come to be in the course of time; that is why the study of history is of such importance.

In keeping with this dynamic understanding of human nature, Burke discloses an attitude to individualism and reason which is distinct from that of the natural-right school. Burke felt that an account of the composition of man which neglects his social nature (or tries to) is radically imperfect. The individual is not a self-sufficient unit which can exist in isolation from society, and society itself, as a consequence, is not composed of a simple agglomeration of these autonomous, isolated units. A community cannot be adequately understood by a simple process of addition; it is a great deal more than the sum of the individuals making it up. And to treat a human being in abstraction from his group is to throw away the chance of thoroughly comprehending what he is, for he is a social creature. Burke's perception of the intimate and necessary connection between man and society involves a drastic revision of the individualism of the natural-right school.

C. E. Vaughan, in describing the transformation which came over western European thought during the middle years of the eighteenth century, saw as its most significant manifestation 'a change from a narrow and cramping conception of man's reason to one far wider and more adequate to his powers'.[37] And he saw Edmund Burke as a prominent figure in the coming of the new order. Whether or not one would wish to call one idea of reason adequate and the other cramping, it is certainly true that Burke's was widely different from the Enlightenment's. When Burke speaks of 'the collected reason of the ages', it is obvious that he means by it something different from the natural reason of the social-contract theorist. To some extent, the distinction can be grasped by what we have said on the other points above. There is not for Burke a given quantum of rational power in every normal man; men vary in their capacities, and some may by character or training be better fitted to undertake those activities which make a heavy call on the rational faculty.[38] In addition to this, the reason of the individual is weak and erratic in comparison with that of the group, whether it be a class or a populace, or a traditional community which has existed time out of mind. Burke seems to have held a hierarchic conception of reason, extending from the uncertain and narrow rational faculty of the individual at the bottom, up through the reason of the 'people' of a country, through the 'collected reason' of a nation's past, through the wisdom of the species, reaching finally up to the pinnacle of rational capacity, the Divine wisdom of God.

The individual is foolish; the multitude, for the moment, is foolish, when they act without deliberation; but the species is wise, and, when time is given to it, as a species it always acts right.[39]

Instead of the Enlightenment human being, naturally equipped to grasp all that is important in the nature of things, and capable of rationally shaping his environment, we have a limited and ignorant man, utterly without knowledge of most things, and with nothing but an obscure comprehension of others. Enlightenment rationalism puts Plato's man outside the cave in the full light of day; but man, from Burke's point of view, is still and necessarily a creature of the dark, living his life by the flickering shadows on the wall.

In the following quotation, we can see Burke making a general attack on the natural-right concept of nature and society. Taking his work as a whole, we must say that 'nature' in some form remains a cardinal idea for him as it does for his opponents, but his 'nature' is far removed from theirs.

The state of civil society . . . is a state of nature; and much more truly so than a savage and incoherent mode of life. For man is by nature reasonable; and he is never perfectly in his natural state, but when he is placed where reason may be best cultivated, and most predominates. Art is man's nature. We are as much, at least, in a state of nature in formed manhood, as in immature and helpless infancy.[40]

'Nature' here no longer suggests simply the primitive, nor the ideal. It is neither man's point of departure, nor his ultimate destination, but both, as well as all the stages in between, so long as they are suitable to man's character and capacities as they have developed up to that point. Edmund Burke's thinking constitutes a significant departure from the natural-right school's idea of nature and of man.

What about Jean-Jacques Rousseau? He is frequently understood to be a natural-right thinker, and we must consider to what extent this is true. Is he firmly established in the natural-right tradition? If not, at what points and in what manner does he differ? How are we to understand his employment of natural-right language and concepts? It will be convenient here, as with Burke, to approach the problem in terms of the prominent features of the theory already noted, namely, its doctrine of human immutability, its individualism, its conception of rights, and its notion of reason.

It is undeniable that there are passages in the writings of Rousseau which would appear to justify the strictures of Sir Leslie Stephen and others who see in Rousseau the apotheosis of natural-right thought.[41] He certainly used the vocabulary and the concepts of the school frequently enough, and what is perhaps his most famous political utterance, 'l'homme est né libre, et partout il est dans les fers', is commonly taken to be a particularly outstanding and dramatic example of the type of assertion which the natural-right theorist can be expected to make.

To understand Rousseau's position, it is necessary to consider his conception of the state of nature, itself a fundamental feature of natural-right thought in the eighteenth century. The usual practice was to show that man in this state had certain 'natural' or essential characteristics and enjoyed certain 'natural' prerogatives, and to insist that these ought to be protected in any rightly constituted community. Positive law operated in the service of natural right. Man's relationship to society was seen in instrumental rather than constitutive terms. Man could be understood as a fairly coherent being independently of any given civil or social order.

It is apparent that Rousseau's natural man is very different. Except for his latent potentialities (which are, admittedly, of great importance), he is little more than an animal,[42] and if one were to set him beside other creatures, one would on the face of it be hard put to it to discover any difference between him and them. Man in a state of nature lives by himself, consorting with members of the opposite sex only periodically to reproduce his kind. He is without language, apparently without reason, and without a moral sense; instead of leading a moral life (for which choice is necessary), he is subject to instinct (or natural necessity).[43] In the *Contrat* it is said that man in his natural state is 'un animal stupide et borné', whereas in society he is 'un être intelligent et un homme'; in this passage there is the clear implication that man's humanity is the product of society.[44] By asserting categorically that 'ce passage de l'état de nature à l'état civil produit dans l'homme un changement très rémarquable', Rousseau is effecting a revision of the natural-right theory of human nature so fundamental that, were it not for the fact that he used the vocabulary and basic concepts of the school, it would sound odd to call it a revision at all.[45] Far from seeing human nature as immutable, Rousseau considers that the transformation to which it is subject in passing from the natural to the civil state could hardly be more profound.

In this light it becomes, I think, fairly clear that Rousseau's individualism must be of a qualified sort when compared to that of the full-blown natural-right thinker. Rousseau rejects the notion that men enter society as coherent units, seeing man and society rather as parts of a single whole. In the only condition in which a man can fairly be said to be independent, that is, outside society, he is not much different from a beast; in order to develop his human character, he must give up his natural liberty for a form of dependence, for a situation in which he must be, and must see himself to be, part of a greater whole :

C'est alors seulement que la voix du devoir succédant à l'impulsion physique, et la droit à l'appetit, l'homme, qui jusques là n'avoit regardé que lui-même, se voit forcé d'agir sur d'autres principes, et de consulter sa raison avant d'écouter ses penchans.[46]

Rousseau describes as the best institutions those 'qui savent le mieux dénaturer l'homme, lui ôter son existence absolue pour lui en donner une relative, et transporter le "moi" dans l'unité commune'.[47]

Leaving aside for the time being the question of Rousseau's relationship to the classical natural-law tradition,[48] we have here also to consider Rousseau's attitude towards a basic feature of the

Enlightenment's version of natural law, that is, its belief in the individual's rational capacity to discern the rights of nature.

Although Rousseau's position was not always clear, it seems to have been his view that man in the state of nature (that is, the individual abstracted from society) was a creature quite unable to recognize natural (which is to say, non-social) rights if such existed and applied to him, and incapable of ordering his life in terms of these rights even if he could recognize them. Rousseau says more than once that 'l'homme Sauvage, privé de toute sorte de lumiéres', is in some sense subject to the rule of instinct, and that it is not until he begins to become a member of a social order that moral notions, concepts of right and wrong, duty and obedience, gradually develop. If natural rights apply to the savage, then they apply in virtually the same way to other beasts as well (that is, without the animal's perception of them as rights)[49] and it is certainly not in this limited sense that most social-contract writers envisage the rights of man. Rousseau's natural man, if he acts in accordance with the law of nature, does so, not by a process of self-conscious acquiescence, but (like other animals) by unconsciously fulfilling the principles of his animal existence.

If one casts Rousseau's conception of freedom in negative terms, one can discern a continuity between natural liberty or independence and political liberty; if a man is free, either naturally or politically, he is not subject to the will of another. But as soon as Rousseau's libertarian theory is viewed in positive terms, the profound difference between the natural and the political conditions emerges. Natural liberty is simply the result of the absence of any enduring relationships with other creatures; political liberty is the product of voluntary submission to rules that one has helped to make. Although it may be that rights of some sort exist in the state of nature and are grounded in the natural man's primitive sense of 'pitié', or in the combination of 'pitié' and 'amour de soi', nevertheless, because of Rousseau's belief that an individual's moral and intellectual faculties can develop only in society, it seems clear that 'natural rights', if there are such things, can be rationally comprehended only by 'l'homme civilisé'; there may be a moral order immanent in the universe, and rights may perhaps apply to 'l'homme Sauvage', to the beasts of the field and the birds of the air, but, if so, these creatures know nothing of them. On this reading, this is so not necessarily because the rights have any logical relation to the social order, but because it is only in such an order that man can develop the character necessary to perceive them. This is a far cry from the usual natural-right view.

It is a commonplace of modern criticism that Rousseau, more than any other eighteenth-century writer, took seriously Pascal's dictum that 'le coeur a ses raisons que la raison ne connaît point',[50] and, indeed, much of Rousseau's effort is aimed at combating what he believed to be the excessive rationalism of the era. For Rousseau, great wisdom is not necessary for the good life; a virtuous existence is much more likely to be achieved if one's natural propensities are developed and reinforced by membership of a traditional social order. In the first *Discours* Rousseau speaks of 'l'heureuse ignorance où la sagesse éternelle nous avoit placés'.[51] In his observations on this work, he rejects the suggestion that 'il est bon de connoître le mal pour apprendre à le fuir', and that 'on ne peut s'assurer de sa vertu qu'après l'avoir mise à l'épreuve' :

Il n'est pas certain que pour apprendre à bien faire, on soit obligé de sçavoir en combien de maniéres on peut faire le mal. Nous avons un guide intérieur, bien plus infallible que tous les livres, et qui ne nous abandonne jamais dans le besoin.[52]

And into the mouth of the Savoyard curate, Rousseau puts the words :

Trop souvent la raison nous trompe, nous n'avons que trop acquis le droit de la récuser; mais la conscience ne trompe jamais; elle est le vrai guide de l'homme; elle est à l'âme ce que l'instinct est au corps.[53]

These are not the sentiments of a natural-right theorist.[54] Rousseau was as aware as Burke that man's reason could be a corrosive and destructive, as well as a creative, force in human life. Both realized that in practical life the satisfaction of men's interests and desires was more important than the convincing of their intellects. Rousseau, unlike his natural-right contemporaries, questions the reliability of the individual's rational faculty and seriously restricts its field of operation.

It would seem fair to say that Rousseau was somewhat more inclined than Burke formally to carry on his intellectual activity within the frontiers of the natural-right school, and to employ some of its major concepts (especially at the outset of his career), but what also appears to be true is Vaughan's remark that 'at least on the more speculative side of the matter, his [Burke's] criticism of the individualists is neither so complete, nor so deep-reaching as that of Rousseau'.[55] By 'individualists' Vaughan meant exponents of what he regards as an 'excessive' individualism, or something closely akin to what we have called the school of natural rights.

Perhaps it is possible to discern in Rousseau's writings a gradual movement away from this mode of thinking in the course of his career. He began by accepting somewhat uncritically many of the popular political ideas of his time (the *Discours sur l'inégalité* has a number of incompatible strains of thought in it), but slowly came to realize that these tended to obscure rather than to reflect accurately his genuine beliefs, and thus sought (not with complete success) to elaborate new and more suitable concepts. If one cannot disengage Rousseau entirely from the natural-right school, neither can one be satisfied with an interpretation that situates him firmly within its confines.

III   Rousseau and Burke, and the Empiricist View of Human Nature

Having looked at the psychological ideas of what we have identified as the rationalist tradition of seventeenth- and eighteenth-century political writing, we must now examine the empiricist view of human nature. We turn away, therefore, from the natural-right school, and its organizing concepts of reason and nature, and direct our attention towards the less coherent empiricist approach, and its dominant ideas of will and artifice.

The relative diffusion and complexity of this approach, when it is compared with the rationalist mode of political thinking, is suggested by the fact that there is no single school of thought, comparable to the rationalist school of natural rights, which typifies this tradition in the early modern period. The school of natural rights would seem to constitute a fairly coherent early-modern political expression of the ancient rationalist tradition, but there is no single place where we can look for the doctrines of political empiricism. Yet Francis Bacon, Thomas Hobbes, the political arithmeticians Sir William Petty and John Collins, Locke of the *Human Understanding* and his follower, Condillac, David Hume, Helvétius, Holbach and Jeremy Bentham – all these men, despite wide variations in ability and style of discourse, provide ample evidence in their writings of an empiricist approach. These men, and many of their contemporaries, can be seen to share certain assumptions about man and political life, and about the character and reliability of planned human activity, and it is primarily these common features of their thought to which we must attend.

Analysis is complicated by two factors. Firstly, it is quite common for a writer to have a foot in both the rationalist and the empiricist camps; he may speak, for example, of man's inherent natural rights, and at the same time profess to believe in the sensationalist psychological theories which were so popular during the period. It is possible, as we have seen, to interpret John Locke in this light. Secondly, during most of the Enlightenment the practical consequences and the demands for reform of the two sets of political attitudes coincided. Kingsley Martin makes this point in connection with utilitarian and natural-law thinking: '... utility and natural law agreed because they were weapons against the same evil ... For the time being ... the two great trends of Liberal thought were in practical agreement.'[56]

There was, during the seventeenth century, a growing interest in the application of science to the natural world. The Royal Society was not formally founded until 1660, and the Académie Royale des Sciences came into being six years later, but groups of scientists in England and on the Continent met regularly to discuss their work during most of the seventeenth century.[57] With the publication of Newton's discoveries in 1687 the authority of the scientific method was assured. Newton's work caused a stir which was felt far beyond the borders of natural science, and men of letters began to feel that the way to gain reliable information about man and society was by the application of scientific techniques to social phenomena. In the preface to *De L'Esprit*, Helvétius writes : 'J'ai cru qu'on devoit traiter la morale comme toutes les autres sciences, et faire une morale comme une physique expérimentale.'[58] Perhaps in part because of the nature of Newton's research, physics (rather than, say, biology) became the model of the early social scientists, and the machine, rather than the plant or the animal, came to be, for those under the influence of Newton, the more popular social analogy.[59] The bent of these scientific writers was thoroughly practical; it has been suggested, for example, that the conditions for the emergence of the first social science, economics, were laid in England towards the end of the seventeenth century in the attempt of practical men to convince their contemporaries that their promotion of certain economic policies was not selfish, but disinterested.[60] At any rate, the fascination with natural science and the attempt to discover a reliable and neutral technique of social research was a characteristic part of the empiricist approach during this period.[61]

Earlier we drew a distinction between 'methodological' and 'epistemological' empiricism in political thinking, and noted that Hobbes falls into the latter category. Fascinated with the procedures of mathematical demonstration, and captivated by their certainty and explanatory 'reach', Hobbes attempted to create a political science with the same virtues. Although he founded no school, his grand conception of man and civil society presents us with not the least vigorous, and certainly the most coherent exposition of epistemological empiricism in early-modern political philosophy. For Hobbes, the world is a place of perpetual movement and man is a creature of sense; civil society is the product of human artifice, and law (which is the command of the sovereign authority) is the maker of justice, not justice the maker of law. This last point places him in direct contradiction to the classical natural-law view. Hobbes's right of nature, the right of man to everything, even to another's body, is not a moral right, as is a right under natural law. Hobbesian natural right is not part of a moral order, but a symbol of the *absence* of a moral order. In the century and a half which followed the publication of *Leviathan*, Hobbes lay like a brooding spirit behind much of European political thinking. Few writers liked him, and few admitted a debt, yet those who ventured on to the slippery slopes of political speculation seemed always to have to take account of him, even if it was only to reject what was taken to be a mean view of human beings and a repressive theory of the state. Michael Oakeshott has written that 'against Hobbes, Filmer defended servitude, Harrington liberty, Clarendon the church, Locke the Englishman, Rousseau mankind, and Butler the Deity.'[62] It seemed frequently that an unacknowledged, and often unconscious debt was owed to Hobbes by many of his intellectual opponents.[63] Condillac, after referring to Aristotle's psychological theory, asserts that 'immédiatement après Aristote vient Locke; car il ne faut pas compter les autres philosophes qui on écrit sur le même sujet',[64] thus only revealing an ignorance of who one of his intellectual ancestors really was.

C*

As for Locke, Condillac's reverence for him is shared by most eighteenth-century men of letters. His psychological writings enjoyed a tremendous vogue, and were of great significance in shaping the particular character of early-modern empiricism. Peter Laslett says of him :

he twisted his fingers round the haft of English intellectual life and got so firm a grasp that it pointed at last in the direction which he had chosen. It was a philosophical reputation which he enjoyed, and it was because of the key position of philosophy that his intellectual domination was possible. Everything else which he wrote was important because he, Locke of the *Human Understanding*, had written it.[65]

In that famous essay Locke takes note of the fact 'it is a received doctrine, that men have native ideas, and original characters, stamped upon their minds in their very first being'.[66] But, he says, it is rather the case that all ideas come from sense experience :

Let us . . . suppose the mind to be, as we say, white paper, void of all characters, without any ideas: How comes it to be furnished? Whence comes it by that vast store which the busy and boundless fancy of man has painted on it with an almost endless variety? Whence has it all the *materials* of reason and knowledge? To this I answer, in one word, from *experience*.[67]

There is in experience a first- and second-order mental activity : sensation, or that which is concerned with the impressions of 'external sensible objects'; and reflection, that which is concerned with 'the internal operations of our minds perceived and reflected on by ourselves'. But there are no innate ideas in the mind of man.

Locke twisted his fingers not only round the haft of English intellectual life, but round that of Europe as well. Sabine has written that Cartesianism in France was 'deliberately supplanted by the philosophy of Locke and the science of Newton' :[68]

With the residence of Voltaire in England between 1726 and 1729, and of Montesquieu ten years later, the philosophy of Locke became the foundation of French enlightenment, and the admiration of English government became the keynote of French liberalism.

In an admiring essay on John Locke in his *Lettres philosophiques*, Voltaire speaks of 'notre Descartes, né pour découvrir les erreurs de l'antiquité, mais pour y substituer les siennes'.[69] In addition to this piece on Locke, a number of letters on Newton, and a good many more on English life and manners, Voltaire devotes one to

Francis Bacon whom he calls 'le père de la philosophie experimentale'.[70] Such writing as this went far towards popularizing on the Continent the work of the three famous Englishmen, Bacon, Newton and Locke. When Jeremy Bentham, in elaborating his utilitarian doctrines later in the eighteenth century, found inspiration in the writings of Helvétius, he was placing himself in debt to a French system of ideas which owed a great deal in its turn to seventeenth-century England.

Empiricist political thinkers in the late seventeenth and eighteenth centuries rejected the doctrine of a transcendental natural law, in part because of their general refusal to accept any notion which did not have a concrete referent in empirical reality. Bentham represents the hard-headed, practical spirit of many such thinkers when he dismisses 'natural and imprescriptible rights' contemptuously as 'nonsense upon stilts'. Their disinclination for metaphysics was matched by a lively interest in psychological and social analysis. In his systematic rejection of the 'chimères' of the priest and the metaphysician, Holbach, for example, reveals both the empiricist's antipathy to transcendental speculation (and hence, to the traditional conception of natural law as a divine moral rule), and also his characteristic interest in the things of this world. Of man he writes :

c'est en vain que son esprit veut s'élancer au delà des bornes du monde visible, il est toujours forcé d'y rentrer. Pour un être formé par la nature et circonscrit par elle, il n'existe rien au delà du grand tout dont il fait partie et dont il éprouve les influences; les êtres que l'on suppose au dessus de la nature ou distingués d'elle-même seront toujours des chimères.[71]

If such thinkers did not accept the view that there is a divine plan immanent in the universe which is discernible as such by man, neither did they entertain the opinion that man himself possesses an innate moral sense pointing out the path of justice. What they observed were certain neutral principles of behaviour which men invariably (or almost always) followed. When they introduce moral language into a political or psychological argument, it can often be seen to involve placing *ex post facto* labels on previously observed tendencies or behavioural patterns. Hobbes reckoned he understood the nature of man and the principles of his operation, and he proceeded to describe as man's 'natural right' the freedom to do what that nature required, i.e. to do *anything* necessary to maintain

motion and avoid death.[72] In the following century Helvétius defined as 'virtuous', 'vicious' or 'permissible' those actions which are
helpful, harmful or of no consequence to the public weal.[73]

There is no room for mystery or complexity in this view of man;
the principles governing his actions are generally understood to be
few and straightforward. Even to speak of 'principles' would seem
to go beyond the more rigorous of the seventeenth- and eighteenth-
century empiricists. Holbach, one of the most uncompromising of
writers, dissolves the common 'active' conception of instinct into a
simple response of the animal (including the human animal) to some
stimulus : 'Ce que l'on nomme l'*instinct* en physique n'est que l'effet
de quelque besoin du corps, de quelque attraction ou répulsion
dans les hommes ou dans les animaux.'[74] Instinct, instead of being
an active, internal drive, is here simply what a creature does when it
is hungry or thirsty; it is a name given to certain observed regular-
ities of behaviour. Holbach writes this in a chapter of the *Système
de la nature* entitled : 'Notre âme ne tire point ses idées d'elle-
même. Il n'y a point d'idées innées.'

The early-modern empiricist saw man in the image of Condillac's
statue or John Locke's *tabula rasa*. Instead of a more or less coherent being living in a state of nature, he found, when he stripped
away all 'artificial' accretions, nothing but a cipher, a virtual
nonentity.[75] The statue comes gradually to life through the application of the sense impressions made on it by the world around it;
it is the characters which the outside world inscribes on the blank
sheet of paper which give the *tabula rasa* its sense and form, and,
in the course of time, produce a human being.

Two issues are particularly helpful in revealing the important
differences between the empiricist's view of human nature and that
of either Rousseau or Burke, namely, the conception of morality,
and the notion of the relationship between man and society. Both
the views of Burke and Rousseau and those of the empiricists
assumed an intimate link between man and the community in
which he lives, but the precise character of that link differed in a
number of important ways. There is, as we have seen, no place for
natural law in empiricist thought; indeed, there seems to be no
room for the traditional concepts of morality in such thinking.
Holbach writes :

On a visiblement abusé de la distinction que l'on a faite si souvent de l'homme *physique* et de l'homme *moral*. L'homme est un être purement physique; l'homme moral n'est que cet être physique considéré sous un certain point de vue. . . .[76]

Elsewhere he asserts that 'l'organe intérieur, que nous appellons *notre âme* est purement matériel'.[77]

In empiricist thought there is a notable secularization of ethics; the concept of right is separated from its transcendent source, and comes to be understood as an index of how people actually feel or think, or how they behave.[78]

John Plamenatz helps to clarify the distance between Rousseau and the empiricists when he specifies the different meanings which Rousseau and David Hume put upon the claim that men become moral in society :

Hume meant only that social experience teaches them what kinds of behaviour are beneficial or harmful, and that the habits of approval and disapproval which encourage or discourage this behaviour are acquired in society. . . . He always spoke of moral rules as if they were rules of efficiency. . . . Rousseau spoke of our being 'transformed' by society. . . . We are altogether different creatures for being social and moral; we pursue ends which it is inconceivable that we should pursue unless we were moral. The rules of morality are not mere rules of efficiency.[79]

As for Burke, it is not to be thought that a man who argues that – 'He who gave our nature to be perfected by our virtue, willed also the necessary means of its perfection – He willed therefore the state'[80] – would accept either the view that moral rules are rules of efficiency, or the view that the state is a contrivance with no other purpose than the fulfilling of human wants. The function of the state is much wider than the mere allocation of benefits; it is an instrument for the moral improvement of mankind, and it must ultimately be judged from that perspective. Rousseau and Burke, then, share a 'conception of men's radical psychological and moral interdependence'.[81] The two issues mentioned above – morality, and man's relationship to his community – are seen here to be intimately intertwined.

For the empiricist, society is not necessary for man's moral perfection (he does not think in these terms), but rather it is an instrument for fulfilling his needs and desires. Plamenatz comments that 'the utilitarians share with Hobbes a complete indifference to the notion of self-improvement as a thing desirable for its own sake'.[82] Empiricist man is inclined to use his fellows in order to achieve his own ends; it is the job of the legislator to arrange things so that the individual, in promoting his own interests, will also promote (or at least not hinder the promotion of) the interests of all the individuals composing the political order.[83]

Empiricist education is a means of inscribing socially acceptable characters on the *tabulae rasae* that make up the state. Rousseau's system of education, as described in *Émile*, is a very different thing, for it is a process which is designed to elicit the full expression of a person's potentialities at each stage of his development; it is a sort of Aristotelian unfolding, a progressive revelation of character. As Joan E. McDonald writes :

Unlike Helvétius, Rousseau accepted the influence of environment only as complementary to the innate potentialities of the individual. Therefore he did not sacrifice the essential nature of man to the possibility of perfection by regarding him as clay to be moulded by the educationist. . . . [84]

The main thing to be taken into account in educating the empiricist individual is his propensity to further his own interest, whereas the being Rousseau and Burke have in mind is a creature of great complexity, whose diverse qualities and needs must be understood and followed as far as possible in providing him with an education.[85] 'The nature of man is intricate; the objects of society are of the greatest possible complexity; and therefore no simple disposition or direction of power can be suitable either to man's nature, or to the quality of his affairs.'[86] Also, Burke's and Rousseau's scepticism with regard to the beneficial effects of increasing individual and social enlightenment sets them off not only from the natural-right school (as we have seen above), but also from the optimistic political empiricists of their time.

As far as the empiricist is concerned, man acts in his own interest.[87] There may be a conflict between, say, his short-term and his long-term interests, or between one pattern of satisfactions and another, but a man can be counted upon to act in his own best interest as he sees it. Neither Rousseau nor Burke accepts this as in itself an adequate explanation of human behaviour; self-interest is a vitally important factor, but it is by no means the only major principle in terms of which individuals act. Altruistic and genuinely public-spirited actions are possible, and can be encouraged when men live in the proper social conditions.

A passage from Alfred Cobban suggests the unity-in-opposition theme which we have been trying to establish in this section with regard to the attitudes of Rousseau and Burke to the empiricist theory of human nature :

Now to be in revolt against that century [the eighteenth] was essentially to be in revolt against a theory of the mind – that superficial psychology of sensations described above. It is in their revolt against the psychological school founded by Locke that Burke, Rousseau and Kant find a principle of union, and it would not be untrue to say that they were all three inspired less by the scientific weakness of this theory than by its inability to satisfy the eternal demand of the human spirit for a sense of reality.[88]

iv   Natural Law and the Theory of Human Nature

We have already[89] examined the attitudes and opinions which Edmund Burke and Jean-Jacques Rousseau held in respect of 'the school of natural rights', which represented what was undoubtedly the most popular mode of social thought in the eighteenth century. Here we shall not be concerned with the two writers' attitudes to any such particular historical embodiment of natural law, but with the general problem of the logical position of natural law in the thinking of Rousseau and Burke; we shall attempt to answer the question of whether either writer can be fairly said to hold a natural-law theory, and, if so, in what sense.

Until fairly recently, it has not been the practice of scholars to find a place for Edmund Burke in the classical tradition of natural law. One popular critical approach in Burke scholarship during most of the last century and a good part of this has taken him to be, in general, a utilitarian,[90] while another favourite (and sometimes related) interpretation of his thought has placed him very loosely in a conservative, historical school. If his work was sometimes admitted to contain natural-right language 'superficially resembling that of his antagonists' which could not easily be explained in terms of utilitarian or conservative, historical presuppositions these 'deviations' were generally accounted for by the fact that Burke was an unsystematic, popular writer who, often engaging in political controversy, simply used what weapons were at hand.[91]

As for Rousseau,[92] a widely held interpretation of his thought and influence has placed him solidly in the French school of natural rights, which in tone and emphasis is distinguishable from the old style of natural-law thought. Scholars who take this view associate Rousseau with the 'political' Locke, with the *philosophes*, and often with the radicals of the French Revolution as well. Another important school of opinion sees Rousseau (like Burke) as a 'precursor' of the nineteenth-century idealists. In this connection, C. E. Vaughan, for example, argues energetically that Rousseau rejected natural law root and branch. Neither interpretation leaves much room for classical natural law in Rousseau, and the second leaves little room for natural law in any form.

But recently there has been something of a shift in both Burke and Rousseau scholarship; critics have begun to draw attention to the natural-law features of each writer's thought. In 1958 Peter Stanlis published the first full-length study of Edmund Burke's use of natural-law concepts, and his book was followed nine years later by another on the same subject written by Burleigh T. Wilkins.[93] Probably the most outstanding natural-law reading of Rousseau has been that of Robert Derathé, whose influential book, *Jean-Jacques Rousseau et la science politique de son temps*, was published in 1950.[94] An instance of the importance with which this study has been regarded by other scholars in the field can be found in Alfred Cobban's complete revision of his study of Rousseau, concerning which he writes :

The need for such drastic alteration has arisen . . . partly as a result of more recent contributions to the study of Rousseau's political thought, particularly in the writings of Professor Roger [sic] Derathé, who has for the first time related Rousseau clearly, and I believe correctly, to his predecessors in the tradition of Natural Law.[95]

Cobban speaks of Derathé 'relating' Rousseau to his predecessors in the tradition of natural law. But it is the particular nature of the relation which must be examined here. Cobban clearly believes that it has been satisfactorily shown that Rousseau was not related to what Derathé calls the *jurisconsultes* simply by virtue of the fact that he had read them, but also because he accepted and employed a conception of natural law recognizably similar to theirs, albeit with some hesitation and with various modifications.[96] What is it that Derathé has in fact shown? In the first place, he has convincingly argued that Rousseau was steeped in the literature of the seventeenth- and early eighteenth-century natural lawyers, and that to appreciate the intellectual past in terms of which Rousseau operated it is necessary not only to consider the work of *les écrivains politiques* such as Hobbes and Locke, but to include as well the great natural-law treatises of Grotius, Pufendorf and Burlamaqui, the critical translations of Barbeyrac, and the theory of sovereignty in Althusius's *Politica*. Derathé says that his aim is to show 'que la doctrine politique de Rousseau est issue d'une réflexion sur les théories soutenues par les penseurs qui se rattachent à ce qu'on a appelé l'*Ecole du droit de la nature et des gens*'.[97] To do this he must demonstrate, as he has done, that Rousseau was in fact familiar with the work of this school and that his political thinking was carried on (at least in part) with this school's doctrines in mind; but he need not maintain that Rousseau was himself a member of that school, and that he accepted their natural-law theories, for his political doctrine could issue out of 'une réflexion sur les théories' even if he was attacking and rejecting them.

Nevertheless, Derathé has a second objective in mind, and that is to find a place for natural law in the writings of Rousseau, or, to put it in other words, to make sense of the numerous passages in Rousseau's writings which assert or seem to imply the existence of a law of nature, by reading them as part of a fairly coherent natural-law theory. In making his case, Derathé restricts himself in the main to Rousseau's psychological and social theory, leaving aside his explicitly political discourse. This is no doubt because, as he himself candidly admits, he is unable to relate Rousseau's theory of the general will to his theory of natural law and individual conscience. He writes :

Chez Rousseau, il y a deux autorités morales auxquelles le citoyen doit se référer pour diriger sa conduite: la volonté générale et la conscience. L'une et l'autre sont 'une règle de justice'.

Ce sont là deux courants de pensée qui suivent chacun leur route, sans jamais se rencontrer. Rousseau aboutit à des conclusions différentes selon qu'il raisonne en politique ou pense en moraliste.[98]

It is acknowledged by Derathé, then, that Rousseau's political thought poses a basic difficulty for a natural-law interpretation of his writings; in Derathé's view, it is when Rousseau 'pense en moraliste' that his adherence to natural law can be substantiated –

hence Derathé's concentration (and ours) on that aspect of Rousseau.

Very briefly, his argument is as follows. Rousseau does not give up the idea of natural law, but in his writings it is placed on a different footing which is more consistent with the rest of his psychological thought. His predecessors in the 'école du droit de la nature' connected the law of nature inextricably with human reason. Rousseau broke this connection, asserting that reason and natural law were related in civil society, but that this law was seated upon another foundation in the state of nature : 'Rousseau est amené à faire une distinction entre le droit naturel primitif, antérieur à la raison et le droit naturel rétabli par la raison.'[99] There are two types of natural law (or, alternatively, two points of view from which natural law may be regarded); there is the 'droit naturel proprement dit', and the 'droit naturel raisonné', the first relating to the state of nature and the second not appearing until the establishment of civil society.[100] The first is founded on the 'instinct de conservation et pitié', and it is a principle in which the animals themselves participate 'en leur qualité d'être sensibles'.[101] As Derathé states that this primitive 'droit naturel' is nothing but another name for 'la bonté naturelle de l'homme',[102] one may perhaps assume that on Derathé's reading of Rousseau other animals possess this quality of natural goodness as well, in the same sense that primitive man does. The second sort is, of course, of exclusively human application, civilized man being the only creature with an active rational capacity.

It must be admitted that this is a very ingenious interpretation, and as one can expect of Derathé, it is very well supported by passages from Rousseau texts. It has the virtue of fitting easily into Rousseau's basic revision of the state of nature in which he rejects the notion of natural sociability, and reduces the constitution of natural man to a few active basic propensities, and a number of latent potentialities. Acording to Derathé, Rousseau's man is 'raisonnable par nature', but 'il ne possède naturellement la raison qu' "en puissance" '; in a natural state, 'il n'a besoin d'autre guide que l'instinct.'[103] The passage from the natural to the social order, in which man develops his rational capacity and comes to have a moral sense, is consistent with this interpretation.[104] 'En passant de l'état de nature à l'état civil, le droit naturel subit la même métamorphose que l'homme auquel il s'applique.'[105] Also, Derathé claims that it provides a moral sanction for the convention instituting society; in his words : 'Rousseau n'aurait pu d'ailleurs rejeter l'idée de loi naturelle sans priver du même coup le contrat social de toute *sanction morale.*'[106] But there are certain serious problems involved in this approach.

Perhaps the principle shortcoming can be uncovered by noticing the character of these 'deux espèces de droit naturel'. Natural law 'dans l'état de nature ... n'était qu'instinct et bonté, dans l'état civil il devient justice et raison.'[107] The gulf between these two things is so profound that it is hard to see why both should be called by the same name, why both should be styled 'droit naturel'. The rational variety is clearly of a moral character, but the other is rooted in instinct and it would seem to be devoid of any moral quality; it looks like another name for natural necessity, and certainly not a description of any mode of behaviour requiring the faculty of ethical choice. Besides, the existence of an active rational capacity is a presupposition of all moral decisions, and Derathé has said that reason, though innate, exists only 'en puissance' in natural man – he does not have the use of it.

This brings up a second difficulty. Derathé appears to reproduce a confusion which is found in Rousseau's thought. He asserts that Rousseau's natural man has need of no guide but instinct (though he has an innate but dormant rational faculty), and quotes such passages as, 'l'Homme Sauvage, livré par la Nature au seul instinct', 'privé de toute sorte de lumiéres',[108] in support of this. But one need only continue the first quotation above from the *Discours sur l'inégalité* in order to point up an apparent confusion in Rousseau's thought, a confusion which is perpetuated in the writing of Derathé. Rousseau writes :

L'Homme Sauvage, livré par la Nature au seul instinct, ou plûtôt dédommagé de celui qui lui manque peut-être, par des facultés capables d'y suppléer d'abord, et de l'élever ensuite fort au-dessus de celle là, commencera donc par les fonctions purement animales.[109]

Rousseau first states roundly man's dependence on instinct alone in the state of nature, and immediately qualifies, or rather replaces, this view with a picture of man compensated for the fact that he does not have instinct by the possession of faculties which at first act in instinct's stead, and afterwards raise him far above the realm of instinct. Is natural man a creature of instinct or is he not?

73

In an earlier passage in the *Discours sur l'inégalité* which is reminiscent of Locke and Condillac, Rousseau argues that there is only a difference of degree between the thinking ability of men and that of animals,[110] and he goes on to say : 'Ce n'est donc pas tant l'entendement qui fait parmi les animaux la distinction spécifique de l'homme que sa qualité d'agent libre.'[111] Man is unique in the animal kingdom by virtue of the fact that he is a free agent. A pigeon will starve to death beside a dish of meat, and a cat by a heap of fruit or grain, because neither is capable of surmounting its natural propensities, but a man is, in some sense, able to choose his instincts : 'La Nature commande à tout animal, et la Bête obéit. L'homme éprouve la même impression, mais il se reconnoît libre d'acquiescer, ou de resister.'[112] Rousseau even goes so far as to say that it is particularly in man's consciousness of his liberty to choose in circumstances in which the animal must obey that his soul's spirituality is displayed.[113]

Now, this mixing together of volition and instinct is the source of much confusion in Rousseau's thought and in the commentaries of scholars, and the matter seems never to have been satisfactorily resolved by Rousseau. Both men and animals reason, he says, the former more effectively than the latter, but a man has the capacity of free choice whereas an animal 'choisit ou rejette par instinct'. But 'instinct', if it is to mean anything, would seem to involve the notion of subjection to some necessary mode of behaviour; it would be eccentric to speak of a bird 'choosing' instinctively not to eat meat, for surely the important thing about this abstinence is that the creature does not recognize that it has any choice at all. The other side of the coin is that if man is provided with a capacity to choose freely, then it seems to be playing with words to say that the mode of behaviour which he is choosing to follow or reject is an 'instinct'. When Rousseau asserts that man, unlike animals, has a 'qualité d'agent libre', he is also unavoidably suggesting that man has a rational faculty which is in some important sense different from that of the animals.[114] Rousseau did not want to admit reason prior to society, but it is hard to accept his choice-of-instinct doctrine as a satisfactory means of resolving his problems.

In the light of this short discussion, there seem to be a number of ways of relating Rousseau's conception of natural law to his conception of human nature, none of them satisfactory. Firstly, the law of nature could be rooted in instinct or in the primitive rational capacity which man shares with the beasts, but this would reduce it to little more than a matter of reflex, animal response, and would strip it of any moral quality, even within society. Secondly, by resorting to what Rousseau does not say but what his ideas seem necessarily to entail, the 'loi de nature' could become a true 'loi de raison', and be founded upon the specifically human rational capacity which we must assume primitive man possesses *even in the state of nature.* This approach would clearly invest natural law with a moral character, but it would do so at the risk of implanting in natural man moral and intellectual capabilities which Rousseau clearly did not want to see put there (except, perhaps, 'en puissance'). Thirdly, there is Derathé's solution which is to ground natural law upon instinct in the state of nature and upon reason in the state of society. Apart from the fact that it is not clear why a non-moral rule of instinct should be called by the same name as a moral law of reason, this interpretation neglects the problems engendered by the confusion of volition and instinct, a confusion which, it has been argued here, is to be found unresolved in Rousseau's thought and which has been perpetuated in the Derathé approach. If it is said that man is governed by instinct alone in the state of nature (reason existing only 'en puissance'), and by reason in society, then there remains the difficulty of explaining the link between the natural and the social conditions, and between Derathé's instinctive and rational types of natural law.

Was Rousseau, then, a natural-law thinker?

At the close of the first of the *Lettres écrites de la montagne* Rousseau remarks upon the difficulty an author experiences in giving a systematic shape to the multitude of ideas which crowd his mind in the act of creation, and the problems encountered in assembling all the parts of a large plan into a coherent and satisfactory whole.[115] We know that he abandoned his *magnum opus, Institutions politiques,* because he felt unable to carry it to a successful conclusion. It is certain that when he came to consider the relations between sovereign states he would have had to cope with the *jurisconsulte* theories of international law, if only to reject them, and, in view of his concept of the general will and the closing lines of the *Social Contract,* perhaps it is not unfair to suggest that this may have been one of the problems he felt unable to clear up to his own satisfaction. As Derathé has recognized, there is an acute tension in

Rousseau's theory; Rousseau himself recognized that he was not good at putting all the pieces together. He seems at times to believe in natural law and he makes the most fulsome declarations of this belief, while on other occasions it is apparent that the law of nature has little or no role to play in his social thought.

It is impossible to be dogmatic about a matter as complex and as fraught with uncertainty as this, but on balance it seems fair to say that the idea of natural law does not have in any way a dominant position in Rousseau's social thought. Certainly Derathé's attempt to establish Rousseau as a natural-law theorist is unsuccessful.

Indeed, Derathé himself says, in describing Rousseau's debt to the *jurisconsultes* that 'il leur doit plus par ce qu'il rejette que par ce qu'il retient de leur enseignement',[116] and adds elsewhere in his book :

On sait que Rousseau s'est fait gloire de défendre en tout la vérité, mais il la défend presque toujours contre quelqu'un. C'est en ce sens qu'il reste le débiteur de ses adversaires, et des jurisconsultes en particulier.[117]

Rousseau was familiar with the doctrines of the prominent seventeenth- and eighteenth-century natural-law thinkers, and he certainly used their tools of political speculation ('état de nature, pacte social, souveraineté'),[118] but he was not by any stretch a *jurisconsulte* and his theory of natural law, if he had one, is so equivocal and obscure that it has never been satisfactorily specified.

In spite of the historical disagreement surrounding Burke's conception of natural law, his views appear at first sight to be clearer than those of Rousseau. This may in part be owing to the disarming effect of contemporary critical agreement in Burke scholarship. Until fairly recently, conventional opinion, advanced and supported by what have been rather disparagingly called 'Benthamite and positivist scholars',[119] has held Burke to be a conservative utilitarian and an opponent of natural law; contemporary scholars, however, have pretty generally adopted the view that Burke was a proponent of natural law and perhaps even something of an anti-utilitarian. Unlike Rousseauist criticism, which has been characterized by continuing fundamental disagreement and wildly conflicting interpretations ever since the eighteenth century, Burke scholarship has been marked by conflicting periods of critical opinion, within which periods there has been fairly wide-spread accord.[120]

One writer who has done much to provide a systematic understanding of Burke as an adherent of natural law is Peter Stanlis. The goal he sets himself is ambitious; he seeks to establish the thesis that 'far from being an enemy of Natural Law, Burke was one of the most eloquent and profound defenders of Natural Law morality and politics in Western civilization'.[121] He argues that Burke is in 'the great classical [natural-law] tradition of Aristotle and Cicero and the Scholastic tradition of St. Thomas Aquinas, Bracton, and Hooker',[122] and to support this view separates Burke's social theory from the conceptions of both the utilitarian school and what he calls the 'eighteenth-century "rights of man" aberration from tradition', exemplified in his opinion by the thought of Rousseau.[123] In describing the natural-right school as an 'aberration' in natural-law thinking, he reveals his commitment to the older tradition, and his belief that something went seriously wrong with the natural-right school.

In making a decisive break between traditional natural law and the school of natural rights, Stanlis relies on the general approach of Leo Strauss, and quotes the following passage from this scholar's book on Hobbes :

We must raise the . . . question, whether there is not a difference of principle between the modern and the traditional view of natural law. Such a difference does in fact exist. Traditional natural law is primarily and mainly an objective 'rule and measure', a binding order prior to, and independent of, the human will, while modern natural law is, or tends to be, primarily and mainly a series of 'rights', of subjective claims, originating in the human will.[124]

Stanlis characterizes this quotation as asking and answering 'the most crucial question concerning the fate of Natural Law in the last three centuries'. Burke, in his opinion, is to be located in the ancient, theological tradition of natural-law thought,[125] from which the natural-right school (represented, in his view, by Hobbes, Locke and Rousseau) is an unfortunate offspring.

Burleigh T. Wilkins also takes Burke to be a natural-law theorist, and in his book, *The Problem of Burke's Political Philosophy*, he attempts to 'make the natural law reading of Burke more acceptable to the scholarly community', by 'taking seriously the major objections to the natural law reading of Burke and by proposing solutions to some of the philosophical difficulties in Burke's thought'.[126] Apart from the consideration of certain test problems in Burke's writings, one of his major objectives is to call into question the validity of what he calls the general 'Strauss-Kirk-Stanlis way of rewriting the history of natural law'[127] which discerns a difference of principle between the traditional view of natural law and the seventeenth- and eighteenth-century school of natural rights, and in particular the interpretation which links Burke to the first and places him in opposition to the second.

He launches his assault at two points. First, he suggests that if one is going to insist upon the discontinuities between the traditional and modern views, it will ultimately prove necessary 'to carry this keenness for diversity back into the classical and Christian conceptions of natural law';[128] Stanlis in particular, argues Wilkins, seriously overstates the monolithic character of this complex and variegated tradition.[129] The second point of attack involves the rehabilitation of John Locke as a traditional natural-law theorist, and not merely a natural-right theorist, and the specific linking of Burke to Locke, and Locke to St Thomas Aquinas : 'I must ... express my preference for two older theses, one asserting the fundamental agreement between Locke and Aquinas where natural law is concerned, the other affirming that Burke's place in the history of political thought is within the Lockean tradition which he alters but does not destroy.'[130]

For present purposes the most pertinent thing to note about Wilkins's study is that, despite strong dissatisfaction with Stanlis's thesis on a number of points, it is in substantial agreement with him on the main issue; Wilkins and Stanlis see Burke's natural-law theory as in large measure (but not entirely) Thomist,[131] that is to say, as belonging to what we have described generally as the classical natural-law tradition.

It is evident that a persuasive case can be made for understanding Burke as a natural-law thinker. Studies of the contents of Burke's library and of the academic programme at Trinity College, Dublin, in the eighteenth century show conclusively that Burke was exposed to the writings of the major ancient and scholastic natural-law philosophers, with the curious exception of Aquinas himself.[132] And references to natural law appear throughout his writings, although it should also be noted that the passages in which the matter is most fully discussed are located in relatively minor works which until recently have not come in for a great deal of scholarly attention.[133]

The placing of Burke in a theological tradition of natural law makes sense in view of his profound religious belief and his trenchant criticism of the natural-right school. References to God, Providence, Omnipotence, Divine Majesty, First Cause, Supreme Judge and so forth are legion in his writings,[134] and leave no room for the suspicion that sometimes comes to mind in the case of Rousseau that his allusions to God are mere 'hat-doffing toward the Deity'[135] with little serious intent or with a restricted strategic purpose. When Burke speaks of natural law issuing from the rational nature of man, a reference to the Creator of the human frame is usually not far away.[136] The ambiguities in Rousseau's view of the relation between natural law and human reason have been noted above, but to the extent that Burke accepted and utilized the concept of natural law in his thinking he clearly took the traditional position, maintaining that it is rooted (by God) in the rational nature of man. In the following comment Wilkins would seem to sum up very well the character of Burke's natural-law belief. Regarding Burke's conception of original justice, Wilkins asks 'whether it is more proper to emphasize the origins of this justice in the Divine Will or to emphasize its harmony with our nature' :

It seems permissible to say, without glossing over the difficulties this involves, that for Burke the ultimate source of original justice is in the Creator and the intermediate source (which may be treated as ultimate in certain practical contexts) is the rational nature of man as created by God.[137]

At the same time this statement also provides a sample of the sort of problems one faces in attempting to come to grips with Burke's natural-law views. For what in fact is the conceptual link between God and man's nature? And what does it mean to say that the latter is 'ultimate' in certain situations? Surely it is ultimate only until a challenge in terms of God's purposes for man is launched; it can then be seen to be subordinate, for the Divine Will is and must always remain the court of final appeal.

These questions raise a more general one which has yet to be answered : given that Burke employs the concept of natural law in some fashion, to what extent is it a 'governing concept' in his thought and how is it to be reconciled with the other concepts which go to make up his social theory? In the absence of detailed argument showing how all the various elements of Burke's social theory can be placed within a single theoretical framework, it is difficult to resist the conclusion that many of the most distinctive features of the Burkean world view – his concepts of utility, expedience, prejudice, prescription, his notion of a distinct national tradition, his denial in at least one place of the possibility of making universally applicable moral and political statements, his acute sense of the radical diversity of human arrangements – that many of these features bespeak an attitude of mind quite alien to that of the typical natural-law thinker, and an understanding of politics and the moral life which is incompatible with the tradition to which Burke is said to adhere.

Much of the energy of those who propose a natural-law interpretation of Burke is expended in suggesting possible connections between one part of Burke's theory and another in a sort of historiographical equivalent to mathematical extrapolation; but everyone admits, I think, that this systematizing is not something in which Burke himself indulged much. He was, after all, much less of a philosopher than Rousseau, and it is therefore not always necessary (indeed, it would be in many cases thoroughly inappropriate) to press his arguments with the vigour with which it is fair to approach many of the arguments of Rousseau or of some other political philosopher. Burke nowhere provides us with a general theory of human nature;[138] his conception emerges in bits and pieces in the course of his writings. While one can, if one wishes, attempt to build up a coherent theory on the basis of the fragmentary statements in Burke's writings, there is no *prima facie* justification for asserting that the theory thus constructed is one which he actually held, or would accept. So his natural-law statements need not always be read as philosophical generalizations; it is frequently necessary to accept them without a too restless search for coherence at the level of first principles. Francis Canavan claims that Burke

did not carry his analysis all the way through to a systematic study of moral principles at their highest and most general level. . . . Burke clearly took the postulates of his moral theory from a natural-law doctrine. But he always approached the doctrine from below, so to speak, that is, from the discussion of a concrete political or legal question. He was therefore content to assume the principles of natural law and was little concerned with analysing and elaborating the theory of natural law as such.[139]

But if this is true, it is also the case that there is as a consequence an inevitable opacity in Burke's thought that bedevils critical discussion. Since Burke himself did not trouble to elucidate systematically his conception of human nature, morality and politics, a critic's attempt at a complete delineation of his world view and the way in which the diverse parts of his system relate to the whole must always remain to some extent conjectural.

All this being said, it is nevertheless apparent that at the level at which Burke can best be understood, he displays a consistency of belief which is not readily discerned in Rousseau. In a letter to Philip Francis, Burke's son, Richard, makes a revealing comment about his father's consistency :

... I must inform you ... that my father's opinions are never hastily adopted, and that even those ideas which have often appeared to me only the effects of momentary heat, or casual impression, I have afterwards found, beyond a possibility of doubt, to be the result of systematic meditation, perhaps of years; or else, if adopted on the spur of the occasion, yet formed upon the conclusions of long and philosophical experience, and supported by no trifling depth of thought. . . . Are you so little conversant with my father . . . as to . . . mistake the warmth of his manner for the heat of his mind?[140]

Burke's writings do exhibit an intellectual (but not an emotional) composure and harmony quite foreign to the work of Rousseau, which habitually contains statements which appear to be at one moment astonishing syntheses, and at the next, unhappy and unresolved paradoxes. Burke is all of a piece; as Morley says, he changed his front, but he never changed his ground.[141]

In summary, then, we may conclude that with respect to the logical position of the law of nature in their thinking, both Burke and Rousseau are equivocal, but for very different reasons. The distinction between Rousseau, the theoretician, and Burke, the practicing politician, is here as elsewhere of considerable importance. Rousseau was never able to get his ideas clear on the subject, though it was not for want of trying; Burke for his part did not choose to set out systematically the whole panoply of his social theory together with its underpinnings, although in the light of what his son says and what we know of his intellectual seriousness, he had in all likelihood established for himself a theoretical position which he found personally satisfactory. Rousseau, though he often employed the concept of natural law, cannot in the final analysis be considered a theorist in that tradition. However, the reader of

Burke receives the distinct impression that if Burke had articulated his views systematically (which he did not), natural law would have provided the foundation on which his philosophy rested; as it is, Burke is clearly not a *philosopher* of natural law, but he must, I think, be counted as one of its *adherents*.

v   Human Nature and the Historical Process

Both Burke and Rousseau had a profound sense of the central role which the historical process plays in the constitution of man, and we must now establish this fact and consider its relation to other aspects of their respective psychological theories. It can be satis-factorily demonstrated that both writers did hold, in fairly large measure, a conception of man as a creature of history; what is rather more difficult to specify, however, is the character of the relationship between this idea and some of their other opinions concerning the nature of man. Both of these issues will come in for some attention here.

In *Émile* Rousseau writes : 'il faut étudier la société par les hommes, et les hommes par la société : ceux qui voudront traiter séparément la politique et la morale n'entendront jamais rien à aucune des deux.'[142] In accordance with this dictum, we shall investigate the linkage between men and the social order in which they live. In particular, we shall be concerned to show that both Burke and Rousseau included as a constitutive element of human nature the operation of social relationships extended over time, that is to say, that their theories of man included the notion of a human community.[143]

Initially, one would be inclined to think that Edmund Burke had a much clearer idea of the role of history in shaping man than did Rousseau. Certainly Burke's vision of the past and his approach to social issues would lead one to expect this. Burke had in his bones the common-law lawyer's sense of the imperceptible 'self-adapta-tion' of institutions, a sense of what might be called 'glacial' political change, and, quite against the popular spirit of his time, he revered the Middle ages and the medieval institution of chivalry.[144] Unlike many of his contemporaries, he did not restrict himself to selecting only the personally congenial portions of the past, but was quite willing to accept *all* past events as having a place in the process of change which leads to the present.[145] In addition, he wrote some history,[146] and he often employed an historical method in his examination of current problems.[147] Rousseau, on the other hand, idealized classical antiquity and regarded the Greek city-states (especially Sparta) and the Roman republic more as models of perfection than as part of the European heritage. He wrote no history as such ('je cherche le droit et la raison et ne dispute pas des faits')[148] and only infrequently could one describe his consideration of problems as 'historical'.

However, if it is accurate to suggest that Burke is more firmly situated in the natural-law tradition than Rousseau, then it is no longer as readily apparent that his conception of man as a creature of history will prove on inspection to be stronger than Rousseau's. For we are not so concerned with their respective 'visions' of the past, as with the extent to which each grasped the notion that the historical process shapes and forms human beings and produces a 'second nature' fully as important and as 'natural' as the first. It is with their explanatory insight that we are concerned here, not with their historical knowledge as such, nor with their images of the past.

There is a passage in the *Reflections* where Burke speaks of 'that wonderful structure, Man; whose prerogative it is, to be in a great degree a creature of his own making'.[149] This statement is followed in the next few pages, however, by statements that appear to take us a long way from the notion of man as self-creator; Burke asserts that political power is a 'holy function' and that those who exercise it are accountable to God,[150] and adds that neither the will of citizens nor that of kings is the standard of right and wrong, but that the legitimizing standard is found in an 'external, immutable law, in which will and reason are the same'. The notion in these passages is that of a Providence which imposes its will upon the world, and to which men are accountable in the performance of their daily affairs.

Some indication is given as to how Burke attempts to reconcile these two ideas of man as self-creator and man as creature of the Creator in a passage which lies nearby, and which has already been noted in another connection. Burke characterizes civil society as that state without which 'man could not by any possibility arrive at the perfection of which his nature is capable, nor even make a remote or faint approach to it.'[151] He goes on to say that God 'who gave our nature to be perfected by our virtue, willed also the necessary means of its perfection – He willed therefore the State'. For our purposes, the important thought here is that of man's virtue perfecting his God-given nature. Burke understands the nature of man, not as a fixed state, but as a process; he refuses to equate the natural with the primitive ('art is man's nature'), associating it instead with a course of development which is consistent with God's plan: 'We are as much, at least, in a state of nature in formed manhood, as in immature and helpless infancy.'[152] 'Nature is never more truly herself than in her grandest forms.'[153] There is a proper mode of human development (entailing society) which man, because of his rational character[154] is able to recognize, and which, because of his moral character, he may choose to follow or not.[155]

Sir Ernest Barker, in describing Aristotle's conception of the law of nature, notes various distinguishable senses in which Aristotle used the word 'natural', and writes:

If we take them all into consideration, we shall see that a 'natural law' will not merely mean a law which is co-extensive with man, or universal: it will also mean a law which has grown concurrently with man, and is, in a sense, evolutionary – yet not so evolutionary but that man's 'art' has co-operated in its growth. The antithesis between natural and conventional, which is only a prima facie antithesis, will disappear; and we shall have a version of an historically developed law which has both a positive quality and a root in the nature of man.[156]

It is a conception of man and nature similar to that which Barker attributes to Aristotle that Burke possesses. In the same part of the *Reflections* as that from which we quoted above, Burke gives his famous description of the social contract as an historical partnership of men and at the same time as a clause in the 'great primaeval contract of eternal society'.[157] God and history are again joined together as they are so often in Burke's writings.

This approach allows Burke to have it both ways, so to speak. On the one hand, he can hold the view that God not only created the world, but that he attends to its general operation, sometimes intervening in the most direct manner in particular historical events.[158] On the other hand, he is able to speak of man being 'in a great degree a creature of his own making'. Human nature (although it can be taken as constant for practical purposes) does indeed change in the course of time, and man himself can discern this in the long run; what does not change is the principle of man's proper development, which may be known in a fragmentary fashion by men, but which is entirely comprehended only by God.[159] There can be both radical historical diversity among the peoples of the world and a universal moral order. Clearly, this doctrine is not without its conceptual difficulties, but Burke did not feel it necessary to pursue them, and it can be substantiated that he did in fact hold these two views.

Burke asserts repeatedly that a government's primary task is to acquaint itself with the wishes and to further the interests of its people, but he is just as emphatic in insisting that the rules in terms of which a government should operate cannot be laid down by the government (or the people) itself. The people can be wrong; in Rousseau's words, 'de lui-même le peuple veut toujours le bien, mais de lui-même il ne le voit pas toujours'.[160] It is the task of government to uphold the true interest of its constituents, even against their transient wishes. Burke says to the Bristol electors (1780):

I . . . maintained your interest, against your opinions, with a constancy that became me. . . . I am to look, indeed, to your opinions; but to such opinions as you and I *must* have five years hence.[161]

It is the duty of the legislator to ensure that public policy satisfies the nature and needs of the people on the one hand, and the eternal demands of right on the other.

In 'just prejudice' one can, according to Burke, see evidence that these two perennial demands have been satisfied in the past. Burkean prejudice is wisdom clothed in circumstance; it 'renders a man's virtue his habit'.[162] Just prejudice weds the universal to the particular, and answers the needs of man and the demands of God. Although some critics see in Burke's ideas of prejudice, prescription and tradition evidence of historicism, an historicist interpretation does not produce a full understanding of his views. In the case before us, inclusion of the word 'just' in the phrase 'just prejudice' gives the show away, by importing some external (and undefined) criterion of right into the evaluation.

There is a remarkable passage in Burke's speech to the Bristol electors in which he speculates that even God himself may be subordinate to the eternal rules of justice:

When we know, that the opinions of even the greatest multitudes are the standard of rectitude, I shall think myself obliged to make those opinions the masters of my conscience. But if it may be doubted whether Omnipotence itself is competent to alter the essential constitution of right and wrong, sure I am, that such *things*, as they and I, are possessed of no such power.[163]

There is, then, this 'diversified but connected fabric of universal justice ... well cramped and bolted together in all parts',[164] but there is also a wealth of human variety on the face of the earth which is the product of history. In Burke's remarks below about the methods of the legislators of old can be seen his opinions regarding both the extent of human diversity (different groups of men constitute, as it were, so many different species of animals), and the means by which this diversity grew up (through the circumstances of civil life) : the legislators, he says,

had to do with men, and they were obliged to study human nature. They had to do with citizens, and they were obliged to study the effects of those habits which are communicated by the circumstances of civil life. They were sensible that the operation of this second nature on the first produced a new combination; and thence arose many diversities among men, according to their birth, their education, their professions, the periods of their lives, their residence in towns or in the country, their several ways of acquiring and of fixing property, and according to the quality of the property itself, all which rendered them as it were so many different species of animals.[165]

The questions to ask in evaluating any theory about man are : 'Does it suit his nature in general? – does it suit his nature as modified by his habits?'[166] Burke does not shrink from speaking of human nature in general; 'human nature' does not strike him as 'an unmanageable or embarrassingly vague concept'.[167] But it is a concept which is appropriate to one type of speculation only, and which must in fact be supplemented with 'nature modified by habit' if a coherent picture of man is to be developed, and particularly if the speculation is to have a practical application.

From a study of his speeches on India, it is clear that Burke believes not only that the ultimate standard of morality is the same in England and on the Indian subcontinent, but also that at bottom Englishmen and Indians are constituted upon the same principles, if only in the sense that they are equally subject to the ordinances of universal justice.[168] Within this very general framework, however, the gulf between the two peoples is enormous, and it is only through a most careful study of Indian manners and social institutions that a European such as Burke can comprehend how they and their society function. As Burke says : 'We know what the empire of opinion is in human nature. I had almost said that the law of opinion was human nature itself.'[169] He asserts that Warren Hastings ought to have governed 'on British principles', but 'not by British forms' :

God forbid; for, if ever there was a case in which the letter kills and the spirit gives life, it would be an attempt to introduce British forms and the substance of despotic principles together into any country.[170]

Hastings should have ruled India with that spirit of equity, justice, protection and lenity which characterizes legitimate British political authority, but the spirit should have been expressed through political institutions appropriate to the country and the people.

Man in a great measure makes himself, then, but, if he is not to deform or distort his nature as time passes, he must make himself virtuously, he must with the use of his reason grasp God's plan for man, and of his own free will subordinate himself to that divine course of development. He is *in* history, subject to its upheavals and vicissitudes, and he must, in whatever particular set of circumstances he finds himself, perfect as far as possible his nature by the exercise of his reason and virtue.

Rousseau, at one point in the *Contrat social*, himself asks one of the questions which lies behind this section of our study : 'Les hommes ont-ils changé de nature?'[171] This query arises in connection with the issue of whether states in his day are capable of holding universal popular assemblies as they have done in the past ('il y a deux mille ans'). His reply on this occasion is indirect; he does not answer yes or no, but contents himself with saying : 'Les bornes du possible dans les choses morales sont moins étroites que nous ne pensons'; a response of implicit and perhaps qualified assent.

However, on the basis of what he wrote on many occasions elsewhere he need not have been so hesitant in his reply, for a basic feature of his social thought was that the nature of man did indeed change with the passing of time, and change very radically at that. The *Contrat* itself, in a much-quoted passage, asserts that the journey from natural to civil society transforms man from 'un animal stupide et borné' into 'un être intelligent et un homme'.[172] In the chapter on the law-giver (II, vii) Rousseau again discusses the transformation of human nature. There he writes :

Celui qui ose entreprendre d'instituer un peuple doit se sentir en état de changer, pour ainsi dire, la nature humaine; de transformer chaque individu . . . ; d'altérer la constitution de l'homme pour la renforcer. . . .[173]

In the Geneva version of the *Contrat*, the equivalent passage for the phrase beginning 'd'altérer' above was : 'Il faut . . . qu'il *mutile* en quelque sorte la constitution de l'homme pour la renforcer',[174] underlining even more vigorously the full extent of the change.

But it is not necessary to depend solely upon the *Contrat social* for evidence of Rousseau's dynamic conception of man. Unlike Burke, Rousseau wrote two works dealing fairly systematically with human nature.[175] In *Émile*, Rousseau speculates about the sort of education appropriate to an individual who is to become a member of society.[176] In the *Discours sur l'inégalité*, he makes a theoretical statement about the changes which must be thought to have taken place in the nature of the human species if man ever existed in a solitary condition and moved from it into a social order.[177] His conception of human nature can be found in its most coherent and self-conscious form in these two-treatises.

Rousseau is, on the whole, quite clear about what he is doing in *Émile*. He says that in order to ensure that his doctrine and proposals are consistent with the nature of man, he has created an imaginary pupil whose development he will chart and whose nature will reveal any gaps lying between his educational theorizing and what is actually practicable.[178] The boy, Émile, is a heuristic device, rather than the image of a real person; he does not exist, nor does anyone quite like him.[179] Mme de Staël's description of *La Nouvelle Héloise* is equally applicable to *Émile* : 'une grande idée morale mise en action et rendue dramatique'.[180] The tutor guides Émile from infancy to young adulthood, and the general approach to his education is clear. In the first pages of the book Rousseau states that we receive education from three major sources : from nature (the inner growth of our organs and faculties), from men (the use we learn to make of this natural growth), and from things (our experience of our surroundings). The first of these is wholly outside human control, the third, partly without and partly within, and the second (to do with the use we make of man's natural growth) is the only source over which we can exercise extensive control. Rousseau asserts that the goal of education is the goal of nature :

Puisque le concours des trois éducations est nécessaire à leur perfection, c'est sur celle à laquelle nous ne pouvons rien qu'il faut diriger les deux autres.[181]

But, he says, the word 'nature' may have too vague a meaning, so it is important to try to define it :

La nature, nous dit-on, n'est que l'habitude. Que signifie cela? N'y a-t-il pas des habitudes qu'on ne contracte que par force, et qui n'étouffent jamais la nature? Telle est, par exemple, l'habitude des plantes dont on gêne la direction verticale. La plante mise en liberté garde l'inclinaison qu'on l'a forcée à prendre; mais la sève n'a point changé pour cela sa direction primitive; et, si la plante continue à végéter, son prolongement redevient vertical. Il en est de même des inclinations des hommes. Tant qu'on reste dans le même état, on peut garder celles qui résultent de l'habitude, et qui nous sont le moins naturelles; mais sitôt que la situation change, l'habitude cesse et le naturel revient.[182]

Proper education, then, entails the provision of an environment which is, as far as possible, appropriate to each stage of a man's growth, and the employment and exercise of the human organs and faculties in a manner which is consistent with their development at any given period in a man's life. There is a natural process of growth in human life which it is not in the power of men to staunch, but only to distort or to foster. Rousseau's well-known insistence upon allowing human beings to be children before they are men[183] arises out of his belief that there is a condition which is appropriate to each stage of a person's life, and distinct needs which must be satisfied at each step of the way if the full realization of human potential is to be achieved. We are not, and ought not to be, in infancy what we are in our youth, nor in young adulthood what we are in old age; otherwise 'nous aurons de jeunes docteurs et de vieux enfants. L'enfance a des manières de voir, de penser, de sentir, qui lui sont propres; rien n'est moins sensé que d'y vouloir substituer les nôtres . . .'.[184] The task of human, as opposed to natural, education is to discover and follow the natural growth of man, and to discover and foster the particular bent of the individual being educated.[185] In the following quotation, Rousseau demonstrates how far his conception in *Émile* is from the view so often attributed to him :

On me dira que je sors de la nature; je n'en crois rien. Elle choisit ses instruments, et les règle, non sur l'opinion, mais sur besoin. Or, les besoins changent selon la situation des hommes. Il y a bien de la différénce entre l'homme naturel vivant dans l'état de nature, et l'homme naturel vivant dans l'état de société.[186]

E. H. Wright has written that for Rousseau 'the natural man is not our first brute forbear, but the last man we are travelling on to be'.[187] It is more accurate to say, I think, that the natural man is the creature at both these stages, and at all the stages in between, so long as he is properly constituted.[188]

The second *Discours* allows us to penetrate more deeply into Rousseau's dynamic conception of man. Although the title, *Discours sur l'origine et les fondemens de l'inégalité parmi les hommes*, suggests a treatment of a specific aspect of human nature, the work itself turns out to be nothing less than (to adopt Mme de Staël's remark) a dramatic presentation of the Rousseauist theory of man. It consists of 'des raisonnemens hypothétiques et conditionnels; plus propres à éclaircir la Nature des choses qu'à montrer la véritable origine'.[189]

Car comment connoître la source de l'inégalité parmi les hommes, si l'on ne commence par les connoître eux mêmes? et comment l'homme viendra-t-il à bout de se voir tel que l'a formé la Nature, à travers tous les changemens que le succession des tems et des choses a dû produire dans sa constitution originelle, et de démêler ce qu'il tient de son propre fond d'avec ce que les circonstances et ses progrès ont ajoûté ou changé à son Etat primitif?[190]

Two points worth noting are here apparent: Rousseau sees a radical transformation of the human constitution taking place with the passing of time; but he also believes that there is something which persists unchanged in this process.[191] At times, to be sure, he describes this identity as a fixed state of being ('un état primitif'),[192] rather than as a principle of growth in accordance with nature, and to this extent would seem to contradict one of the major principles of *Émile*, that a man can be natural in society as well as in the so-called state of nature.

However, the inconsistency in his thought can be accounted for, and the doctrine of the second *Discours* can be shown to be not fundamentally at odds with that of *Émile*. Throughout his life Rousseau's antipathy to large, impersonal cities was matched by a warm affection for (and, to some extent, an idealization of)[193] the simple community and the placid, innocent, natural people it alleged-ly produced.[194] His imagination, therefore, was readily kindled by the primitive and the simple, less readily by the conventional

and the relatively intricate. So, although most of his political speculation has to do with the latter, there is about his writings an air of
emotional inconsistency – a tone of sombre pessimism when he
speaks of political society and nostalgic admiration when he turns
to the state of nature – which has bedevilled Rousseau scholarship
since the eighteenth century and which has fostered many popular
misconceptions of his thought.[195]

In the second part of the *Discours sur l'inégalité* Rousseau describes some of the stages of existence through which men must have
passed on their journey from a condition of pre-social independence
to a social and eventually political order.[196] Rousseau makes it quite
clear that these are merely typical instances or models abstracted
from a continuous process of change which it is not possible to
document in full. In speaking of the slowly changing first stage
Rousseau writes :

Je parcours comme un trait des multitudes de Siécles, forcé par le tems qui
s'écoule, par l'abondance des choses que j'ai à dire, et par le progrès presque
insensible des commencemens; car plus les événemens étoient lents à se
succeder, plus ils sont prompts à décrire.[197]

This belief that the historical process itself is a basic explanatory
factor in understanding the constitution of man is evident throughout the entire treatise, but nowhere is it more explicit, especially in
its relation to the changing nature of man, than in the following
passage which is to be found in the closing pages of the work :

En découvrant et suivant ainsi les routes oubliées et perdues qui de l'état
Naturel ont dû mener l'homme à l'état Civil; en rétablissant, avec les positions intermédiaires que je viens de marquer, celles que le tems qui me
presse m'a fait supprimer, ou que l'imagination ne m'a point suggérées;
tout Lecteur attentif ne pourra qu'être frappé de l'espace immense qui
sépare ces deux états. C'est dans cette lente succession des choses qu'il verra
la solution d'une infinité de problèmes de morale et de Politique que les
Philosophes ne peuvent résoudre. . . . En un mot, il expliquera comment
l'âme et les passions humaines s'altérant insensiblement, changent pour
ainsi dire de Nature; pourquoi nos besoins et nos plaisirs changent d'objets
à la longue. . . . L'homme Sauvage et l'homme policé différent tellement
par le fond du coeur et des inclinations, que ce qui fait le bonheur suprême de
l'un, réduiroit l'autre au désespoir.[198]

In this passage, where Rousseau also speaks of 'le Genre-humain
d'un âge n'étant pas le Genre-humain d'un autre âge',[199] one cannot

fail to be struck with the profoundly important part which the historical process has to play, but in Rousseau's mind it cannot of itself provide a full explanation of the constituting of man. In Cartesian style, Rousseau in the *Discours sur l'inégalité* attempts to strip away all the conditional accretions from the human frame and arrive at the essentials of human nature.[200] 'Méditant', as he says, 'sur les premiéres et plus simples opérations de l'Ame humaine', Rousseau discerns in natural man two principles of behaviour prior to reason ('amour de soi' and 'pitié'),[201] as well as the quality of free agency and the faculty of self-improvement ('perfectibilité' or 'la faculté de se perfectionner'). The considerable ambiguities in his treatment of these immanent characteristics (some of which have been discussed above, especially in the previous section) and the place of reason in Rousseau's scheme need not detain us at this time, for what is important to note just now is that these essential qualities of human nature are operative in one form or another throughout the life of the human species and are *not* historical products. Man is not merely clay to be pressed into whatever shape the historical process makes possible; he possesses certain internal drives, and it is the conjunction of these drives with the exigencies of history which make him what he is at any particular time. In this important respect, then, Rousseau clearly cannot be regarded as a precursor of nineteenth-century historicism.

Rousseau coins the word 'perfectibilité' to describe one of his qualities, but it is not at first clear why he does this, for immediately after introducing this idea into the treatise Rousseau proceeds to emphasize the possibility that this faculty may allow man at times to sink 'plus bas que la Bête même' : 'Il seroit triste pour nous d'être forcés de convenir, que cette faculté distinctive, et presque illimitée, est la source de tous les malheurs de l'homme.'[202]

However, it appears that perfectibility may be an early and perhaps less fully elaborated conception of the principle of development which has already been noted in *Émile*, except that in this case it relates to the human race, rather than to a single individual. To call this human faculty 'perfectibility' is to suggest that there is some norm in terms of which improvement of the human condition can be measured; and to assert at the same time that this same faculty might be the source of all human ills seems to imply that the change which is inherent in the notion of self-improvement is contingent upon the human will, or circumstances, or both. There is a condition which is appropriate to man at each point in the history of the species, but it is up to man to choose whether or not he will accept it or strive to achieve it. Harold Höffding writes that Rousseau in his main works

arrived at a clear insight already enjoyed by Shaftesbury, of the relativity of the conception of nature no less than of civilization. When any civilization meets the given conditions of life it effects an unfolding of the latent possibilities without undermining the power of life, and then it is natural. Asserting that true civilization must correspond to the actual stage attained, and so drawing the conclusion that there can be no absolutely universal civilization . . . he had virtually conceded that there is no universally true 'nature'.[203]

What, it might be asked, is the criterion for deciding whether man at any given stage in his development is fulfilling his potentialities? It is possible, in closing this discussion of Rousseau's views regarding human nature and the historical process, to suggest very briefly what criterion there might be.[204] At the end of the *Discours sur l'inégalité* Rousseau enumerates the manifold differences between natural and civil man, and then turns to 'la véritable cause de toutes ces différences' :

Le Sauvage vit en lui-même; l'homme sociable toûjours hors de lui ne sait vivre que dans l'opinion des autres, et c'est, pour ainsi dire, de leur seul jugement qu'il tire le sentiment de sa propre existence.[205]

The natural man enjoys an interior balance which renders him impregnable to all but the physical assaults of his fellows (and physical pain is often less to be feared than mental torment);[206] 'l'homme sociable', however, depends upon the opinions of others even to the extent of self-definition, and he is, as a result, painfully vulnerable, and quite unable to experience the peace and respose of his fellow in the state of nature. It is for this reason that Rousseau ranks pride ('amour-propre') as the greatest of social evils,[207] and much of his writing is occupied with the search for conventional means of re-establishing man's natural harmony within civil society. This harmony once achieved, man will be a natural man in whatever condition he finds himself, and civil society will become a natural state.

The following sentiment of the placid eighteenth-century historian, Edward Gibbon, although it relates strictly to wealth, is perfectly in accord with Rousseauist doctrine : 'According to the scale of Switzerland, I am a rich man; and I am indeed rich, since my income is superior to my expense, and my expense is equal to my wishes.'[208]

Rousseau, using the vocabulary of freedom, puts it this way: 'L'homme vraiment libre ne veut que ce qu'il peut, et fait ce qu'il lui plaît. Voilà ma maxime fondamentale.'[209]

If the word 'natural' is taken to mean 'what is fitting to man's nature', rather than 'what is primitive' or 'what is ideal in the abstract', then we can say that Rousseau feels it is possible for man to live naturally inside as well as outside society.[210] Rousseau's insight in this respect is similar to, though perhaps not so profound as Burke's. In the Geneva manuscript Rousseau suggests that it is in 'l'art perfectionné' that men are to look for 'la réparation des maux que l'art commencé fit à la nature'.[211] Edmund Burke makes the point succinctly and unambiguously 'art is man's nature'.

Rousseau, then, realized that artifice can be natural, that society, an apparent artifact, is natural when it releases and fulfils the potentialities of mankind, when it makes possible the psychological and social harmony of men. It is worthwhile recalling here that Rousseau's golden age was itself a simple, *social* order, and it would surely be foolhardy to claim that this image of perfection so dear to Rousseau's heart was in his opinion 'unnatural'. The trouble for Rousseau was that he rarely if ever discovered his European contemporaries living 'naturally' in this sense, whereas in his mind's eye he was always able to imagine 'l'homme Sauvage' enjoying this happy condition.

Edmund Burke took the view that it is the task of men to work at perfecting their God-given nature and attached to this view the derivative belief that there exist vast historical diversities in human nature within the universal framework of God. Rousseau, in his more secular view of man, at times (especially in *Émile*) saw the psychological necessity for human beings to develop their potentialities, and at other times (especially in the *Contrat*) saw the political necessity for men to be radically transformed. His objective in each case was the same, that is, the psychological and social 'balance' of men, but he frequently shifted his emphasis (and perhaps unwittingly altered his opinions) in searching for the means of achieving it. Although he would not deny that man is the creature of God, his analysis of the predicament of mankind and his prescription of a possible cure are both much more consistently mundane than are Burke's

VI Independence and Moral Freedom

We may now turn to the question of liberty in the psychological thinking of Rousseau and Burke. Our general objective in this section is twofold : to show that both Burke and Rousseau make a distinction between what might be called 'independence' and 'moral freedom', and to uncover the extent to which the thinking of the two men in respect of the second concept, moral freedom, is similar. As working definitions, we shall take 'independence' to mean freedom of action as such and to entail the absence of social and moral restraints of any sort,[212] and 'moral freedom' to mean freedom of action subject to rules and to entail the absence of other than moral restraints.[213]

That Rousseau does in fact distinguish between independence and moral freedom is, I think, quite clear. He elucidates the character of each in the process of giving an account of l'homme Sauvage' and 'l'homme civilisé', independence relating to the former, and moral liberty (at least as a goal or possibility) relating to the latter. Natural liberty (what Rousseau calls in one place 'cette parfaite indépendance et cette liberté sans régle')[214] is the property of man in his most primitive condition, that is, *before* he becomes a member of any community.

In the Geneva manuscript Rousseau describes the lot of man in this primitive condition in the following terms :

... chacun resteroit isolé parmi les autres, chacun ne songeroit qu'à soi; nôtre entendement ne sauroit se développer; nous vivrions sans rien sentir, nous mourrions sans avoir vécu: tout nôtre bonheur consisteroit à ne pas connoitre notre misère; il n'y auroit ni bonté dans nos coeurs ni moralité dans nos actions, et nous n'aurions jamais gouté le plus délicieux sentiment de l'ame, qui est l'amour de la vertu.[215]

Independence, then, is 'liberty without rule' and is the possession of a creature who is destitute of social relationships, unencumbered by any sort of enlightenment, and ignorant of the guiding principles of human behaviour – a creature with neither goodness in his heart nor morality in his actions, as Rousseau says.

In the *Contrat* (I, viii) Rousseau contrasts the freedom and property ownership which one finds in civil society with the natural

95

liberty and mere possession which is the best one can hope for in a state of nature. Natural liberty, he says, 'n'a pour bornes que les forces de l'individu'; possession he describes in Hobbesian language as constituting 'un droit illimité à tout ce qui le tente et qu'il peut atteindre'.[216] It is to be noted that in the case of both natural liberty and the natural right to 'property' the restraints on a man's freedom of action are solely physical. What a man *can* do, he may do, for self-preservation is nature's first law.[217]

This version of natural right seems to rule out natural law in its traditional form as a moral rule binding on all men. Nevertheless, an instance of Rousseau's apparent acceptance of the traditional view of natural law may be found in the eighth of his *Lettres écrites de la montagne* where he is engaged in underlining the fundamental connection between law and liberty:'Il n'y a donc point de liberté sans Loix, ni où quelqu'un est au dessus des Loix : dans l'état même de nature l'homme n'est libre qu'à la faveur de la Loi naturelle qui commande à tous.'[218] This, it seems obvious, is an expression of traditional natural-law thinking, and the liberty of which he is speaking is clearly what we have been calling moral freedom; but we have given our reasons for thinking it difficult to find a place for Rousseau in the natural-law tradition.[219]

In the same passage Rousseau provides a crisp account of the distinction he sees between independence and moral freedom :

On a beau vouloir confondre l'indépendance et la liberté. Ces deux choses sont si différentes que même elles s'excluent mutuellement. Quand chacun fait ce qu'il lui plait, on fait souvent ce qui déplait à d'autres, et cela ne s'appelle pas un état libre. La liberté consiste moins à faire sa volonté qu'à n'être pas soumis à celle d'autrui; elle consiste encore à ne pas soumettre la volonté d'autrui à la nôtre.[220]

This is, one might say, Rousseau's first principle of liberty, moral or political; subjection to the will of another is the worst possible sort of bondage.

Let us consider now more directly the nature of Rousseau's conception of moral freedom. One of Rousseau's major preoccupations was the need for institutions and procedures which would re-establish in civil society man's natural self-sufficiency, or, more precisely, which would liberate him from dependence on or submission to the wills of other men. Through utter reliance upon a political order *of a certain sort* (if it could only be achieved), man would achieve a harmony or balance which Rousseau felt the civilized man he saw about him lacked, and he would enjoy in civilized form a freedom from other persons' will such as he had once enjoyed in the state of nature.[221]

Rousseau admired 'l'homme sauvage' primarily because of his internal coherence; he led a rude, beast-like existence, but at least he was not in contradiction with himself (a favourite expression of Rousseau) – or, to use a word which has come into wide use since Rousseau's day and which expresses a thoroughly Rousseauist idea, he was not 'alienated', either from himself or from society.

A quotation from a political fragment exemplifies this recurrent theme well :

Ce qui fait la misère humaine est la contradiction qui se trouve entre notre état et nos desirs, entre nos devoirs et nos penchans, entre la nature et les institutions sociales, entre l'homme et le citoyen; rendez l'homme un vous le rendrez heureux autant qu'il peut l'être. Donnez-le tout entier à l'état ou laissez-le tout entier à lui-même, mais si vous partagez son coeur vous le déchirez. . . .[222]

Rousseau, then, was attempting to take away man's contradictions, 'rendre l'homme un', but in a condition that would make possible the full development of his faculties rather than in one that presupposed the total absence of such development. Moral liberty constitutes an important dimension of this civilized ideal.

It is possible to stipulate two negative requirements which Rousseau argues must be fulfilled before a man can be considered morally free : first, a man must not be subject to the will of another, and second; he must not be subject to his 'lower nature'.[223] This negative characterization reveals a parallelism in Rousseau's thought between independence and moral liberty, for a state of independence fulfils these two conditions as well. Natural man is not subject to the will of others because he is solitary; and he is not subject to his 'lower nature' because in his pre-social state the notion of a lower and a higher nature simply does not apply to him. He does not possess the qualities (reason, consciousness of self, morality and the 'social vices' such as pride and greed) which must be assumed to exist if this concept is to have any significance. It is when independence and moral liberty are described *positively* (as in the first paragraph of this section) that the full extent of the difference between the two is apparent.

No doubt the most basic point with regard to the first requirement (that a man must not be subject to the will of another) is the
logical necessity that a man must have freedom of will if he is to
be a moral agent.[224] As it is a necessary condition of moral action,
it is considered by Rousseau to be a defining property of man.

Renoncer à sa liberté c'est renoncer à sa qualité d'homme, aux droits de
l'humanité, même à ses devoirs. . . . Une telle renonciation est incompatible
avec la nature de l'homme, et c'est ôter toute moralité à ses actions que
d'ôter toute liberté á sa volonté.[225]

Rousseau gives extended and eloquent descriptions of the sense
in which he feels that civilized man is in bondage to others. In the
second *Discours* he describes the process by which man lost his
primitive independence. Although the transformation begins with
the appearance of the first human associations, the turning point in
this lengthy journey from nature to political society is the rise of
systematic specialization of labour which Rousseau typifies as the
age of metallurgy and agriculture; the plough, which is made by
one person and used by another, is the symbol of this secular fall of
man : 'ce sont le fer et le bled qui ont civilisé les hommes, et perdu
le Genre-humain.'[226] Characteristically, it is the moral effect of
this revolution that upsets Rousseau :

. . . dès l'instant qu'un homme eut besoin du secours d'un autre . . . les
vastes forêts se changérent en des Campagnes riantes qu'il falut arroser de
la sueur des hommes, et dans lesquelles on vit bientôt l'esclavage et la misére
germer et croître avec les moissons.[227]

One might argue that this reliance on artifacts is a dependence
on things rather than on men, but Rousseau took this to be a
superficial view of the situation. If a farmer needed a plough to till
his fields, and did not have the skills to make one for himself, then
this was a dependence on *men*, in this case on the blacksmith or
the ploughwright. If Rousseau had had any developed conception
of a vast and impersonal market economy, he would have rejected
the view that a man in such a system could feel himself to be subject to impersonal economic laws rather than to the wills of other
(especially wealthier) men.

But men in a social order suffer from a vastly more radical kind
of dependence than that involved in being by turns producer and
consumer. As men moved from the natural to the social condition,
their nature itself began to change. Men began to live through the

eyes of their fellows and to value themselves and their abilities in
the light of the opinions of other men. One might say there was a
market economy in human worth; a person's value or 'price' was
determined by the esteem in which he was held by others, and the
market judgement was one in which the individual himself generally
concurred. Men ceased to be whole and self-sufficient, and 'amour-
propre', a relative, social faculty, supplanted the primitive, absolute
quality of 'amour de soi'; it became in the interest of men to appear
what they really were not :

Etre et paroître devinrent deux choses tout à fait différentes . . . de libre et
independent qu'étoit auparavant l'homme, le voilà par une multitude de
nouveaux besoins assujéti, pour ainsi dire, à toute la Nature, et surtout à
ses semblables dont il devient l'esclave en un sens, même en devenant leur
maître; riche, il a besoin de leurs services; pauvre, il a besoin de leurs
secours. . . .[228]

Man is not only materially dependent on his fellows, but spiritually
dependent as well.

Notwithstanding Rousseau's sombre analysis of the predicament
of mankind, he makes it quite clear that there can be no turning
back in search of an arcadian past;[229] indeed, his analysis itself is
enough to suggest this, for man's character is transformed in human
communities, it is socialized, and Rousseau knows of no process of
de-socialization. 'L'homme civilisé' suffers a crippling personal
dependence upon the will and opinion of other men, and on
Rousseau's analysis men in society be they poor or rich, weak or
powerful, live in slavery. Since a return to the state of nature is out
of the question, how might social man achieve moral liberty (in the
first sense of freedom from subjection to another's will), and hence
an escape from his predicament? Rousseau, both in his life and in
his writings, explored various possibilities.

From time to time he himself tried to find a way out by simply
isolating himself as much as possible from his fellows in a sort of
civilized version of a return to nature; one could hardly be in subjection to another if there were no 'others' around.[230] Rousseau
provided cogent theoretical reasons in his various publications why
this would not work, and as it turned out it worked no better in
practice than in theory; society would not leave him alone, and he
would not leave society alone.

Taking seriously his own strictures to the effect that man is irrevocably a social creature, Rousseau also addressed himself to the problem of improving his life within a social order. For example, he believed that a trade, preferably a simple manual one, was helpful in securing a man against his fellows. If a man possessed some socially necessary skill which did not require much capital investment, then he could move about easily, either from place to place or from employer to employer, and in a sense impose his own conditions of life and work, rather than have them imposed upon him.[231] He also espoused the life led in simple, farming communities; where families approach self-sufficiency, where the tenor of life is unvaried and tradition strong, it is not human will but human habit that rules.[232] Finally, a more drastic remedy is to be found in the stringent restriction of personal desire. A man without desire would be utterly independent of human society; therefore, reduce desire, and increase freedom, at least in the sense of the absence of social dependence : 'D'où vient la faiblesse de l'homme? De l'inégalité qui se trouve entre sa force et ses désirs. . . . Diminuez donc les désirs, c'est comme si vous augmentiez les forces.'[233]

All these constitute what might be termed minor themes in Rousseau's thought on liberty, and it is significant that each involves the limitation of desire.[234] None of them, in fact, seems at first sight to sit easily with the principle of the free development of human faculties. Here, then, is the stoic Rousseau.

However, there were times when Rousseau believed that this line of thought was unsatisfactory. There was something pinched or crabbed about the simple limitation of human faculties and human wishes. In *Émile*, he writes :

En quoi donc consiste la sagesse humaine ou la route du vrai bonheur? Ce n'est pas précisément à diminuer nos désirs; car, s'ils étaient au-dessous de notre puissance, une partie de nos facultés resterait oisive, et nous ne jouirions pas de tout notre être. Ce n'est pas non plus à étendre nos facultés, car si nos désirs s'étendaient à la fois en plus grand rapport, nous n'en deviendrions que plus misérables: mais c'est à diminuer l'excès des désirs sur les facultés, et à mettre en égalité parfaite la puissance et la volonté. C'est alors seulement que, toutes les forces étant en action, l'âme cependant restera paisible, et que l'homme se trouvera bien ordonné.[235]

There is in Rousseau, then, a more positive strain of thought which is similar to themes mentioned above to the extent that the achievement of moral freedom involves an element of restraint or limitation. However, rather than there being a limitation imposed on desire or development, there is an *ordering* of desire and development, and (a crucial point in Rousseau's ethics) this ordering is self-imposed. If men voluntarily regulate their behaviour then they can be understood to be morally free, but it is indispensable that they *themselves* frame the rules, otherwise they will be subject to the rules (the will) of another, and so unfree. It is this central Rousseauist doctrine that Kant fastened upon, and it is this moral doctrine, too, that carries us straight into politics, for when Rousseau addressed himself to the question of how men in communities can frame rules for themselves which all can abide by, he realized that the answer must be political. As he says in describing the development of his social thinking, 'j'avais vu que tout tenait radicalement à la politique'.[236]

The second of Rousseau's two requirements for moral freedom which we said we would consider was that a man must not be subject to his 'lower nature'. This idea of freedom is founded on the general contention that man has a lower and a higher (usually rational) nature, and that it is the task of the latter to order and control the passionate, irrational side of man. It has clear affinities, for example, with Plato's doctrine of justice in the soul, and with much Christian moral philosophy. This recurrent Rousseauist theme, entailing the division of the self, appears in both Rousseau's moral and political thought.[237] Maurice Cranston calls this the theory of 'rational freedom'[238] and Isaiah Berlin terms it 'positive liberty'.[239]

Émile's religious mentor, the 'vicaire savoyard', gives classic expression to the sentiment which lies behind this doctrine of moral freedom :

J'ai toujours la puissance de vouloir, non la force d'exécuter. Quand je me livre aux tentations, j'agis selon l'impulsion des objets externes. Quand je me reproche cette faiblesse, je n'écoute que ma volonté; je suis esclave par mes vices, et libre par mes remords; le sentiment de ma liberté ne s'efface en moi que quand je me déprave, et que j'empêche enfin la voix de l'âme de s'élever contre la loi du corps.[240]

In the *Contrat* Rousseau describes 'la liberté morale' specifically in terms of 'rational freedom'; it is that, he says,

qui seule rend l'homme vraiment maître de lui; car l'impulsion du seul appetit est esclavage, et l'obéissance à la loi qu'on s'est prescritte est liberté.[241]

And Émile's tutor asserts :

C'est une erreur de distinguer les passions en permises et défendues, pour se livrer aux premières et se refuser aux autres. Toutes sont bonnes quand on en reste le maître; toutes sont mauvaises quand on s'y laisse assujettir.[242]

A final quotation opens before us a predicament in personal relationships similar to the forced-to-be-free situation in politics, and suggests the difficulties into which one who holds this doctrine of moral freedom can sometimes be led. Émile, approaching maturity, has what is in effect a failure of nerve, and cries out to his tutor :

O mon ami, mon protecteur, mon maître, reprenez l'autorité que vous voulez déposer au moment qu'il m'importe le plus qu'elle vous reste. . . . Je veux obéir à vos lois, je le veux toujours, c'est ma volonté constante; si jamais je vous désobéis, ce sera malgré moi: rendez-moi libre en me protégeant contre mes passions qui me font violence; empêchez-moi d'être leur esclave, et forcez-moi d'être mon propre maître en n'obéissant point à mes sens, mais à ma raison.[243]

It is difficult to see how a man could be considered free in such a condition. True enough, his soul may be properly ordered,[244] but this is achieved at the expense of his free agency; he becomes subject to another's will, and has the 'right' pattern externally imposed on him. His dependence is intensely personal. In this case, there is an incompatibility between the achievement of freedom in the first sense (freedom from another's will) and freedom in the second sense (freedom from the dominance of one's lower nature). Such an incompatibility does not arise until the 'ordering agent' ceases to be the person himself, or some part of him, and becomes another person or persons. This is an issue to which we shall return later.[245]

Let us turn now to Edmund Burke. Two general questions need to be asked in examining Burke's conception of moral freedom, and in evaluating the degree to which it is similar to Rousseau's. Firstly, does Burke (like Rousseau) distinguish between independence and moral freedom? Secondly, does he conceive of moral freedom in terms similar to those of Rousseau? More specifically, is it possible to discern in his writing two different dimensions of moral liberty, namely, freedom from subjection to the will of others, and freedom from one's lower self?

As for the first question, it seems clear that if Burke did make a distinction between freedom of action as such and freedom according to rules, he did so in terms rather different from those of Rousseau. We have seen that Rousseau makes this distinction via his conception of natural and social man, and we know that this state-of-nature style of argument was as a rule foreign to Burke.[246] However, we shall argue that Burke *did* make a distinction between these two kinds of freedom, and that this distinction issues out of his separation of theoretical and practical knowledge.

We have examined certain leading features of Burke's epistemological doctrine elsewhere,[247] and have emphasized the crucial role it plays in his social and political thought. Here we shall argue that, at least in respect of liberty and natural rights, the category of 'theoretical knowledge' performs in Burke's thinking an analytical function similar to that which the state-of-nature concept plays in Rousseau's. As a consequence, it enables Burke to consider (and reject) the claims of revolutionary theorists and others that 'absolute liberty' and the 'metaphysic rights' of man constitute practicable and desirable objectives of social policy. And 'abstract liberty', as we shall see, has certain characteristics in common with Rousseau's natural independence.

Abstract or theoretical liberty in Burke's mind is liberty *per se*, liberty in abstraction from everything else, and Burke readily admits that, '*abstractedly speaking*', liberty is to be considered a good (though he takes care to add that government, the political antithesis of liberty, is in the same light to be considered a benefit).[248] But this is to take a politically naive view of a principle, 'as it stands stripped of every relation, in all the nakedness and solitude of metaphysical abstraction'.

The questions continually at the back of Burke's mind are : What if 'learned and speculative men' (or giddy sophists, for that matter) *do* reflect on the concept of liberty in the abstract? What possible bearing do these reflections have on actual political freedom? In proportion as they are metaphysically true (that is to say, purified of any extraneous concepts), they are morally and politically false (incomplete and incapable of being applied).[249] Liberty, as he says, 'must be limited in order to be possessed'.[250]

Burke, then, distinguishes in this way between simple independence (the principle of liberty *per se*) and moral freedom, and dismisses the former as an inadequate conception. In a letter to M.

Dupont, Burke gives it as his opinion that, of all the loose terms in the world, 'liberty' is the most indefinite, and proceeds to specify what he does *not* mean by the word. Liberty, he says, is not 'solitary, unconnected, individual, selfish liberty, as if every man was to regulate the whole of his conduct by his own will. The liberty I mean is *social* freedom'.[251] Liberty, as freedom of action without social or moral restraint, is not a concept which Burke can accept.

A difference between Rousseau and Burke is apparent. Because of the social-contract tradition in which Rousseau was writing, there is an inevitable ambiguity as to whether his natural man was meant to be an empirical description or a theoretical device, and consequently a lack of clarity regarding the empirical status of the natural man's independence or liberty. With Burke's conception of abstract liberty there can be no such doubt; it was a purely speculative condition without any claim to empirical reality.[252] What is more, it is a condition which Burke rejected as conceptually inadequate and in its influence morally objectionable, whereas natural liberty for Rousseau was a feature of a primitive condition which Rousseau at times idealized, even though he realized it was utterly inapplicable to civilized man.

We have seen in our discussion of abstract liberty what Burke does *not* mean by freedom. Let us now examine the positive side of the matter, what Burke does mean by freedom, and attempt to come to some conclusion regarding his degree of similarity to Rousseau on this point.

Burke as a rule makes little attempt to separate what we have termed moral and political liberty, and consequently the analytical distinction between the two is difficult to make, often more difficult than in the case of Rousseau. As he was in most of his discussions of liberty concentrating on political events, we shall attempt to provide here only sufficient evidence to bring out the similarity of the two men's moral theory, and will leave further discussion to the following chapter where political liberty is discussed.

Like Rousseau, Burke maintained that the only liberty possible for civilized man was a 'liberty inseparable from order'.[253] However, unlike Rousseau, he asserts that we are all born in subjection to law, to the law of nature, and it is by virtue of this universal moral framework that we are free. Burke writes:

We may bite our chains if we will, but we shall be made to know ourselves, and be taught that man is born to be governed by law; and he that will substitute *will* in the place of it is an enemy to God.[254]

No man can lawfully govern himself according to his own will, much less can one person be governed by the will of another.[255]

Apart from his theoretical reasons for insisting that liberty and order were inseparable. Burke felt that in practice liberty could not be sustained over a period of time on any other basis. It had to be limited to be possessed, and the utopian attempt to realize it absolutely could only lead to its loss or distortion : 'there is an extreme in liberty, which may be infinitely noxious to those who are to receive it, and which in the end will leave them no liberty at all.'[256] In addition, Burke regarded freedom as simply one good among others, not as the greatest or the only good.[257] Therefore, he was at pains always to consider liberty in a moral context composed of other goods having fully as valid claims to satisfaction.

What Burke sought, then, was what he called 'a manly, moral, regulated liberty',[258] a freedom of men equal under the law :

What is liberty without wisdom, and without virtue? It is the greatest of all possible evils; for it is folly, vice, and madness, without tuition or restraint. Those who know what virtuous liberty is, cannot bear to see it disgraced by incapable heads, on account of their having high-sounding words in their mouths.[259]

Did Burke also subscribe to the conception of moral freedom in the second sense in which we have used the term in this section, that is, in the sense of a man being free from the illicit domination of his lower nature? We shall show that this is a feature of his thought, although it does not hold as prominent a position in his doctrine of freedom as it does in Rousseau's.

Certainly Burke took the view that there is a proper hierarchy in the constitution of man, that his rational faculty ought by rights to rule his appetitive nature. But to say that Burke accepts the doctrine of a proper ordering of the soul is not in itself sufficient to justify us in saying that he regards such an ordering as a state of moral freedom. However, there are a few places in which he does make it clear that he is not averse to regarding such an ordering in this light. For example, in a *Letter to a Member of the National Assembly* Burke asserts :

Men are qualified for civil liberty in exact proportion to their disposition to put moral chains upon their own appetites. . . . It is ordained in the eternal constitution of things, that men of intemperate minds cannot be free. Their passions forge their fetters.[260]

And in a letter Burke speaks of men who have forfeited their rights and privileges by the abuse (or lack of use) of their rational faculties :

To men so degraded, a state of strong constraint is a sort of necessary substitute for freedom; since, bad as it is, it may deliver them in some measure from the worst of all slavery, – that is, the despotism of their own blind and brutal passions.[261]

This statement is strikingly similar to Rousseauist doctrine. For men who are spiritually deficient, paternal control and guidance may be necessary; political activity in an imperfect world must often involve the positive *making* of men and citizens, not merely the neutral regulation of their relationships.

'The worst of all slavery is the despotism of one's own blind and brutal passions' : 'l'impulsion du seul appetit est esclavage' – both Burke and Rousseau have a clearly recognizable strain of 'rational freedom' running through their thought. However, Rousseau differs from Burke in his greater inclination to speak occasionally of discipline or coercion as if it were freedom, 'true' or 'real' freedom.[262] It is perhaps worth noting that Burke in the quotation immediately above describes constraint as 'a sort of necessary substitute for freedom', not as freedom in a different and more lordly guise. For his part, Rousseau puts into the mouth of Émile what amounts to an equivalent of the forced-to-be-free principle; keep me, says Émile, from being the slave of my passions : 'empêchez-moi d'être leur esclave, et forcez-moi d'être mon propre maître.'

In this section we have tried – without ignoring the differences – to disclose very briefly the similarities between Burke's and Rousseau's doctrines of moral freedom.[263] We have argued that each makes a distinction between 'independence' and 'moral freedom', and that two themes may be discerned in each writer's conception of the second : namely, that moral freedom entails freedom from another's will, and that it entails freedom from one's lower nature.

3

The State and the Citizen in Rousseau and Burke

1 Introduction

Both Burke and Rousseau were figures of enormous importance in eighteenth-century political debate. Edmund Burke's contribution to European letters was predominantly political, and he is remembered today primarily for his magisterial pronouncements on the great affairs of state which confronted England during his lifetime. Although his forays into other literary pursuits very often met with success, they nevertheless leave one with the impression of a man searching for his 'métier', or leaving it momentarily; these excursions occurred early in his career, and the various topics taken up were not as a rule extensively explored or frequently returned to.[1] A letter of 1746 or 7 suggests the academic uncertainties of the young man; Burke charts his course from his first intellectual interest, which he calls his 'furor mathematicus', through a 'furor logicus', a 'furor historicus', and finally to a 'furor poeticus'.[2] A few years later he writes in connection with the legal studies which he had taken up : 'at least, I have this comfort; that tho' a middling poet cannot be endured, there is some quarter for a middling lawyer.'[3] As it happened, Burke turned out to be, not a middling lawyer, but a powerful orator and a superb political writer.

Rousseau's literary history has a very different shape. Like Burke, he began his career with a multitude of schemes buzzing in his head, but unlike Burke, he continued throughout his life to explore widely divergent intellectual activities, to try out projects of all sorts, to take up, and put down, and take up again a number of topics of recurrent interest. Indeed, his curious mind roved the fields of speculation even more widely than he himself wandered over the face of Europe. Concurrently with the publication of his

107

most important political works, Rousseau was placing before the public other writings on a variety of subjects, most of which enjoyed an enormous success. It is not possible to say whether Rousseau was best known in his day as a political writer, a novelist, an educationist, or a composer; he was renowned in all fields. But certainly his political publications received great attention and occasioned violent controversy, and they have continued to do so down to the present day, although not always for the same reasons.

The general question which we have before us in this chapter, then, is : what sort of political thinkers are Rousseau and Burke? What is the character of their political thought and to what extent is it similar? More particularly, we shall be trying to specify their answers to a number of questions about the citizen and the political order, some of them of primarily local eighteenth-century interest, others of more enduring concern to ages before and since. First of all, there are the two classic questions of seventeenth- and eighteenth-century political speculation, questions which are in fact distinguishable but which during that period tended to be confused. How did a political order come into being? What makes it legitimate? Then there are a number of particular issues round which controversy turned. How can we best understand the notions of a subject or a citizen, and those of a 'prince' or a legislature? Are there occasions in which a citizen can rightfully rebel against the political authority? If so, how does one judge when a given political order is illegitimate and rebellion a proper course of action? What is the nature of liberty? of law? What sort of relationship is there between them? What is the proper role of reason, and of what might be called 'public spirit', in political affairs? How significant is a country's history in its present political life, and what sort of influence does it have (or ought it to have) over political action? What kind of reform is possible for some of the problem-ridden eighteenth-century European states? It is in coping with the answers of Rousseau and Burke to such questions as these that most of this chapter will be taken up. As with the previous chapter, the discussion will open with a look at the school of natural rights, this time at its political theory and at the attitudes of Burke and Rousseau to that theory.

II   Rousseau and Burke, and the Political Theory of the
     School of Natural Rights

The position of John Locke's political thought in the natural-right
tradition was briefly examined in the second part of each of the
two previous chapters. As the leading ideas of this tradition became increasingly popular among men of action in the eighteenth
century, and more widely used in political controversy, the cautious
intricacy which marked Locke's speculation was gradually supplanted by bolder and coarser forms of argument, more suited to
the promotion of specific political programmes. The explanatory-
prescriptive ambiguity marking the *Second Treatise* disappears, as
the obvious programmatic function of natural-right discourse in the
latter half of the eighteenth century declares itself more openly.

A Lockean circumspection is still evident in the following quotation from the American Declaration of Independence (1776), but
the liberal, reformist goals of most natural-right adherents ensured
that this was in general a minor theme :

Prudence, indeed, will dictate that Governments long established should not
be changed for light and transient causes; and accordingly all experience
hath shown, that mankind are more disposed to suffer, while evils are suffer-
able, than to right themselves by abolishing the forms to which they are
accustomed. But when a long train of abuses and usurpations, pursuing
invariably the same Object, evinces a design to reduce them under absolute
Despotism, it is their right, it is their duty, to throw off such Government,
and to provide new Guards for their future security.[4]

Thomas Paine's political ideas point up in the sharpest terms
what might be called the late eighteenth-century vulgarization of
Locke.[5] Indeed, perhaps Paine's only major shortcoming as a representative of popular natural-right thought is the way in which he
carried each idea to its logical extreme; his utterly uncompromising simplicity approaches caricature. Paine's breathtaking individualism does, however, help to bring out some of the theory's
leading features.

When a number of natural men decide to combine together the
result is the state, conceived by natural-right thinkers as a collection of individuals whose significant distinguishing mark is not so
much a distinctive language or history, but the bond of association
itself which makes the collection *this* state rather than another. 'A
nation', says Paine, 'is composed of distinct, unconnected individu-

als';[6] it is simply the sum of all the autonomous units which make up a given political order. The legislative decisions (if fully democratic) of such a collection of individuals are, to employ Rousseauist vocabulary, the result of the will of all rather than of the general will.

Political society is constituted for the benefit of the natural man, and in particular to foster and protect the individual in the exercise of his natural rights. The standard by which civil society is judged and the goals for which it is created lie outside politics; they are natural.[7] With writers in the natural-right tradition, there is no talk of the change from 'un animal stupide et borné' to 'un être intelligent et un homme', which comes over man as he moves from a natural to a political condition. For them, the human being has always been 'un être intelligent et un homme', and his rights, even in the civil state, are granted to him by nature. With regard to this point Paine writes :

Hitherto we have spoken only . . . of the natural rights of man. We have now to consider the civil rights of man, and to show how the one originates from the other. Man did not enter into society to become *worse* than he was before, nor to have fewer rights than he had before, but to have those rights better secured. His natural rights are the foundation of all his civil rights. . . . Every civil right has for its foundation some natural right pre-existing in the individual.[8]

With such a doctrine as this, it is clear that the creative role of government is virtually nil. Government is no longer the contingent good which it was for Locke, but a 'necessary evil', to use a phrase of Paine which has become commonplace in the language. Government is something to be confined within strict areas, hedged in with prohibitions, and limited to the performance of certain specific functions.

The conditions in which men could rightfully attempt to overthrow a government they deemed unjust were ultimately a matter for each individual to consider rationally for himself. Just as every generation was assumed to be 'competent to all the purposes which its occasions require',[9] so the citizen's capacity to reason was taken as adequate to reveal to him when it was his right, and indeed his duty, to resist the political authority. Edmund Burke does not deny that there are occasions when civil disobedience is the duty of good men, but such a course of action, in his opinion, ought 'not to be agitated by common minds'.[10] For the natural-right thinker, however, there are no common minds in the sense which Burke intends; there are instead minds competent to all necessary purposes. Unlike British statesman, natural-right adherents are not at all 'afraid to put men to live and trade each on his own private stock of reason'.[11] That is precisely what they are trying to do.

Lacking in much natural-right thought of this sort is a realization of the importance of other than strictly politico-legal connections between men. That men may be united by common language, by common customs, and by long association seems to be of relatively minor significance (or else productive of downright evil) to the exponent of natural rights. The possible beneficial political effects of such relationships are lost on them. Here as elsewhere, Tom Paine states the position of the school in its most extreme form :

Every age and generation must be as free to act for itself, *in all cases*, as the ages and generations which preceded it. The vanity and presumption of governing beyond the grave, is the most ridiculous and insolent of all tyrannies.[12]

It is to the present, and not to the 'musty records and mouldy parchments'[13] of the past, that one must refer, in order to discover what are the prerogatives of the living.

It is not necessary to spend much time elaborating Edmund Burke's position with respect to the political doctrines of the natural-right school, particularly in the light of what has already been said in the previous two chapters.[14] One of the main practical purposes for which he wrote some of his most famous speeches and essays was to refute the claims of this school of thought, and to neutralize its practical effects. In a speech of less than ten pages on the reform of the system of representation in the House of Commons, the heart of Burke's objections to the political theory of natural rights can be seen, as well as his specific rejection of three of the most salient features of the school, namely, its conception of individualism, of rights, and of rationalism. A short quotation relates to the first two points :

They who plead an absolute right cannot be satisfied with anything short of personal representation, because all *natural* rights must be the rights of individuals; as by *nature* there is no such thing as politic or corporate personality . . . they lay it down that every man ought to govern himself, and that where he cannot go himself he must send his representative; that all other government is usurpation; and is so far from having a claim to our obedience, it is not only our right, but our duty, to resist it.[15]

Here Burke is arguing that a claim of natural right is based on an extreme individualism which is ultimately subversive of all civil government. His reaction is to reject the claim of right ('our constitution is a prescriptive constitution ... whose sole authority is that it has existed time out of mind'), and to show up the serious inadequacies of the doctrine of individualism ('a nation is not an idea only of local extent, and individual momentary aggregation; but it is an idea of continuity, which extends in time as well as in numbers and in space').[16] As for the question of rationalism, he points out his agreement with the natural-right school that in respect of a claim of right, the weakest are at one with the strong:

the meanest petitioner, the most gross and ignorant, is as good as the best; in some respects his claim is more favourable on account of his ignorance; his weakness, his poverty, and distress, only add to his titles; he sues *in forma pauperis*; he ought to be a favourite of the court.

But to Burke it is obvious that this is the case, not because of some presumed quantum of reason that each man possesses (indeed, he emphasizes the serious inequalities in this respect), but because of the moral equality of all men before the law. Men are morally, not rationally equal. It is in contradiction of this assertion of the adequacy and equality of individual reason that Burke makes his well-known remark that the individual is foolish, the multitude, for the moment, is foolish, when they act without deliberation, but the species is wise and, given time, always acts rightly.

Jean-Jacques Rousseau, although he has at first glance the appearance of a natural-right theorist, is in most important aspects of his political thought far removed from that school. We suggested earlier that Rousseau appears to move gradually further and further away from natural-right doctrine in the course of his career. His elaboration of the notion of a general will is of importance here, for it is certainly a concept which is difficult to reconcile with natural-right principles. It embraces in a single framework the two distinct natural-right notions of the 'individual' and the 'state'.[17] Men are both rulers and ruled : citizens, in their exercise of sovereign power, and subjects, in their subjection to law. Rousseau is putting aside the natural-right antithesis, rejecting its belief in a sort of caretaker government, and providing an obvious creative role for the political order. A sentence from J. D. Mabbott sums up Rousseau's thinking on this point, and separates his doctrine from that of the Hegelians :

Where the State had . . . been shown [by Rousseau] to be not only a natural but a liberating and a moralizing institution, it was made by Hegel and his followers to absorb into itself the whole of freedom and morality.[18]

We have already noted above[19] the gulf which lies between the Rousseauist concept of rights and that of the natural-right school itself and have given as an example of Rousseau's thinking on the subject his separation of natural independence from civil liberty. The general will establishes the rules of political right, and so the conditions of political freedom. In the *Discours sur l'économie politique*, he says : 'C'est à la loi seule que les hommes doivent la justice et la liberté. C'est cet organe salutaire de la volonté de tous, qui rétablit dans le droit l'égalité naturelle entre les hommes.'[20]

In the general will, too, we have the institutional expression of the rational desire of the community. It is, of course, a will for the common good, but, accurately to promote the ends of the community, a distinct form of intelligence is required. Men must be fitted for political life; as Rousseau says, 'former des citoyens n'est pas l'affaire d'un jour; et pour les avoir hommes, il faut les instruire enfans'.[21] Indeed Rousseau's difficulty in believing that the members of an un-formed nation can successfully discern their own good makes it necessary for him to introduce in the *Contrat social* the almost divine lawgiver. But it remains clear that, where the general will exists, and is properly expressed, it constitutes an understanding and definition of the good far superior to that of the individual citizen or ruler on his own.[22] In all three points, then, in which we have noted the natural-right school's distinctive position – in the matter of individualism, rights, and reason – Rousseau's concept of the general will, to mention no other feature of his political thought, entails a demonstrably different set of assumptions about the nature of politics.

As for the radical aspect of the eighteenth-century school of natural rights, Rousseau's political works, despite certain revolutionary passages (and we have seen that even Edmund Burke can sound revolutionary upon occasion),[23] in general tend to counsel moderation and tolerance of mild social injustices, and even at times appear to encourage a sort of political quietism. With respect to this point, we must emphasize once again the distinction to be made between Rousseau's speculation about the ideal and his consideration of the actual. One need not agree with Beaulavon that to determine the conditions of a just state is to point out the road to those who love justice,[24] but, if an ideal condition is mistakenly taken to be a short-run practical possibility, it may have revolutionary effects in political life, though it was designed to have no such influence. In Alfred Cobban's words, 'the explanation of the co-existence of extreme principles and conservative practical ideas is that Rousseau has a clear sense, though he does not put it so explicitly as Burke, of the distinction between the right and the possible'.[25] The following passage from the second *Discours* is an example of his moderate thinking :

. . . c'est surtout la grande antiquité des Loix qui les rends saintes et vénérables . . . en s'accoutumant à négliger les anciens usages sous prétexte de fair mieux, on introduit souvent de grands maux pour en corriger de moindres.[26]

It is not, then, satisfactory to view Rousseau as a member of the school of natural rights; he frequently employed the idiom and some of the concepts of the school, as did a great many prominent political writers in the eighteenth century, but his particular understanding of the world of politics led him down a different path. And it is not, I think, possible to accept C. E. Vaughan's contention that Rousseau began an individualist and ended up a collectivist. His early *Discours sur l'inégalité* is not solidly in the individualistic natural-right tradition (witness his particular theory of the state of nature),[27] and the *Contrat social*, in which Vaughan discerns a collectivist Rousseau, still makes use of a number of the conventions of the school. The truth in Vaughan's assertion would seem to lie in the fact that Rousseau became increasingly dissatisfied with the abstract individualism of the natural-right school, and realized that, in order to achieve his goal (i.e. conditions fully satisfactory for the individual), other and less 'individualistic' arrangements were necessary.

Rousseau was influenced by this popular style of political argument, just as were other writers (like Burke) whose sympathies clearly lay elsewhere, and he was subject to this influence in some degree all the way through his writing career, but it is clear, I think, that in most important political matters, the ideas of the school did not in the end content him, and that when he used them, he took them up only to transform or to supersede them.

III   Rousseau and Burke, and Empiricist Political Thought

The distinction between Rousseau and Burke on one side, and many political empiricists on the other, might be suggested in a rough way by the disparity of mood characterizing their respective approaches to political analysis.[28] The latter shared with the natural-right school a self-confident, optimistic, innovatary spirit quite in keeping with the scientific temper of the period. They had a sense of the novelty of their age and their activities, a feeling of infinite possibility and a happy assurance that they could tackle most things with success.

They were inclined to conceive the study of moral and political life in terms of natural science, and the practitioners of both the empirical and the deductive methods in social analysis reckoned the practice of politics to be something that could be reduced to a technique. Hobbes asserted boldly that civil philosophy was 'no older than my own book *De Cive*',[29] and, on the inductive side of things, we find in John Collins's social research an example of the barren empiricism which was part of the early history of the Royal Society, and which was spawned by an immoderate faith in technique.[30] The ordering of men in society was understood to be a relatively straight-forward affair, or at any rate an activity which did not require the sophisticated experience and knowledge and the constant attention traditionally associated with it. Once a systematic legal code was formulated, Jeremy Bentham believed, revision would be required no more than once in a hundred years, 'for the sake of changing such terms and expressions as by that time may have become obsolete'.[31]

This faith in man's rational capabilities did not take the shape of an appreciation of what man had done in the past, but rather an optimism about what man can do in the present. Having at last (in the eighteenth century) got at the truth about man, it is now possible to build society anew, but this time, consciously, rationally, upon the correct principles. Although European history (especially that of the 'dark ages') has little in it to be proud of, there are now, thanks to the discoveries of the Enlightenment, grounds for optimism about the future.[32]

Now, neither Rousseau nor Burke shared the steadfast optimism characteristic of many of their contemporaries, and neither had much confidence in the capacity of panaceas to better the lot of mankind. Rousseau's falling out with his *philosophe* friends symbolizes this divergence of intellectual paths. They felt that human improvement was possible, but by no means certain. Rousseau, for his part, was highly pessimistic, and saw about him evidence of decline, and Edmund Burke, although he thought he could discern a gradual advance in most European institutions and particularly in the constitutional history of England, was filled with foreboding and depression by the French Revolution.[33] In Burke's writings on the Revolution can be seen his objections to all attempts to renovate a political community according to abstract principles which do not take into account the concrete details of the situation. Rousseau objects to the Abbé de Saint-Pierre's method on similar grounds :

C'est ici, ce me semble, qu'on retrouve le défaut ordinaire à l'Abbé de Saint-Pierre qui est de n'appliquer jamais assés bien ses vues, aux hommes, aux tems, aux circonstances, et d'offrir toujours comme des facilités pour l'exécution d'un projet, des avantages qui lui servent souvent d'obstacles. Dans le plan dont il s'agit, il vouloit modifier un gouvernement que sa longue durée a rendu déclinant, par des moyens tout à fait étrangers à sa constitution présente. . . .[34]

In describing the empiricist's approach to politics there can be no talk of his spending 'his life on his knees before the great mystery of social life', as Cobban has picturesquely spoken of Burke.[35] Society, for Holbach, or Hume, or Bentham is no living institution 'amongst whose leviathan bowels he fears to probe with murderous scalpel'. Such sentiments would be dismissed by them as so much mystical nonsense. Society is a public device to serve private advantage, and its performance of this task can be measured with fair precision, for the interests of citizens are on the whole readily discernible. They did not appreciate as did Rousseau and Burke the profoundly socializing force of a civil order, nor the 'tacit dimension' of community life; for them, law was an instrument to be used to achieve certain technical objectives.

These are a few of the temperamental and thematic disparities lying between Rousseau and Burke and their empiricist contemporaries. It is not surprising that each has so often been identified with the reaction to the Enlightenment. The rather similar reaction of these two men, so different in their social and political experience, was the sign of a serious shift of emphasis and approach in the political speculation of Europe.

IV   The Traditional Political Community

Edmund Burke's traditionalism is an aspect of his thought which is as well known and as much dwelt upon as any in his work, and descriptions of it 'may be found in a hundred text books on the history of conservatism'.[36] Indeed, the problem one encounters in documenting Burke's traditionalist doctrine is in the very abundance of evidence; one hardly knows where to start. His traditionalist views are at the very centre of his conception of society, and hence appear and reappear everywhere in his writings. His idea of the European political order is typical :

The states of the Christian world have grown up to their present magnitude in a great length of time, and by a great variety of accidents. They have been improved to what we see them with greater or less degrees of felicity and skill. Not one of them has been formed upon a regular plan or with any unity of design. As their constitutions are not systematical, they have not been directed to any *peculiar* end, eminently distinguished, and superseding every other. The objects which they embrace are of the greatest possible variety, and have become in a manner infinite. In all these old countries, the state has been made to the people, and not the people conformed to the state.[37]

It is not, therefore, necessary to explore this aspect of Burke's thought at length, and the bulk of this part of the study will be devoted to determining the character of Rousseau's attitude to the past and to a country's political tradition. What does need to be considered in the case of Burke, however, is the outer limit of his traditionalist doctrine, a limit which is in effect defined by his belief in a superordinate moral authority whose dominion extends over every political community. It is within this universal moral frame that history must be taken to operate, and it is this feature of Burke's thought which most conclusively separates him from the company of those who see in such historical products as nations the ultimate authority of all moral and political activity.[38] The relationship between history and natural law with respect to human nature has already been explored above. With regard to politics, certain opinions which Burke held reveal conclusively his acceptance of a regulating principle superior to all political orders.

For example, he firmly believed that neither the prince nor the people are capable of themselves, in their legislative capacity, of creating right. As he says, 'all human laws are, properly speaking, only declaratory; they may alter the mode and application, but have no power over the substance of original justice'.[39] Not only the government, but the people themselves, even *all* the people, can be wrong in their perception of public advantage and can institute an unjust law; when this is the case, the law is without authority and invalid. In *The Tracts on the Popery Laws*, Burke considers this issue, and in the clearest language asserts the existence of a transcendent authority. One passage may be quoted at length :

But if we could suppose that such a ratification [of a law directed against the community] was made, not virtually but actually, by the people, not representatively, but even collectively, still it would be null and void. They have no right to make a law prejudicial to the whole community, even though the delinquents in making such an act should be themselves the chief sufferers by it; because it would be made against the principle of a superior law, which it is not in the power of any community, or of the whole race of man, to alter – I mean the will of Him who gave us our nature, and in giving impressed an invariable law upon it. It would be hard to point out any error more truly subversive of all the order and beauty, of all the peace and happiness, of human society, than the position that any body of men have a right to make what laws they please; or that laws can derive any authority from their institution merely and independent of the quality of the subject-matter.[40]

It is clear that Burke believes it hardly possible that a people could knowingly legislate against itself, but, even if it could, laws created in such a manner would be illegitimate.

Burke's position on civil rebellion reveals his attitude in this matter from another point of view. Although much of the most impassioned rhetoric in his writings is devoted to a denunciation of those who are carrying out some actual rebellion (the case of the French Revolution is obvious), Burke does not deny the right of rebellion as such. Most actual civil disorder is unjustified, and the vast preponderance of revolutionaries have misunderstood the political situation and dangerously misconceived their duty. Nevertheless, little as Burke liked to draw attention to the fact, he had to admit that there were situations in which a country's citizens could justifiably rebel. He notes, for example, that in his view the

Americans during the War of Independence ('that rebellion', as he calls it), were purely on the defensive, and stood in the same relation to England, as England did to James II, in 1688.[41] Burke contented himself with saying that these occasions occurred very rarely, and that one should approach such a state of affairs with the most cautious reluctance :

As it was not made for common abuses, so it is not to be agitated by common minds. The speculative line of demarcation, where obedience ought to end, and resistance must begin, is faint, obscure, and not easily definable.[42]

Without attempting therefore to define, what never can be defined, the case of a revolution in government, this I think may be safely affirmed, that a sore and pressing evil is to be removed, and that a good, great in its amount and unequivocal in its nature, must be probable almost to certainty, before the inestimable price of our own morals, and the well-being of a number of our fellow-citizens, is paid for a revolution.

Being a Whig politician with the customary reverence for the Glorious Revolution of 1688, Burke would have found it awkward to claim that no right of rebellion existed, and indeed such a claim would not have been consistent with his other views.

There have been many reputable and erudite critics of Rousseau who have held that his appreciation of the importance of tradition and a customary way of life in the functioning of the state was either exiguous or non-existent. We referred in the first chapter to Sir Leslie Stephen's remark that, in the opinion of Rousseau, politics is 'a quasi-mathematical science'.

History and observation are simply irrelevant ... Society will be put together on a geometrical plan, without reference to idiosyncrasies of man and races, or to their historical development.[43]

C. E. Vaughan, too, who enjoys a justifiably prominent position in Rousseau scholarship, has claimed that, although Rousseau 'was right in holding that the civil state, in some form, is essential to the moral life of man',

he was wrong in assuming that either the civil state, or the sense of duty, could ever have sprung to birth in a single moment; that it was possible for them to be anything but the slow growth of time. Time, however, is just what he was not willing to give. . . . The good is always, in his view, the birth of a single moment, the product of a single effort.[44]

E

But there have been, since Rousseau's own day, some critics who have seen that he was indeed willing to give time, that he was quite ready to grant that the historical process was a vital category in explaining the composition of peoples and states. His contemporary, Grimm, for example, was critical of what he understood to be Rousseau's simple analogy between the life of the species and the life of the individual man ('l'espèce humaine, selon notre auteur, a, ainsi comme l'homme individual, ses différens ages....'),[45] and Mme de Staël, in her frankly admiring letters on Rousseau, describes an aspect of his political thought, as she understood it, as follows :

Mais l'esprit humain n'a point fait en un moment le pas immense de l'état sauvage à l'état civilisé; les idées se sont lentement développées; les circonstances ont quelquefois fait naître des institutions si heureuses que la pensée doit en envier la gloire au hasard. La plupart des gouvernements se sont formés par la suite des temps et des événemens, et souvent la connoissance de leur nature et de leur principe a plutôt suivi que précédé leur établissement.[46]

More recently, such scholars as Harald Höffding, E. H. Wright and Jean Starobinski have stressed the traditional aspect of Rousseau's political thought.

Vaughan's claim that Rousseau assumed the civil state and the sense of duty to be always the birth of a single moment is demonstrably incorrect. Rousseau certainly accepted the view that the conception of right and wrong had emerged out of habitual human association and that many different nations and political orders had in fact been thrown up by the historical process. However, Vaughan makes a statement a bit later in the same passage which, although superficially similar, is nevertheless very different in its implications, and is worth pausing to consider. After stating roundly that 'the idea of development is essential to a true theory of Right', he says : 'it is because that idea was entirely foreign to his mind that the theory of Rousseau is so imperfect.'[47] What Vaughan appears to be talking about here is the requirements of a theory of political obligation, and his statement raises two questions. Is the idea of development essential, or, indeed, even appropriate to a theory of Right? Whatever the answer to the first question, did or did not Rousseau hold such an idea as a part of his theory of obligation?

Now, it is important to realize that these questions (which are faced in Part VII below) are different in kind from the issues to which we are addressing ourselves in this section. Rousseau's theory of obligation can be separated from his views regarding the historical variety of states; to assert that Rousseau held a particular theory of obligation does not in itself provide a warrant for saying that he accepted or rejected any particular conception of political tradition (and vice versa). The *Contrat social*, on which claims of Rousseau's a-historical or anti-historical frame of mind are usually based, has as its primary objective the consideration of 'les principes du droit politique'. So long as Rousseau is occupied with this task, history, seen as a factor accounting for the actual emergence and character of peoples, is irrelevant, and to criticize Rousseau on these occasions for neglecting the actual political experience of nations is to miss the point of what he is doing.[48] He is, as he says, taking 'les hommes tels qu'ils sont, et les lois telles qu'elles peuvent être',[49] but his discussion of 'laws as they might be' does not in itself tell us what picture he holds of 'men as they are', still less does it tell us how he reckons men came to be what they are, though it does imply certain general principles of human behaviour.[50]

However, even within the *Contrat* itself, Rousseau quite clearly acknowledges the existence of great differences between countries and peoples. Although the chapters in the treatise dealing with the social contract, sovereignty, the general will and legislation are those which receive the greatest critical attention, it ought not to be forgotten that a considerable portion of the *Contrat* is made up of what might be called eighteenth-century social science, and here Rousseau discloses his awareness of the historical variety of the human species,[51] and of the necessity of constructing institutions suitable to the particular habits and customs of a given people.[52]

Elsewhere, there is ample evidence of a traditionalist view of the state. It is illuminating, for example, to consider what Rousseau has to say about the lawgiver, the great man who incorporates a people out of a mass of unconnected individuals.[53] His profoundly creative function in the *Contrat*, his role as 'le méchanicien qui invente la machine' instead of 'l'ouvrier qui la monte et la fait marcher', has often been noted. At the end of Book II, Rousseau shows that in his view the 'Législateur' is not so much a maker of laws as the founder of a community[54]

Je parle des moeurs, des coutumes, et surtout de l'opinion; partie inconnue à nos politiques, mais de laquelle dépend le succès de toutes les autres: partie dont le grand Législateur s'occupe en secret, tandis qu'il paroit se borner à des réglemens particuliers qui ne sont que le ceintre de la voûte, dont les moeurs, plus lentes à naitre, forment enfin l'inébranlable Clef.[55]

And in the *Économie politique* Rousseau insists :

Formez donc des hommes si vous voulez commander à des hommes: si vous voulez qu'on obéisse aux loix, faites qu'on les aime, et que pour faire ce qu'on doit, il suffise de songer qu'on le doit faire. C'étoit là le grand art des gouvernemens anciens. . . .[56]

In his *Considérations sur le gouvernement de Pologne* Rousseau has a section entitled 'Esprit des anciennes institutions' in which he discusses the practices of three great legislators of old that he often admired : Moses, Lycurgus and Numa. He writes that Moses

forma et executa l'étonnante entreprise d'instituer en corps de nation un essain de malheureux fugitifs . . . Pour empêcher que son peuple ne se fondit parmi les peuples étrangers, il lui donna des moeurs et des usages inaliables avec ceux des autres nations. . . .[57]

Lycurgus, he says, undertood the task of legislating for a servile and vice-ridden people, and hence had to use a firm hand; he had to impose 'un joug de fer' upon the Spartans,

mais il l'attacha, l'identifia, pour ainsi dire, à ce joug en l'en occupant toujours. Il lui montra sans cesse la patrie dans ses loix, dans ses jeux, dans sa maison, dans ses amours, dans ses festins.

Numa, not Romulus, says Rousseau, was the true founder of Rome. Those who take him to be simply the author of rites and religious ceremonies badly misjudge him, for it was Numa who ensured that the imperfect work of Romulus would be lasting :

Ce fut Numa qui le rendit solide et durable en unissant ces brigands en un corps indissoluble, en les transformant en Citoyens, moins par des loix, dont leur rustique pauvreté n'avoit guère encor besoin, que par des institutions douces qui les attachoient les uns aux autres et tous à leur sol en rendant enfin leur ville sacrée. . . .

The same spirit informed the method of all the ancient legislators :

Tous chercherent des liens qui attachassent les Citoyens à la patrie et les uns aux autres, et ils les trouvérent dans des usages particuliers. . . .

These 'usages particuliers' included religious ceremonies, games and physical training, and public spectacles recalling the history and exploits of the country.

Certain features of Rousseau's conception of the lawgiver may now be pointed out. Rousseau is obviously concerned primarily, not with laws, but with 'moeurs'.[58] The great men who found durable communities are in the main occupied with the way of life which the citizen leads, rather than with a formal structure of laws. There appears to be a reciprocal relationship between great political leaders and 'moeurs' – perhaps also between laws and 'moeurs'. The more deeply rooted and healthy are the morals and modes of behaviour of the people, the less need there is for a creative national patriarch, or for an elaborate system of laws and decrees. In situations where a traditional way of life and a sense of community membership are weak or little developed, however, the need for a legislator is acute and his potential sphere of action is much larger. Strong laws and leaders can create or foster 'moeurs', just as 'moeurs' can help to insure the emergence of suitable laws and good leaders. Montesquieu's aphorism, quoted by Rousseau, comes to mind : 'Dans la naissance des sociétés ... ce sont les chefs des républiques qui font l'institution, et c'est ensuite l'institution qui forme les chefs des républiques.'[59]

Rousseau's legislator is usually responsible for incorporating a people who have been living in a natural or a corrupt environment, and his function is so supremely difficult that Rousseau at times cannot bring himself to believe that it is within the compass of mankind. 'Il faudroit des Dieux pour donner des loix aux hommes.'[60] 'C'est une fonction ... qui n'a rien de commun avec l'empire humain....' G. D. H. Cole is no doubt correct in suggesting that the legislator's 'place, in a developed society, is taken by the whole complex of social custom, organization, and tradition that has grown up with the State', but it is going rather too far to say that the legislator as such is 'the spirit of institutions personified.'[61] This is certainly a way of making sense of what Rousseau says, and it does seem at times to be what his argument 'requires', but nevertheless when Rousseau speaks of the 'Législateur' it is generally pretty clear that he has in mind a single great man, an identifiable Moses, Lycurgus, or Numa.

The function of Rousseau's lawgiver, then, is at least as much moral as political. He must adjust his policies to suit the peculiarities of the people he is dealing with, but he must also mould the character of the people to the political order which he is creating. Burke's description of Agricola's *method* would not be uncongenial to Rousseau, although the idea of a nation which once enjoyed a savage liberty being reduced to a polite and easy subjection could not be expected to find favour with him :

Agricola reconciled the Britons to the Roman government by reconciling them to the Roman manners. He moulded that fierce nation by degrees to soft and social customs . . . he subdued the Britons by civilizing them; and made them exchange a savage liberty for a polite and easy subjection. His conduct is the most perfect model for those employed in the unhappy, but sometimes necessary, task of subduing a rude and free people.[62]

If the legislator's labours are successful, the result is not so much a state with an enviable system of law and political institutions, as a patriotic community which, because of its strong traditional way of life, is able to withstand the shocks which bad political leaders and mediocre laws can give it. Such a community is, in a manner of speaking, protected by tradition against political extremism; it enjoys an internal non-political stability.

When Rousseau himself was asked to become a lawgiver for Corsica and Poland, he accepted only with considerable reluctance, and his approach (especially in the case of Poland) reveals something more about his conception of the traditional political community. He was able to tackle the problem of Corsica with guarded optimism because, as he says, 'les Corses sont presque encore dans l'état naturel et sain',[63] and are hence in a condition 'qui rend une bonne institution possible'.[64] Nevertheless, it is clear that he possessed a very modest conception of his role and abilities in this practical field :

Je veux leur dire . . . mon avis et mes raisons avec une telle simplicité qu'il n'y ait rien qui puisse les séduire, parce qu'il est très possible que je me trompe et que je serois bien fâché qu'ils adoptassent mon sentiment à leur préjudice.[65]

Poland is a different and more difficult case, for it is a large and venerable European state which cannot in any way be described as being almost 'dans l'état naturel et sain'. In this case Rousseau abdicates the position of 'législateur' to become simply a 'conseiller',[66] and in this capacity aims to give only 'vues générales, pour éclairer non pour guider l'instituteur'.[67] He is painfully aware of the limitations of theory, when it is to be applied to an actual situation with which the theoretician has no first-hand experience. In the very first paragraph of the *Considérations* he says that he knows of no one better equipped to plan Polish political reform than Count

Wielhorski, and the reasons he gives for this statement are important. Count Wielhorski, he writes,

joint aux connoissances générales que ce travail exige toutes celles du local
et des détails particuliers, impossibles à donner par écrit, et néanmoins
necessaires à savoir pour approprier une institution au peuple auquel on la
destine. Si l'on ne connoît à fond la Nation pour laquelle on travaille,
l'ouvrage qu'on fera pour elle, quelque excellent qu'il puisse être en lui-
même, péchera toujours par l'application, et bien plus encore lorsqu'il
s'agira d'une nation déja toute instituée, dont les gouts, les moeurs, les
préjugés et les vices sont trop enracinés pour pouvoir être aisément étouffés
par des semences nouvelles.[68]

This passage, with its acute sense of the radical distinction between
theoretical and practical knowledge, and of the many uncertainties
and vicissitudes that dog the steps by which a theory is realized in
practice, is surely worthy of Burke. Coming as it does at the very
beginning of the *Considérations*, it sets the tone of the entire work,
and suggests the kind of intelligibility which Rousseau believed
could be expected from it.

Two major themes in the *Considérations* are relevant to the
present discussion. The first, patriotism, will receive explicit attention in the next section; at this stage it is enough to point out
Rousseau's preoccupation with ensuring that the Poles' vigorous
sense of attachment to their own country and manners is sustained
and nurtured. Rousseau sees patriotism not only as a force which
will protect a country against its enemies,[69] but also as an internal
principle of unity and stability which can fuse the ends of the
citizens with the goals of the state.[70] There are numerous hints in
the *Considérations* of that sense of exclusiveness and xenophobia
which was to become a characteristic of nationalism in a short
time.[71] Rousseau builds up a picture of a people which is united by
common language, mores, customs and history, and which defines
itself, at least in part, in terms of its distinctiveness, its historical
differences from other peoples.[72]

The second major theme which helps to clarify his doctrine of
political traditionalism is his cautious approach to reform and his
reluctance to advocate anything approaching a radical or rapid
change. The infinite variety of social life and the hallowed categories of time and place did not generally arouse in Rousseau
the poetic response they so frequently excited in Burke, but they
are nevertheless part of a profoundly important aspect of Rousseau's

thought, evidence of which can be found throughout his work. This theme, which appears as early as the first *Discours*, recurs throughout his political writings : 'Quand il est question d'éstablissemens politiques, c'est le tems et le lieu qui décident de tout.'[73] In his study of Poland, Rousseau approaches political reform with great hesitation, and his recommendations of change are singularly moderate. Rousseau at the outset apostrophizes the Poles thus :

Brave Polonois, prenez garde; prenez garde que pour vouloir trop bien être vous n'empiriez votre situation. En songeant à ce que vous voulez aquerir, n'oubliez pas ce que vous pouvez perdre. Corrigez, s'il se peut, les abus de votre constitution; mais ne méprisez pas celle qui vous a faits ce que vous étes.[74]

Je ne dis pas qu'il faille laisser les choses dans l'état où elles sont; mais je dis qu'il n'y faut toucher qu'avec une circonspection extrême.[75]

And at the conclusion of his work, Rousseau speaks of the spirit in which he undertook the task :

Peut-être tout ceci n'est-il qu'un tas de chiméres, mais voila mes idées . . . quelque singularité qu'on leur trouve, je n'y vois rien, quant à moi, que de bien adapté au coeur humain, de bon, de praticable, surtout en Pologne, m'étant appliqué dans mes vues à suivre l'esprit de cette République, et à n'y proposer que le moins de changemens que j'ai pu pour en corriger les défauts.[76]

Rousseau's conception of the nature of reform, his notion of piecemeal trial-and-error improvement extended over a long period of time, bears many marks of similarity with Burke's ideas. In Part XIII of his *Considérations*, entitled 'Projet pour assujettir à une marche graduelle tous les membres du gouvernement', he writes :

Sur ce plan, gradué dans son execution par une marche successive qu'on pourroit précipiter, ralentir, ou même arrêter selon son bon ou mauvais succés, on n'avanceroit qu'à volonté, guidé par l'expérience . . . et cela avec l'avantage inestimable d'avoir évité tout changement vif et brusque et le danger des revolutions.[77]

In the 'Conclusion' he notes that 'il faut necessairement un certains tems pour sentir l'effet de la meilleur réforme et prendre la consistance qui doit en être le fruit'.[78] And, like Burke, he is willing at times to tolerate customs and institutions which theoretically he can regard only as positive abuses, because he realizes that their removal or radical reformulation would only make the general situation worse.[79]

Edmund Burke's profound and poetic conception of political tradition is one of the most prominent features of his thought, and it has not been considered necessary to give more than a few instances of it in this section. But while it is not possible seriously to contest the presence of a traditionalist view in Burke's thought, critics have denied the existence of such a view in the writings of Rousseau. A primary objective of this part of the chapter has been to show that this is not an adequate understanding of the matter. We need not assert that Rousseau's idea of the traditional political community occupies anything like the salient position in his writings that Burke's does in his; this is clearly not so, partly because Rousseau's preoccupations were not the same as those of Burke, and partly because of a genuine divergence of thought. But two claims may be lodged at this point : firstly, Rousseau's conception of political tradition is fairly coherent and evidence of it can be found throughout his most important political treatises; and secondly, it bears certain notable similarities to the more elaborate doctrine of Edmund Burke.

v   The Limitations of Reason : Public Spirit and Public Institutions

The idea of a traditional political community, as it is conceived by Rousseau and Burke, contains in germ much of what is to be discussed here, for it involves within itself a modest assessment of the role of the individual's rational faculty in political activity, and a concomitant emphasis on many of the springs of political action which we are indicating by the term 'public spirit'.

This phrase, it will be immediately apparent, is not a precise expression and is not susceptible to clear definition. It is a generic term designed to include within it such phenomena as patriotism, customary allegiance to the practices and institutions of a country, the affection men feel for what is old and familiar in the public realm, and the 'halo effect' of emotions in which reverence for one object casts its light upon other proximate but unrelated objects (as, for example, adherence to a set of religious institutions may predispose citizens in favour of the political order established in their country). 'Public spirit' in general is intended to characterize

E*

the non-intellecutal side of a person's response to political institutions, leaders and events. These phenomena may arise spontaneously in the course of time, but in the opinion of both Burke and Rousseau it is unusual for them to emerge in this way in a form suitable to the maintenance of a just state.

Much of Burke's concern with public spirit issues out of his recognition of the need for effective controls on anti-social behaviour and the unlicensed expression of selfish interests, a need which in Burke's mind exists not only because of the intrinsic merits of a community in which selfishness does not reign, but also because of the very limited practical effectiveness of law and the enforcement of law. Laws reach only a little way, whereas public spirit penetrates into the very soul of the citizen. Laws must not be designed simply to satisfy some abstract principles of justice; they must meet the concrete problems of a particular community with its own peculiarities and biases. Procrustes, Burke says, shall never be my hero of legislation;[80] laws must follow the bent of the people if they are to be obeyed, and legislation, if it is to be used as an instrument of improvement, must guide and amend the inclinations of the citizenry by a series of small steps over a long period of time, rather than confront directly the predispositions of the community with 'a sudden jerk of authority' in an unexpected and contrary direction.[81] In his criticism of abstract reason and his discussion of instinct and of what is natural in politics,[82] Burke establishes a position for public spirit which is based not just on its practical utility, but on the positive moral contribution which it makes to civilized life.

Burke's view of the respective functions of reason and public spirit is grounded in certain epistemological assumptions that he makes. A man without traditions or habits of behaviour to draw on, if such a thing were even possible, would be incapable of investing what happened to him with significance and consequently of regulating his conduct. His actions would have no consistency or general direction. Because such a man would be forced to rely solely on abstract reason, his rational faculty would be of no help to him, for a man cannot subject his entire life to reason, self-consciously deliberating and deciding upon every course of action at every step of the way; he must continually and unthinkingly draw on his experience and fall back on habitual modes of conduct. Consider what Burke says about prejudice :

Prejudice is of ready application in the emergency; it previously engages the mind in a steady course of wisdom and virtue, and does not leave the man hesitating in the moment of decision, sceptical, puzzled, and unresolved. Prejudice renders a man's virtue his habit; and not a series of unconnected acts. Through just prejudice, his duty becomes a part of his nature.[83]

While Burke would argue that the complete realization of the mistaken ideal of the fully rational life is simply an impossibility, he would also contend that to work from a false model will be to distort and corrupt one's life and to cause needless harm in the world. Indeed, this is precisely what he accuses the French revolutionaries of doing, the best of whom, he says, are 'only men of theory'.[84] We shall return to these matters in a moment. Two Burkean principles, however, are already clear.

First, a man in his ordinary activity and in his political life must necessarily base his life on 'moeurs' of some kind, and it is important both for him and his community that he be able to rely on beneficial 'moeurs', that is to say, assumptions and customs that will sustain his well-being and foster order and justice in the society. Secondly, and closely related to this, the world of politics is not functionally distinct from the larger social realm. Burke does not share with, say, Hobbes, Locke or James Mill, the liberal conception of a state with certain limited, definable purposes which, once achieved, give men the freedom and security necessary for the private development of private interests. The relationship between the political and the social in Burke's thought is intimate and far-reaching; good political institutions and beneficial social practices draw on and support one another, and the function of politics is not simply to keep the peace, but to improve mankind.

At one point in the *Contrat social*, Rousseau discusses the executive authority of the state which is responsible for carrying out the decisions of the sovereign, and asserts that each member of the executive or government has three distinct types of will: first, the personal will which he possesses as an individual and which serves his own interest; second, the will of the partial association to which he belongs, in this case the government; and third, the sovereign will of the state itself, which he has as a citizen. Rousseau argues that the natural order of priority of these three wills in a person is based on how directly or immediately each relates to his personal interest; hence the personal will comes first and the general or sovereign will last. However, in a just state the required order of priority is precisely the reverse; the general will should always be at the top of the list.[85]

This analysis, which may be generalized to all citizens in a state, indicates the problem for which public spirit provides part of an answer. The natural hierarchy of priorities has to be reordered; men have to be transformed so that personal selfishness will not make political relationships either impossible or structurally unjust. Patriotism specifically, but more broadly the whole range of emotional commitments a citizen may feel for the state, will help to make the public self predominate and thus assist in creating the conditions necessary for a stable and legitimate political order.[86]

Rousseau is of course often described as a thorough anti-rationalist,[87] and it is not difficult to see why this claim has been made. Three reasons come to mind. Firstly, there are a fair number of passages in his works which cannot seriously be read as anything other than an attack on the rational faculty itself.[88] Then there are more numerous occasions in which Rousseau does not wish to deny the importance of reason as such, but to deny it its place of prominence in human nature, and to elevate other faculties or characteristics which he thinks have been ignored or downgraded. In this mood, Rousseau is not so much anti-rational as 'pro' something else.[89] Finally, there is Rousseau's congenital tendency to state straight away whatever point is on his mind in the most dramatic manner possible, often paradoxically, and thereafter to elucidate, to qualify, and sometimes to revise or even to reject. This has quite understandably engendered much critical confusion, and has started readers on a wide variety of false scents.[90]

However, even when, at the outset of his writing career, he answered with an apparently unqualified 'no' the question, 'Si le rétablissement des Sciences et des Arts a contribué à épurer les moeurs?', it can be seen upon a careful reading of the first *Discours* that his position was not as unequivocal as his contemporaries took it to be. It is not until the end of the work that his qualifications become explicit, but even earlier on in the treatise his attacks seem often to be directed, not against human reason and artifacts as such, but against the abuse of them and against the vices which they ostensibly foster – luxury, deception, excessively fastidious taste, and so forth. In the last few pages, Rousseau makes his views quite clear, and puts forward a notion of a sort of Platonic aristocracy of intelligence.[91] He applauds those great and original minds ('les Verulams, les Descartes et les Newtons, ces Precepteurs du Genre-humain')[92] who have been able to advance human knowledge, and who have had no need of masters, and asserts that princes ought not to refuse the counsel of those best equipped to give it.[93] What he objects to here, it becomes apparent, is the common situation in which difficult matters of speculation come to be 'agitated by common minds'.[94] Men are variously endowed with capacities and abilities, and they ought to engage in those activities which are appropriate to their own peculiar make-up: 'Tel qui sera toute sa vie un mauvais versificateur, un Geométre subalterne, seroit peut-être devenu un grand fabricateur d'étoffes.'[95]

However, this drastic intellectual inequality is in Rousseau's opinion balanced by moral equality. One of Rousseau's most basic moral principles was that men did not need great knowledge in order to lead a virtuous life.[96] This is a major theme in the first *Discours*, and it is taken up again and again in other works. Knowledge is not virtue for Rousseau, nor is wisdom the prerequisite of the good life. The seat of morality, one might say, is in the heart, not in the mind, and conscience speaks directly to man, without the clumsy intervention of reflection.[97] As for the citizen, his specifically political virtue is expressed in conscientious participation in formulating the general will, and in obedience to law. It remains of course a serious question whether the often paternalistic means of achieving what is politically good are compatible with the individual's moral or political autonomy.

Indeed, ignorance ('l'heureuse ignorance où la sagesse éternelle nous avoit placés')[98] can often be a positive aid to virtuous behaviour:

Jusqu'alors les Romains s'étoient contentés de pratiquer la vertu; tout fut perdu quand ils commencerent à l'étudier.[99]

The closing lines of the first treatise are devoted to driving the point home:

O vertu! Science sublime des ames simples, faut-il donc tant de peines et d'appareil pour te connoître? Tes principes ne sont-ils pas gravés dans tous les coeurs, et ne suffit-il pas pour apprendre tes Loix de rentrer en soi-même et d'écouter la voix de sa conscience dans le silence des passions?[100]

Virtue is not the reward of a life-time of intellectual struggle and moral effort; it is rather a happy state, a free gift of nature, which is all too easily corrupted by the experience of life. Therefore, what is required of a man is not so much a positive seeking after virtue and the eradication of evil, but the preservation of his innocence of vice. Émile was to be subjected to a sort of negative education in which the wrong things were kept away from him until he had reached a stage of maturity which enabled him to cope with evil and temptation.[101]

Earlier in the study we saw that, although Rousseau's conception of reason is not always easy to specify, in his opinion the rational faculty in man so long as he is living in a pre-social condition is either very weak or else existent only as a potentiality, and that it is only when man begins to live among his fellows that it starts to assume a force and definable character of its own. An instance of the consequent limited effectiveness of reason can be seen in what Rousseau has to say about the formation and working out of community life in the early stages of social development. In the *Discours sur l'inégalité* the institution of a society based on law is pictured as a trick which the rich, banding together, play upon the poor and dispossessed. The latter react to the duplicity as follows :

Tous coururent au devant de leurs fers croyant assûrer leur liberté; car avec assés de raison pour sentir les avantages d'un établissement politique, ils n'avoient pas assés d'expérience pour en prévoir les dangers; les plus capables de pressentir les abus étoient précisément ceux qui comptoient d'en profiter. . . .[102]

Because of the difficulty of explaining how an ignorant mass can somehow constitute itself into a coherent political society, there is frequently in Rousseau's presentation a single man or a small minority of far-seeing individuals who assist in the working out of political life, and a large ignorant majority who follow their lead. In the *Contrat social* it is the lawgiver who performs this critical role, and the fact that his is a tutelary or educative, more than a legislative function suggests the condition of the people who are the beneficiaries of his efforts. In outlining the general problem which necessitates the lawgiver, Rousseau makes it clear that the heart of the difficulty is to be found in the uncivilized nature of the common man, and in particular in his lack of intellectual penetration; Rousseau writes in the Geneva manuscript :

. . . comme l'art de généraliser ainsi ses idées est un des exercices les plus difficiles et les plus tardifs de l'entendement humain, le commun des hommes sera-t-il jamais en état de tirer de cette maniére de raisonner les régles de sa conduite, et quand il faudroit consulter la volonté générale sur un acte particulier, combien de fois n'arriveroit-il pas à un homme bien intentionné de se tromper sur la régle ou sur l'application et de ne suivre que son penchant en pensant obéir à la loi?[103]

The problem, here, as Rousseau points out, is that 'nous ne commençons proprement à devenir hommes qu'après avoir été Citoyens'.

It is clear from the discussion in the final version of the *Contrat* that the mass of people have, as it were, the energy and the desire necessary for the founding of a political society; this must be so, because the lawgiver's programme can only be presented to, not forced upon, the people, who must then approve or reject it. But they lack the creative genius, the patience, and the sense of occasion and direction which the legislator supplies. The wishes of the people are akin to a natural force blindly searching for the good ('De lui-même le peuple veut toujours le bien, mais de lui-même il ne le voit pas toujours'; 'le public veut le bien qu'il ne voit pas');[104] the legislator must harness this public desire, shape and define it, direct its flow, and finally transform it from a natural into a political force. Whether the men who are the subjects of this management are viewed individually or in the mass, it is the inadequacy of the rational faculty which is crucial: 'Il faut obliger les uns [the individuals] à conformer leurs volontés à leur raison; il faut apprendre à l'autre [the public] à connoitre ce qu'il veut.'[105]

With the achievement of this individual and public enlightenment there will be a union of understanding (that which the legislator has been concerned to foster) and will (the primitive force or raw material which the people themselves directly supplied), and there will be harmony among the individuals and a maximum of strength in the state.[106] In order to arrive at this happy situation the lawgiver must radically change ('altérer' or 'mutiler') the nature of man by means of education, persuasion (but never force), and deception, and in general he must by the exercise of his 'sublime reason' make up for the rational deficiencies of 'le vulgaire'.[107]

But his task is broader than this. Although the development of citizen rationality is of central importance, it is part of the larger issue of forming human character itself. In the *Économie politique*, Rousseau writes:

S'il est bon de savoir employer les hommes tels qu'ils sont, il vaut beaucoup mieux encore les rendre tels qu'on a besoin qu'ils soient; l'autorité la plus absolue est celle qui pénétre, jusqu'à l'intérieur de l'homme, et ne s'exerce pas moins sur la volonté que sur les actions.[108]

If the lawgiver is helping to set up a political order *de novo*, or if he is legislating for an uncorrupted people, one of his major preoccupations must be to ensure the continuance within civil society of those conditions which sustain the practice (but not the study) of social virtue; he must adjust laws to salutary 'moeurs'. If, however, he has to cope with an 'old' or corrupt political community (and age and corruption generally go hand in hand), then it is important for him to encourage the implementation of a system of law which will 'restore' ancient virtue; he must reform degenerate 'moeurs' with good law. Rousseau has a lively awareness that it is human character as a whole, and not just human reason, that forms the basis of the state; 'les Gouvernemens humains avoient besoin d'une base plus solide que la seule raison'.[109] Rousseau, in fact, far from being a proper object of the Burkean attack on excessive and misplaced rationalism, would not disagree with Burke's belief that (especially in the eighteenth century) it is more often the meddlesome, restless spirit of rational criticism which causes ills in a country than it is its old abuses and familiar prejudices.[110]

It is clearly unsatisfactory to relate Rousseau's 'loi' to reason and 'moeurs' to public spirit, although Rousseau at one point does say of the 'magistrat' that 'sa raison même lui doit être suspecte, et il ne doit suivre d'autre regle que la raison publique, qui est la loi'.[111] But it is certainly safe to say that 'moeurs' – custom, habit, manners, morals – appeal primarily to the non-rational side of man, while law, or rather the lawmaking process, entails conscious, purposeful activity; it is clear that one cannot 'make' morals in the sense that one can make laws.[112] It is necessary here to think in terms of 'the lawmaking process' rather than 'law' because certain Rousseauist doctrines blur the distinction between law and custom, by suggesting the manner in which present law can with the passing of time assume the character and force of custom, and perhaps also (though this is less certain) by suggesting the manner in which custom can gradually come to be invested with the authority of law.[113]

Regarding the first procedure (the transformation of law into custom), Rousseau's admission that tacit acceptance by the sovereign of an old law constitutes legitimization makes it clear that the differences between a traditional practice and a law which is generations old must be slight and at times practically indiscernible. In the third book of the *Contrat* there is a passage which in its reverence for antiquity has a distinct flavour of Burke:

Pourquoi donc porte-t-on tant de respect aux anciennes loix? C'est pour cela même. On doit croire qu'il n'y a que l'excellence des volontés antiques qui les ait pu conserver si longtems; si le Souverain ne les eut reconnu constamment salutaire il les eut milles fois révoquées. Voilà pourquoi loin de s'affoiblir les loix acquierent san cesse une force nouvelle dans tout Etat bien constitué; le préjugé de l'antiquité, les rend chaque jour plus vénérables. . . .[114]

In such a passage as this (which it should be noted, comes from the *Contrat* itself) Rousseau comes very close to accepting the notion of the prescriptive validity of ancient laws, their binding force over subsequent generations, and reveals a Burkean attitude to the sympathetic prejudice with which one should approach them. The general will seems here almost to be provided with a temporal dimension, and politics in a 'mature' country appears to be an activity which is engaged in the maintenance and repair of a relatively coherent national heritage rather than in a series of national reincarnations. Consider for instance the following fragment: 'Dans tout pays où les moeurs sont une partie intégrante de la constitution de l'Etat, les lois sont toujours plus tournées à maintenir les coutumes qu'à punir ou récompenser.'[115]

With respect to the second procedure (the transformation of custom into law), Rousseau on one occasion specifically rejects what might be called the prescriptive theory of political obligation,[116] *apparently* so dear to the heart of Burke,[117] in which might, with the passing of time, is gradually turned into right, and custom becomes over the years invested with the same authority as law. Nevertheless, in so far as he breaks down the distinction between law and custom he appears to be approaching this theory. In the quotation just above laws are venerated *because* they are old, and they seem to derive as much of their authority from previous decisions of the sovereign in ages gone by, as they do from their acceptance by the current general will. In short, old laws with their roots in the past have 'une force naturelle'[118] which is more comprehensive and penetrating than the persuasive power of today's decisions of the general will. It should also be noted that according to a passage just quoted above 'moeurs' themselves are sometimes a part of the constitution of a state.

Finally, we might include here a remark which Rousseau makes in the 'Dédicace' of the *Discours sur l'inégalité* shortly after saying that given the choice he would not have wished to inhabit 'une République de nouvelle institution, quelque bonnes loix qu'elle pût avoir' for fear that the system of government and the people might not be suited to one another: 'J'aurois donc cherché pour ma Patrie une heureuse et tranquille République dont l'ancienneté se perdît en quelque sorte dans la nuit des tems....'[119] In this striking image Rousseau suggests that a legitimate political order can exist for which there is no record or memory of a unanimous covenant setting society up. There may or may not have been an actual contract, but the facts are lost in the mists of time. Now, this need cause no difficulty if one interprets his social-contract argument as an explanatory model of political obligation. Such an historical conception simply suggests that *in fact* time can produce right, and can cloak 'governments that were violent in their commencement'[120] in the vestments of legitimate political authority. That is to say, it is easier to believe that in practice a just state will emerge in the course of a long period of time than that it will be the birth of a single moment, although it remains equally true that the recognition of a state as just is not based on how long that state has existed. To the question, 'Why should I obey the sovereign?', it is not satisfactory to answer, 'because it has existed a long, long time'.

Rousseau's theory of political obligation, however, in no way affects our contention that Rousseau realized the practical limitations of reason in the carrying on of political life and the practical necessity of the factors we have gathered together under the term 'public spirit'. We shall close this discussion of Rousseau with the following gloomy political fragment:

L'erreur de la plupart des moralistes fut toujours de prendre l'homme pour en être essentiellement raisonnable. L'homme n'est qu'un être sensible qui consulte uniquement ses passions pour agir, et à qui la raison ne sert qu'à pallier les sottises qu'elles lui font faire. [121]

This was an error that Rousseau was not usually inclined to commit; as can be judged from the sombre tenor of the above passage, it was more frequently in the opposite direction that he tended to travel.

Edmund Burke's distrust of the rational faculty, whether in the field of political analysis or political action, is a salient feature of his thought often noted by commentators, as is his reliance upon the non-rational sources of political activity.

In a sense Burke circumscribed reason's field of action by redefining the concept of reason itself. C. E. Vaughan was thinking along these lines when he wrote that:

To Burke, reason is no longer the purely passive and analytic faculty of Locke and his disciples; it is a creative faculty, which draws upon the darker and more mysterious, no less than upon the more definite and conscious, elements of man's experience.[122]

But the process of redefinition extends farther than this, particularly when Burke is thinking of political affairs and the capacities of citizens; reason in these circumstances is not simply a characteristic of individual human beings, but a quality of human groups as well.

Now, at this point it might be objected that Burke is not limiting but expanding the role of reason, and in a sense this is true; however, in redefining it, he is in effect changing the concept into something else, for it is clear that the 'reason' of a nation is something quite different from the 'reason' of a man, and the effect (and often the major purpose) of this redefinition is to emphasize the limitations of reason, *as it is commonly understood*:

We [the British] are afraid to put men to live and trade each on his own private stock of reason; because we suspect that this stock in each man is small, and that individuals would do better to avail themselves of the general bank and capital of nations and of ages.[123]

The individual's small private stock of reason needs to be supported and supplemented by the rational capital of nations.

It would appear that in the latter case the term 'reason' is designed to convey some such meaning as the total stock of human experience, the 'wisdom' of the species ('wisdom' here suggesting all that makes up customary or traditional patterns of behaviour). But a consequence of this line of argument is to undermine the autonomy of individual citizen rationality which involves in part reasoning abstractly according to some accepted procedures, that is to say, what Burke sometimes typifies as 'airy speculation'.[124] It is to the serious political limitations of this sort of thought that both Rousseau and Burke attempted to call attention. When Burke referred, and especially when he referred disparagingly, to an individual's 'reason' it was generally this human faculty that he had in mind.

It must be admitted that Burke has the habit of investing such words as 'reason', 'rational', 'speculation', 'philosophy' and so forth, with connotations of praise or blame, according to his opinion of the sort of activity which is being described and the skill with which it is being carried on. In a speech on parliamentary reform, Burke candidly admits as much:

I do not vilify theory and speculation – no, because that would be to vilify reason itself. *Neque decipitur ratio, neque decipit unquam.* No; whenever I speak against theory, I mean always a weak, erroneous, fallacious, unfounded, or imperfect theory....[125]

His statements about the rational faculty, then, generally have an obvious normative content, and much of his argument is devoted to disclosing that the conception of reason in a given political theory (with which he disagrees) is downright wrongheaded and decidedly out of harmony with the 'great principles of reason and equity', or the 'eternal rules of justice and reason' (with which Burke is in profound agreement).[126]

Nevertheless, to admit this is not to undermine our contention that Burke seriously limits the rational faculty's field of operation. The fact that he finds so much bad theory about him Burke is able to explain with the help of the principle that the authority of reason over men is comparatively weak, and its utility in their affairs relatively narrow. Reasoning has a valid place in social studies, but it is an activity which is of limited scope, and which it is very difficult to engage in successfully.

The characters of nature are legible, it is true; but they are not plain enough to enable those who run, to read them. We must make use of a cautious, I had almost said a timorous, method of proceeding.[127]

Men often act right from their feelings, who afterwards reason but ill on them from principle: but as it is impossible to avoid an attempt at such reasoning, and equally impossible to prevent its having some influence on our practice, surely it is worth taking some pains to have it just, and founded on the basis of sure experience.[128]

Burke's statement that men often act right from their feelings, who *afterwards* reason but ill on them from principle brings up a very important aspect of his conception of the rational process. He thinks that his rationalist opponents (he names such men as

Voltaire, Helvétius and Rousseau)[129] have the idea that a man works up a theoretical system out of whole cloth, as it were; they recognize no predecessors, and count themselves the disciples of no one – they believe themselves to be original thinkers. It is Burke's belief that the notion of originality in social thought is the result of a serious misconstruction of the manner in which the human mind operates. In his view, theory is drawn from practice, and a man carries on (he *must* carry on) his thinking within some intellectual context or heritage. As speculation and theorizing are activities which cannot be avoided, it is well to have a clear understanding of what one is doing when one is thinking abstractly in order to be able to do it better and to be able to avoid unhappy practical misadventures. A false step in the classroom involves mere error, but a false step in the legislature involves public evil.[130] Hence his famous statement :

It seems to me a preposterous way of reasoning, and a perfect confusion of ideas, to take the theories which learned and speculative men have made from that government, and then, supposing it made on those theories, which were made from it, to accuse the government as not corresponding with them.[131]

This view of theory and practice is clearly connected with his notion of a country's heritage and his traditional style of practising politics.[132] In connection with it, two further points may be mentioned. Firstly, he believes that, since speculation is a derivative of practice, the most potent way of proving or invalidating a social theory is to set it up against practice; as he says, one of the ways of discovering a false theory

is by comparing it with practice. This is the true touchstone of all theories which regard man and the affairs of men – does it suit his nature in general ? – does it suit his nature as modified by his habits?[133]

He also notes in a reply to Charles Fox on the subject of French affairs that there are occasions when 'our feelings contradict our theories; and when this is the case, our feelings are true, and the theory is false.'[134]

Secondly, as we pointed out earlier, an exercise in political reason, especially if it stays close to actual political life and does not ascend into philosophy, must match in subtlety the political 'reality' which it is designed to cope with or consider. Political action, and thought related to political action, are matters of detail, of time and occasion, and of experience.[135] Simplicity, in these circumstances, is not a virtue, but an ignorant failing; it is 'the offspring of cold hearts and muddy understandings'.[136]

When I hear the simplicity of contrivance aimed at and boasted of in any new political constitutions, I am at no loss to decide that the artificers are grossly ignorant of their trade, or totally negligent of their duty. The simple governments are fundamentally defective, to say no worse of them.[137]

From projects conceived and undertaken in an appropriate spirit there arises, 'not an excellence in simplicity, but one far superior, an excellence in composition'.[138]

Edmund Burke, then, views human communities in the light of history; they are what they have become over a long period of time, or if, as in the case of the American colonies, they are newly constructed entities, they are nevertheless composed of individuals who come from somewhere and who hence have an identifiable past. The rebellious colonists are first and foremost Englishmen, and Englishmen of a particular sort,[139] and properly to understand the nature of their discontent and the consequent political adjustments which must be made to effect a reconciliation, it is necessary to examine the English 'pedigree of this fierce people'[140] in conjunction with the local circumstances which obtain in North America.[141]

A citizen's traditional way of life is a more potent force in determining his behaviour than is the exercise of his fragile and uncertain rational faculty.[142] As we have noted, Burke makes this point in part by redefining the concept of reason itself; he rationalizes the idea of a national heritage so that it becomes the 'collected reason of ages'[143] in which an individual can participate but which he can never fully master.[144] The transmission of knowledge, of this collected reason, is not, in Burke's view, restricted simply to the sphere of explicitly formulated rational instruction, to the domain of formal education. It should rather be understood as what the sociologist calls 'the process of socialization'; it is the subtle procedure by which a child grows into a civilized adult, and includes 'teaching' ways of thinking and acting by example, and absorbing them by unconscious imitation.[145] So, to understand man properly, one must realize that the greater part of his life is composed of customs and habits which have never been subjected to the scrutiny of reason, which are indeed 'second nature'. It is not that man acts irrationally, but that he acts unreflectively, and this unreflective behaviour is in fact much more rational than behaviour which is based solely or primarily on design or technique.

At the end of our discussion of Rousseau we quoted a political fragment in which he attacks the majority of moralists for assuming man to be basically rational, whereas in fact he is a creature of sensation and passion who uses reason to help get himself out of the difficulties into which his unthinking impetuosity hurries him. Edmund Burke could almost be drawing the appropriate political conclusion from this judgement when he writes that 'politics ought to be adjusted, not to human reasonings, but to human nature; of which the reason is but a part, and by no means the greatest part.'[146]

vi Political Liberty

Edmund Burke's strongest attack on Rousseau occurs in the *Letter to a Member of the National Assembly* (1791), and it is interesting to note how many of the criticisms which he directs at the Genevan and his revolutionary 'disciples' are criticisms which Rousseau himself raised with equal force in connection with contemporary French society.[147] The ground of Burke's case against Rousseau is his alleged pernicious moral influence : 'Rousseau is a moralist, or is he nothing.' Burke's contention is that Rousseau ('the great professor and founder of the *philosophy of vanity*') has effected a moral revolution in Europe by overturning the traditional Christian hierarchy of values – by replacing humility with vanity, and by elevating right above duty, will above reason.

Under the old dispensation, the political effect of virtuous behaviour was to make men modest in their evaluation of their own abilities, tolerant of a less than perfect state of affairs, realistic in the demands they made of a political system; the new Rousseauist morality, according to Burke, had just the contrary effect; it made men vain, impatient and visonary. Of the revolutionary legislators Burke writes :

Their great problem is to find a substitute for all the principles which hitherto have been employed to regulate the human will and action ... They have therefore chosen a selfish, flattering, seductive, ostentatious vice, in the place of plain duty. True humility, the basis of the Christian system ... they have totally discarded.

It would appear that Burke's judgement of Rousseau in this passage was formed primarily on the basis of his life, rather than his works. At any rate, this is what Burke concentrates on – Rousseau's abandonment of his children to the foundling hospital, his turbulent visit to England under Hume's guidance, his well publicized personal failings and vices. The only piece of writing specifically mentioned by Burke in this passage is *La Nouvelle Héloïse*; the only other implied is the *Confessions*. However, towards the end of the discussion he does consider Rousseau's writings as a whole, and gives it as his opinion that 'the *general spirit and tendency* of his works is mischievous ...'.

On the face of it, it is not difficult to appreciate how Burke could believe that Rousseau's *political* doctrines are of a piece with his life and literary productions, all of them together dissolving traditional moral bonds and encouraging disorder and licentious behaviour. Rousseau's most important political idea, was, after all, 'la volonté générale', the general *will*. Burke was adamant that the dominion of will was as much to be feared in politics as in moral life :

I have ever abhorred, since the first dawn of my understanding to this its obscure twilight, all the operations of opinion, fancy, inclination, and will, in the affairs of government, where only a sovereign reason, paramount to all forms of legislation and administration, should dictate. Government is made for the very purpose of opposing that reason to will and caprice, in the reformers or in the reformed, in the governors or in the governed, in kings, in senates, or in people.[148]

Burke's intense antipathy to the sovereignty of will could hardly be more clear; but I think an elucidation of what Burke meant by 'will' and what Rousseau meant by the same term will help to clarify, not only their conception of the political role of volition, but also the extent to which there is a gulf between their respective doctrines of political liberty. When Burke spoke of 'will' pejoratively, what he customarily meant was the domination of appetite over reason within the individual soul, or (in the political realm) the rule by a man or men whose moral composition was disordered in this way – 'the arbitrary pleasure of one man'.[149] The clear implication was that of irrational, short-term, inconstant government, either personal or political. A citizen under such a government found himself subject to the arbitrary decisions of other men, the very reverse of proper government, and the very situation which political society was designed to prevent.

Society requires not only that the passions of individuals should be subjected, but that even in the mass and body, as well as in the individuals, the inclinations of men should frequently be thwarted, their will controlled, and their passions brought into subjection. This can only be done *by a power out of themselves*; and not, in the exercise of its function, subject to that will and to those passions, which it is its office to bridle and subdue.[150]

Despite first impressions to the contrary, a major preoccupation of Rousseau's political thought, as of his moral thought, is the profound need of mankind for an order in which 'will' *in Burke's sense* will not dominate. Given his doctrine of the general will, such a contention may at first sight seem implausible, but it was precisely through the medium of 'la volonté générale' that Rousseau hoped to achieve his objective. The general will bears no resemblance to the selfish, particular will of individuals, as Rousseau goes to considerable lengths to make clear.[151] It is Rousseau's answer to what he regards as the fundamental problem of politics, the reconciliation of liberty and obedience.[152] At one point in the *Contrat* Rousseau makes a distinction between the citizen as the maker of law and the citizen as the subject of law.[153] It is mainly in respect of the citizen as law-maker that the legitimacy of the legislative process is demonstrated. We may here most usefully consider the question of liberty, however, specifically from the perspective of the subject, assuming for the moment that the necessary requirements of legitimate law-making have been fulfilled.

From this second perspective, it is evident that the point of Rousseau's argument is to secure the member's political liberty within society, that is, to free him from arbitrary decrees and personal or private will. Utter dependence on a just system of law is political freedom; dependence on persons is bondage.[154] The subject in Rousseau's polity looks up to laws and not to rulers, and laws, says Rousseau, consider 'les sujets en corps et les actions comme abstraites, jamais un homme comme individu ni une action particuliére'.[155] Man does not feel himself to be a slave to the laws of natural science; neither will he feel himself to be in bondage to the laws of a just state. What Rousseau is attempting to do, through the proper arrangement of thoroughly artificial institutions, is to reestablish in politics the impersonal and objective conditions of the state of nature.[156] It is in this condition that a man is free and – equally important – feels himself to be free.

In the closing lines of the *Reflections* Burke, not without justification, describes himself as one 'almost the whole of whose public exertion has been a struggle for the liberty of others'.[157] This suggests his approach to the problem of political liberty; his interest in liberty was occasioned by contemporary political problems, and his response to them, although by no means untheoretical, was predominantly practical. His usual line of argument (for example, in considering American or French affairs) was to take the British constitution, whose distinguishing feature was in his opinion its concrete embodiment of free government,[158] as a model and consider the issue in terms of it. It is in Burke's elaboration of his conception of British freedom that one can discover his general views on social and political liberty.[159]

The British constitution on Burke's interpretation achieves in practice what Rousseau sought to achieve theoretically, that is, the reconciliation of two apparent opposites, liberty and obedience :[160]

To make a government requires no great prudence. Settle the seat of power; teach obedience; and the work is done. To give freedom is still more easy. It is not necessary to guide; it only requires to let go the rein. But to form a *free government*; that is, to temper together these opposite elements of liberty and restraint in one consistent work, requires much thought, deep reflection, a sagacious, powerful, and combining mind.[161]

It is this reconciling of liberty and restraint that is the glory of the British political system and the goal that will elude the French revolutionaries. With the above quotation of Burke in mind, one can appreciate his accurate prediction of both the anarchic and the authoritarian phases of the French upheaval; it is easy in his view to have one or the other, but supremely difficult to combine both.

There is an important section in the *Reflections* in which Burke argues that it is the practice of the British people to regard their liberties as an 'entailed inheritance' derived from their forefathers, and to be transmitted by them to their posterity.[162] By treating political freedom as if it were property Burke is trying to bring into relief a number of points which he feels are in danger of being neglected. In the first place, he wishes to outflank the natural-right thinkers by showing that their appeals to nature are irrelevant in considering practical political liberty. Secondly, he wants to demonstrate the concrete, particular character of liberty in the 'real world'. Thirdly, he is suggesting that 'considering our liberties in the light of an inheritance'[163] produces an orderly, temperate attitude of mind conducive to the secure and continued enjoyment of a liberal way of life. Finally, and related to each of the previous points, Burke is giving his interpretation of the means by which the English have successfully combined the two principles of liberty and obedience in a harmonious pattern of free government.

Burke is patently aware of the rarity of such a political system and of its value, and, in keeping with his discussion of liberty as a 'blessing and a benefit, not an abstract speculation',[164] he more than once declares his belief that there are many forms or patterns which a liberal state may take.

I am not so narrowminded as to be unable to conceive that the same object may be attained in many ways, and perhaps in ways very different from those which we have followed in this country.[165]

... social and civil freedom, like all other things in common life, are variously mixed and modified, enjoyed in very different degrees, and shaped into an infinite diversity of forms, according to the temper and circumstances of every community.[166]

Despite the individuality of principles when they are embodied in a given country, Burke says that there are certain signs which are reliable indications of whether a country is free. Before congratulating France on her recent acquisition of liberty, Burke states, it would be wise to enquire

how it had been combined with government; with public force; with the discipline and obedience of armies; with the collection of an effective and well-distributed revenue; with morality and religion; with the solidity of property; with peace and order; with civil and social manners.[167]

Most of what Burke says as described above may be understood as an application of the general principle to which he consistently adheres, namely, the principle that freedom can exist only in a context of order.

... liberty, the only liberty I mean, is a liberty connected with order; that not only exists along with order and virtue, but which cannot exist at all without them. It inheres in good and steady government, as in its substance and vital principle.[168]

Elsewhere he specifies more particularly his meaning by calling it 'social freedom' :

It is that state of things in which liberty is secured by the equality of restraint. A constitution of things in which the liberty of no one man, and no body of men, and no number of men, can find means to trespass on the liberty of any person, or any description of persons, in the society. This kind of liberty is indeed but another name for justice; ascertained by wise laws, and secured by well-constructed institutions.[169]

Liberty is secured by an equality of restraint; 'la liberté consiste moins à faire sa volonté qu'à n'être pas soumis à celle d'autrui'.[170] Political liberty is, then, as it is for Rousseau, liberty under the law.

In Part vi of the previous chapter we discussed briefly Rousseau's forced-to-be-free paradox from the point of view of moral liberty; here we shall look at its political ramifications and make certain comparisons with Burke's doctrine.[171] The problem which Rousseau's paradox purports to solve is roughly as follows.

The citizen (as legislator) participates in the making of a decision of the general will which is in the common interest of the members of the state. However, the same citizen (as subject) sometimes finds that it is in his particular or selfish interest to flout or evade the requirements of the general will, as they are expressed in law. There are two obvious situations in which this could occur. Firstly, a citizen might find that in the lawmaking process he is a member of the minority that voted against the law, and hence have reservations about abiding by the decision.[172] Secondly, a member of the majority might simply have second thoughts about the decision when it came to be applied, or he might calculate that it is in his personal interest to disobey the law covertly so long as he can be sure everyone else will obey it.

In either case, the sovereign (of which the citizen [as legislator] is a part) coerces the citizen (as subject) in order to make him live up to his legislative agreements. When this happens, the citizen (as subject) is being forced by himself (or rather, by a body of which he is a member) to be free, that is, to deny his merely selfish, short-term interests and to follow the common, long-term interests to which he has already freely agreed in his capacity as a member of the sovereign and in the advantages of which he shares.

The crucial difference between the moral doctrine of 'rational freedom' and this political doctrine of 'enforced freedom' is that the former entails a sort of internal domination (a man rules over himself), whereas the latter involves coercion applied to a person from outside, from another person or persons.[173] Rousseau's argument as outlined in the paragraphs above is that so long as a law is legitimate, that is, in part, so long as it is a rule which the subjects have had a hand in formulating, then legally applied force may in certain circumstances be understood as a condition of political freedom. Strictly speaking, Rousseau's notorious paradox is self-contradictory, but he himself was surely aware of this, and a host of commentators have tried to uncover the meaning which they take to be embedded in this extraordinary assertion. The chapter of the *Contrat* in which the statement appears is, of course, a favourite passage for critics who see Rousseau as a totalitarian, but I should like to suggest two possible interpretations of the paradox which are very far from being totalitarian in implication, and which both, in my opinion, make sense in the light of what Rousseau says elsewhere.

The first and more general interpretation issues out of Rousseau's contention that political liberty is necessarily related to a system of law. 'Independence' is Rousseau's term for the type of freedom that a man can have in a state of anarchy. But moral and political liberty entail the existence of moral or legal rules, and consequently of rights and duties. In the case of law, where there is not universal recognition and obedience there must be enforcement, and enforcement of a particular law with respect to a particular offender may be necessary to maintain a system in which freedom can flourish. This is of benefit not only to society, but also to the individual lawbreaker because he is being obliged to live up to the requirements which make his political freedom possible.

The second interpretation may be outlined specifically from the point of view of the coerced individual; it hinges on the concept of the divided self, and the distinction between one's private or particular will and one's general will. John Plamenatz, in a discussion of Rousseau's paradox, notes that men speak of rules *restraining* them, but of passions *enslaving* them.[174] Men frequently experience the sense of being in thrall to their appetites, and of recognizing and accepting rules of conduct, but being unable to follow them. For a person in this situation, the enforcement of conformity to stipulated rules of conduct may not seem an infringement of liberty, but a release from bondage to forces over which the individual has inadequate control. The disobedient subject of a legitimate state is compelled to follow his general will (as expressed in the legislative process), and to deny the dictates of his particular will. This is, then, the direct political parallel to the moral dilemma Émile found himself in when he appealed to his tutor to compel him to be master of himself.[175] But in political life the tutor's place is taken by the laws of the land.

This general line of thinking is discernible in Burke's writings also, and it is occasionally articulated in a most striking fashion. There is more than a hint of it in Burke's conception of representation and the proper role of governors.[176] Burke argues that a popular representative ought to prefer his own reasoned judgement to the will of his constituents, if an occasion arises in which the two come into conflict.[177]

[A representative's] unbiassed opinion, his mature judgment, his enlightened conscience, he ought not to sacrifice to you, to any man, or to any set of men living. . . . Your representative owes you, not his industry only, but his judgment; and he betrays, instead of serving you, if he sacrifices it to your opinion. . . . If the local constituent should have an interest, or should form an hasty opinion, evidently opposite to the real good of the rest of the community, the member for that place ought to be as far, as any other, from any endeavour to give it effect.[178]

When it appears evident to our governors that our desires and our interests are at variance, they ought not to gratify the former at the expense of the latter.[179]

Rousseau would certainly fall in with Burke's notion of a citizen's 'better' interest which the government persuades or guides him into following, but what he would not be able to accept is the separation of rulers and ruled in the idea of representation. He believed it was nonsense to say that the people ruled through their representatives; Rousseau directed a telling shaft at the *philosophes'* favourite empirical model of good government and at the constitution that Burke so much revered when he wrote that the English think they are free, but in fact, with the exception of general elections when the people choose their rulers, they are nothing better than slaves.[180]

We have already alluded to a passage in Burke's *Letter to a Member of the National Assembly* in which he argues that there must be a controlling power upon man's appetite, and that the weaker the internal restraints are, the stronger must be the political.[181] His description there of passions as 'fetters' carries with it the clear implication that political constraints, in the case of unruly subjects, become a condition of political liberty.

In the *Reflections* Burke is more explicit. He argues that man, in exchanging a savage for a civil state, makes an agreement :

That he may obtain justice, he gives up his right of determining what it is in points the most essential to him. That he may secure some liberty, he makes a surrender in trust of the whole of it.[182]

Burke then proceeds to argue that government is designed to provide for the 'wants' of men, including 'the want, out of civil society, of a sufficient restraint upon their passions'. This control can in the nature of things only be carried out by some external power, and so it is, Burke says, that 'in this sense the restraints on men, as well as their liberties, are to be reckoned among their rights'. To speak of a citizen's right to be restrained, as Burke does, is to formulate a notion of the relation between force and liberty with notable Rousseauist overtones.

Indeed, the two writers shared a recognizably similar insight into the function of coercion in politics. Both recognized the obvious point, its practical necessity, and the consequent need to justify it and regulate its use; each laboured to demonstrate that there are circumstances in which force can be recognized as a positive benefit, not merely for society as a whole, but for the individuals coerced themselves. But much more important, both Rousseau and Burke as libertarians felt the need to justify the legal application of force *in terms of liberty itself*. They were not content to argue that men gained so much in the way of security and well-being from the rule of law that the forfeiture of their liberty was well worthwhile. Men obviously did gain in this way, but a major contention of both writers was that men who lived under the rule of law lived freely, and lived freely as a consequence of the rule of law.

Far from accepting the Hobbesian doctrine that liberty 'dependeth on the silence of the laws',[183] the two writers were on the whole much closer in spirit to the following sentiment of John Locke.

For law, in its true notion, is not so much the limitation as the direction of a free and intelligent agent to his proper interest, and prescribes no farther than is for the general good of those under that law. Could they be happier without it, the law, as an useless thing, would of itself vanish; and that ill deserves the name of confinement which hedges us in only from bogs and precipices. So that however it may be mistaken, the end of law is not to abolish or restrain, but to preserve and enlarge freedom. For in all the states of created beings capable of laws, where there is no law, there is no freedom.[184]

Political liberty could not, in the opinion of either, be adequately understood as living simply in the silence of the laws; on the contrary, it 'inheres in good and steady government, as in its substance and vital principle'. In the *Économie politique* Rousseau wrote a paean of praise for law, which runs in part as follows :

Par quel art inconcevable a-t-on pû trouver le moyen d'assujettir les hommes pour les rendres libres? . . . de faire valoir leur consentement contre leur refus, et de les forcer à se punir eux-mêmes, quand ils font ce qu'ils n'ont pas voulu?. . . .ces prodiges sont l'ouvrage de la loi. C'est à la loi seule que les hommes doivent la justice et la liberté.[185]

The complex relationship of law and liberty in the writings of both Rousseau and Burke is the product of two basic assumptions which they have in common : first, that there exists radical human imperfection in the world; and second, that this imperfection is susceptible to improvement by the application of human intelligence and will. This humanist attitude is of great importance in understanding their ideas about politics and man. Burke's approach to the problem is grounded ultimately in his Christian religious beliefs, whereas Rousseau's is more secular, as can be seen in the sociological analysis of the fall of man in the second *Discours* and his completely secular account of the conditions necessary for man's improvement in the *Contrat*. Despite this difference, they share a view of politics as a creative activity whose function is not simply to regulate, but to moralize and liberate mankind. Liberty is not something which it is possible to characterize simply by its empirical presence or absence in a political system; it is a goal which may be realized gradually with the developing maturity of man.

An imperfect citizenry requires vigorous moral and political leadership for its improvement. John Stuart Mill himself justified the paternalistic rule of a political elite both for primitive communities and, more surprisingly, for the England of his day,[186] and there is a readily identifiable strain of paternalism in the writings of Burke and Rousseau as well. The two general situations in which paternalism and the application of force may be justified in terms of libertarian values are, first, where an individual's rational nature is dominated by his appetites, and, second, where a community has not developed the capacity to rule itself in an enlightened fashion. Burke speaks to both conditions, and speaks for Rousseau as well as himself when he writes : 'When a state of slavery is that upon which we are to work, the very means which lead to liberty must partake of compulsion.'[187]

vii The Problem of Political Obligation

As Burke appears to accept a 'prescriptive' theory of political obligation,[188] and Rousseau specifically rejects it,[189] grounds for comparison in such a matter seem, on the surface, to be discouragingly slender.

However, I think it can be shown conclusively that Burke did *not* believe that the mere turning of the ages was sufficient to 'mellow into legality' a despotic or arbitrary regime, although he does certainly argue that the historical process has an important part to play in the creation and maintenance of a just political order.[190] Briefly, it is Burke's view that, in terms of *right*, the long, peaceful history of a state gives it a presumption in its favour; that is to say, it is a good deal more likely than not that the government is legitimate, although this need not necessarily be the case.[191] In terms of *fact*, an awareness of a peaceful history on the part of the subject has a beneficial political effect; it inclines him to believe that the government is just and its rulings good, and in this way perpetuates and enhances the stability of the state.

There is a passage in one of the opening speeches on the impeachment of Warren Hastings[192] in which Burke vehemently attacks the doctrine that 'arbitrary power' (the rule of mere human will) can be justly held or justly transmitted : 'Those who give and those who receive arbitrary power are alike criminal; and there is no man but is bound to resist it to the best of his power, wherever it shall show its face to the world.'[193]

As a part of this argument Burke makes it clear that a government which was 'violent in its commencement' cannot, through its mere continued existence, come into a just title. He describes the right to rule as 'this great gift of government, the greatest, the best, that was

F

ever given by God to mankind', and considers how this right may be obtained :

The title of conquest makes no difference at all. No conquest can give such a right; for conquest, that is force, cannot convert its own injustice into a just title, by which it may rule others at its pleasure.[194]

He then, somewhat surprisingly in the light of what has just been quoted, describes conquest as the 'more immediate designation of the hand of God' and argues that it entails for the conqueror, not the free exercise of uninhibited power, but 'all the painful duties and subordination to the power of God, which belonged to the sovereign whom he has displaced'. A conqueror, then, may obtain the right to rule, but not by virtue of conquering, or of conquering and holding; something else is required. 'Men intrusted with power' ought, in their use of it, 'to conform to principles, and not to draw their principles from the corrupt practices of any man whatever'.[195]

But if Burke refuses to accept a prescriptive theory of political obligation, he also rejects decisively the social-contract theory as it is upheld by contemporary writers. The core of his objection to this justification of political rule is to be found in his profound conviction that legitimate government can never entail the straightforward dominance of human will. Of the social-contract school Burke writes :

They always speak as if they were of opinion that there is a singular species of compact between them and their magistrates, which binds the magistrate, but which has nothing reciprocal in it, but that the majesty of the people has a right to dissolve it without any reason, but its will.[196]

In outlining his own view concerning what turns a collection of human beings into a moral union,[197] Burke exploits the social-contract notion of voluntary agreement or choice, but radically transforms it : it is, he says, a matter of choice, but 'not of one day, or one set of people, not a tumultuary and giddy choice; it is a deliberate election of ages and of generations'.[198]

Burke felt that there was a serious inadequacy or artificiality about the popular theory justifying government. The inadequacy, he felt, lay primarily in the description of political obligation in terms of the metaphor of a legal contract, that is, an act of agreement drawn up with the terms specified. Such a metaphor implied a point in time at which the contract was 'signed', and a number of specific, identifiable parties to the agreement. What is more, it suggested that the failure of one of the parties to honour the agreement in some particular could render the entire contract null and void. Such implications as these, it seemed to Burke, were singularly inappropriate in an account of the grounds of political obedience.

Burke also decisively rejects a third account of political obligation, the theory of divine right, which was once held, he says, by 'those exploded fanatics of slavery, who formerly maintained, what I believe no creature now maintains, "that the crown is held by divine hereditary and indefeasible right" '.[199] Since this theory was discredited by the time Burke wrote, he pauses only long enough to dismiss it as absurd.

So far, it is apparent that Edmund Burke did not hold a prescriptive theory of political obligation, although he sometimes appeared to, that he did not hold a social-contract theory in its popular eighteenth-century form, although he employed the vocabulary of the school, and that he emphatically did not hold a divine-right theory in any form. It now falls to us to give a brief description of the theory to which he *did* in fact adhere.

It would not be possible to elaborate a fully coherent account without fathering on Burke a theory which he may or may not have held, but which he at any rate never made explicit. It is undeniable that he never gave a systematic account of his view of political obligation; it is equally undeniable that his political utterances presuppose some theory (or theories) of obligation, and that he thought these utterances were consistent. As he says of himself in the third person, 'if he could venture to value himself upon anything, it is on the virtue of consistency that he would value himself the most. Strip him of this, and you leave him naked indeed'.[200] Our immediate task, then, is to chart the main lines of his theory, in so far as his writings warrant. This is best begun by attempting to uncover the basic reasons why he found each of the three theories alluded to above wrong or inadequate.

His dismissal of the first (prescriptive) account would seem to arise from his view that it is not possible to derive right from fact, at least not in this simple, direct way.[201] The main reason why Burke cannot accept the second (social-contract) account is because he does not believe that the erection and/or the justification of a political order can be the result of a simple act of will of a collection of individuals. This is to misconceive the nature of a political community and hence the requirements of justification. It is false to argue that the state is simply the product of conscious human design, of artifice pure and simple;[202] 'the state ought not to be considered as nothing better than a partnership agreement in a trade of pepper and coffee, calico or tobacco, or some other such low concern, to be taken up for a little temporary interest, and to be dissolved by the fancy of the parties.'[203]

Burke regards the third (divine-right) account as an 'exploded' theory, and hence does not trouble to explain in detail his reasons for rejecting it, but this much at least is apparent, that he views as the argument of despots the theory that there are by nature rulers (kings) and subjects, and that the former derive their right to rule solely from their place in a line of succession. This constitutes an attempt to argue that not only the state and its structure of government are decreed by God, but so also is the particular royal succession in a country, and both are thus built into the very nature of things. It is claimed that there is in effect a *natural* right to rule and a consequent natural duty of subjects to obey. Burke felt that in actuality, this theory meant the political domination of will, the will of the king. Here is what he says on the subject :

These old fanatics of single arbitrary power dogmatized as if hereditary royalty was the only lawful government in the world, just as our new fanatics of popular arbitrary power maintain that a popular election is the sole lawful source of authority. The old prerogative enthusiasts, it is true, did speculate foolishly, and perhaps impiously too, as if monarchy had more of a divine sanction than any other mode of government; and as if a right to govern by inheritance were in strictness indefeasible in every person, who should be found in the succession to a throne, and under every circumstance, which no civil or political right can be.[204]

If legitimate government is neither natural nor artificial, then what is it? Burke, it would seem, is maintaining that it can be viewed from both points of view, and, indeed, that it must be so viewed, if it is to be properly understood. If we were to choose on Burke's behalf an image of politics, it would be, not the image of God's absolute rule over the earth, nor that of law and contract, but the image of a language.[205] A language is, so to speak, coexistent with man; it is natural in the sense that its origin, like man's, is lost in the mists of time, and over the ages it has assumed a distinctive character which no man could have predicted or planned. A child does not choose his tongue, any more than a citizen chooses his native land; each is his before he knows he could have had another.[206]

But if it is natural in this sense, it is artificial in another. Although all men must have a native language or country, they may in the course of their life choose another, or they may consciously adapt and reform the one they have. It is through the interaction of volition and circumstance that a distinctive linguistic or political character emerges. However, it is naive to think that a single man or a single generation can drastically alter the terms of political life or the structure of a language; at any particular moment the bulk of things is given. It is through the operation of choice extended over time ('the deliberate election of ages and generations') that human influence is brought to bear on human conditions. By this device, by art 'working after the pattern of nature',[207] the classical distinctions between art and nature, between will and reason, are broken down and it becomes possible for what Burke regards as a truer conception of man to emerge.

It is instructive to note Burke's attitude to rebellion which he consistently asserts is a legitimate course of action in certain unusual circumstances.[208] It is not a single breach of justice or a solitary act of oppression on the part of the rulers that justifies such an extreme measure; it is rather the citizen's sober recognition over a period of time that the government is irretrievably corrupt, systematically evil, or, as Burke says, 'utterly incorrigible'.[209] He insists on the obvious point that rebellion is a last resort, and argues that the result of such an action is always uncertain, whereas the fact that it will entail *some* evil is not. He is, on the whole, reluctant to discuss the abstract conditions in which an uprising is justified : 'times, and occasions, and provocations, will teach their own lessons.'

The speculative line of demarcation, where obedience ought to end, and resistance must begin, is faint, obscure, and not easily definable. It is not a single act, or a single event which determines it. Governments must be abused and deranged indeed, before it can be thought of; and the prospect of the future must be as bad as the experience of the past.[210]

Rebellion, then, should be viewed as a sombre and melancholy duty, rather than as an abstract right.

By what criteria is a government to be judged just or unjust? When we press Burke vigorously for an answer, we find ourselves faced with ambiguity and obscurity. The ultimate appeal must presumably be to natural law, and it seems that in the final analysis each individual must make up his own mind about whether the government has contravened original justice, and, if so, whether it has done so systematically or occasionally.

As for the connection between natural law and the practical moral principles which are embedded in such Burkean conceptions as expedience, prescription, and just prejudice, Burke nowhere provides an adequate account. He *asserts* the connection, but he does not explain it. For example, in the *Reflections*, Burke voices his agreement with the French lawyer, Domat, who tells us 'with great truth', that prescription is 'a part of the law of nature',[211] but he does not tell us how this is so. He defines the 'prescription' which justifies British political institutions by saying that it is a deliberate election of ages and that, although the individual and the multitude (acting precipitately) are foolish, the species is wise and, given sufficient time, always acts rightly.[212] But this would seem to justify all old governments and no new ones. Can there be an old (prescriptive) government which is corrupt, and, if so, how is its corruption to be recognized? Can there be a new (non-prescriptive) government which is just, and, if so, how is it to be recognized as legitimate?[213] One would be inclined to say that such judgements must be made in terms of divine natural law, but if this is the case, what function does 'prescription' play? Prescription itself must be evaluated by the standards of natural law.

In one of his writings on Ireland, Burke claims that, although the 'immediate and instrumental cause of the law' may be the governing power, 'the remote and efficient cause is the consent of the people, either actual or implied; and such consent is absolutely essential to its validity'.[214] And in speaking of the controversy about the duration of Parliament, he says:

I most heartily wish that the deliberate sense of the kingdom on this great subject should be known. When it is known it *must* be prevalent. It would be dreadful indeed, if there was any power in the nation capable of resisting its unanimous desire. . . .[215]

However, immediately following upon the first quotation relating to Irish affairs Burke asserts categorically that, if the people, even explicitly and directly (i.e. not via representatives), should enact a law that is unjust, then it is null and void, as contravening natural law. Presumably, he who adopted unconstitutional measures to oppose this popular decision would in these circumstances be acting rightly. It would seem, then, that the deliberate sense of the people must be prevalent *only when it is consistent with natural law*; otherwise not. Burke's customary way round these difficulties was simply to assume that 'deliberate' practice, and the 'proper' expression of popular desire simply were not in conflict with the requirements of natural law.

We shall not explore the obscurities and ambiguities in the Burkean doctrine of political obligation any farther. Not surprisingly, on this subject he was more forceful and concrete in attack than in exposition and he was by conviction reluctant to indulge in the latter anyhow. If we have not been able to discover a coherent theory of obligation in Burke's writings we have nevertheless found it possible to recount Burke's criticism of contemporary theories and to suggest the direction in which his thought was flowing. The direction is symbolized, I think, by the analogy that most appropriately illuminates Burke's ideas about the grounds of the just state; membership in a state is like membership in a linguistic community, and a theory of obligation must reflect this if it is to be convincing.

There are of course, many obvious and important differences in the approaches of Burke and Rousseau to the problem of political obligation. For one thing, it was an issue which Rousseau attacked *as a problem*, indeed as the most important problem of politics, whereas Burke came at it incidentally in the course of doing something else. Unlike Rousseau, 'Je cherche le droit et la raison et ne dispute pas des faits',[216] Burke in almost all of his political writings *is*, as it were, 'arguing about fact', and it is in the context of this factual argumentation that Burke considers 'le droit et la raison'. Also, it appears that Rousseau believed there was only one absolutely legitimate form of political society ('il y a mille maniéres de rassembler les hommes, il n'y en a qu'une de les unir'[217]); Burke always maintained that there were various paths to justice, although presumably the principles composing the criterion are general; in civil society, he says, the specific conventions 'in each corporation, determine what it is that constitutes the people, so as to make their act the signification of the general will'.[218]

And at the centre of Rousseau's conception of just law is the idea that a man can recognize as legitimate and morally binding those political regulations which he has had a hand in formulating, which he, in a manner of speaking, has prescribed to himself. This fundamental democratic, participatory feature of Rousseau's theory of political obligation sets him decisively apart from Burke.[219] Nevertheless there are certain features of Rousseau's theory relevant to this comparative study which might be mentioned.

Rousseau is of course generally regarded as a social-contract theorist, but it is important to consider the precise function which the concept of a social contract plays in his work. Rousseau utilizes the concept in two of his major political writings, the *Discours sur inégalité* and the *Contrat social* itself. In both places it is employed to account for the establishment of law, but its nature in each case is very different. In the *Discours* Rousseau is describing the process by which men moved from a natural to a civil state, and argues that at a given point in this process (after a wretched state of war has supervened) men make an agreement to live under a rule of law.[220] But this contract, as universally desirable as it appears on the surface, is in reality a cunning scheme of the rich to protect their own possessions and to enslave the poor: 'Telle fut, ou dut être l'origine de la Société et des Loix, qui donnérent de nouvelles entraves au foible et de nouvelles forces au rich.'[221]

It is clear that Rousseau here is not describing the grounds of just law, but the mechanism which may have brought into existence (unjust) actual civil society. Employed in this manner, it is an undeniable intrusion into his story which is the account of a *process* of change. As John Plamenatz asserts: 'it explains nothing that could not be better explained without it ... It is altogether out of place.'[222] Perhaps the only thing which it might be taken to explain is Rousseau's insight that *all* human associations, whether they be accounted legitimate or not, rest in part on the consent of the members. The poor, after all, agree to the proposal of the rich and it is their freely given, though misguided assent which makes the political association possible.

In the *Contrat social* the contract is made necessary by the style of argument Rousseau was employing. It is something of a formal device issuing out of the assumption that it is possible to conceive of man living in an extra-social state of nature, and therefore necessary (given Rousseau's moral views) to maintain that man must have agreed to enter a political order. If man once lived in a state of nature, then there must initially have been unanimous agreement setting just civil society up.

As we noted earlier, if this style of argument is clearly recognized as an explanatory model rather than an actual account of a just polity, then there need be no basic objection to its use, but the confusion which plagues this kind of thought, both among its practitioners and among its critics, shows the difficulties and dangers which this particular approach to politics makes it hard to avoid. We have argued that Edmund Burke saw the difficulties in this way of thinking, and we want to suggest here that Rousseau was not unaware of them either. It can be argued that it was at least partially because Rousseau perceived the unreality of the contract style of thought that he developed his doctrine of the general will. A 'contract' implies an act made once at some point in time and subsequently adhered to; this is an implication inappropriate to the nature of an association of civil society which persists over generations, and into which future citizens are born. Nativity is not a matter of choice.

The general will replaced act with process. It is not possible to conceive of 'la volonté générale' as an event which takes place once and is fixed and finished; it is rather a procedure for making laws, a procedure which must be followed on each occasion that a law is made. Rousseau set his sights high. In order to have a legitimate political order, it was not sufficient, in his opinion, that there be a popularly agreed-to consitution of some description, giving some legislative body the right to make laws, and the citizens the duty to obey them. Rousseau, because of his stringent moral views, was led to insist on a specific form for the sovereign body, that is to say, an assembly of all citizens. A citizen was not obliged to obey a law unless he had had a voice in its formulation – not simply a voice in designating the body authorized to make law, but a voice in the actual lawmaking itself.[223] And this requirement makes sense independently of any convenant originating civil society. It would be possible in Rousseau's scheme, I think, for an existing corrupt society to become legitimate by commencing to fulfil the requirements of the general will; and it would certainly be possible for a just state to lapse into illegitimacy by ceasing to do so.

Now, by replacing the social contract with the general will as the legitimizing concept, Rousseau is attempting to disentangle himself from the conventions of the social-contract school and in particular from the historical-theoretical ambiguities which are invariably associated with it. In an attack on Grotius for justifying one fact by another, Rousseau writes : 'Il n'est pas question de ce qui est, mais de ce qui est convenable et juste, ni du pouvoir auquel on est forcé d'obéir mais de celui qu'on est obligé de reconnoitre.'[224] He is suggesting that the actual manner in which a state was formed is not relevant in considering its legitimacy; its origins may be lost 'dans la nuit des tems'.[225] What is relevant is the recognition on the part of the citizens that in some significant sense[226] all have a part in the making of decisions which affect all. A state cannot be invested with just political authority unless the sovereign is composed of the subjects : 'ces mots de *sujet* et de *souverain* sont des corrélations identiques dont l'idée se réunit sous le seul mot de Citoyen.'[227] (These issues will be discussed in somewhat greater detail in the second part of the concluding chapter.)

In our discussion of moral and political liberty we considered the distinction between a will which relates to the individual, short-term selfish interests of a man, and a will which relates to those public interests which he holds in common with other men. The 'volonté générale' represents Rousseau's attempt to give institutional expression to man's efforts to satisfy the second type of interest. A decision of the general will, Rousseau maintains, will be in the best interests of the community as a whole, and of each individual member as well.[228] It is a decision-making procedure which is both general in its source and general in its application;[229] that is to say, its expression requires the participation of all the citizens of the state and it deals with all members fairly. It is, then, in sum, a means of discovering and giving effect to the 'real sense of the people'.[230]

We have claimed above that the ultimate 'validating concept' for Edmund Burke was the law of nature; the positive law of the state was in the last analysis to be judged in the light of the universal rule of God. How this divine law was to be related to such Burkean notions as prescription and just prejudice remains, as we have seen, unclear. The very different concept which does equivalent duty for Rousseau is the general will. Its relationship to a law of nature, which Rousseau occasionally seemed to accept, is alike obscure.

In this matter of political obligation, one might say that the similarities which exist in the writings of the two men are to be discovered by comparing what we have identified as the minor theme of one with the major theme of the other.[231] That is to say, one might compare Burke's natural-law doctrine (major theme) with Rousseau's equivocal thought on the same subject (minor theme), or one might set Burke's notion of a prescriptive constitution in which there is a 'deliberate election of ages and generations' (minor theme) beside Rousseau's idea of a general will (major theme).

When the two writers consider how *in practice* states can emerge which may justly command the obedience of their subjects, then their traditionalist ideas often bear a strong resemblance. It seems possible that the experience of Poland taught Rousseau in a more concrete fashion than before that 'les bornes du possible dans les choses morales sont moins étroites que nous ne pensons',[232] but it served primarily to strengthen and mature an insight which he had had for years. In history, there is variety, eccentricity, change, often immense change; in 'le droit politique', there is generality and unity. It is not a view with which Burke would have disagreed.

In considering the grounds of the legitimate state, it is evident that both Rousseau and Burke were moving away from what they took to be the abstract individualism of the social-contract school, and were trying to give an account of politics which would do justice to what they felt was a seriously neglected aspect of social life. If one thinks in the simplified terms of 'society' and 'individual' for a moment, one might say that they were insisting on the importance of the first of these notions in achieving an adequate understanding of the second. Their general point was that neither could be understood in abstraction from the other, that even the provisional separation of the two for purposes of analysis would result and had in fact resulted in serious (and, Burke would say, practically speaking, dangerous) theoretical misconceptions of politics and morals.

4

Summary

1   On Life and Style

The previous chapters of this study have provided a comparative account of the social and political doctrines of Jean-Jacques Rousseau and Edmund Burke, based on the plentiful evidence that exists to support the contention that they are in many notable respects in basic agreement with one another. If the affinities are as extensive and in many cases as important as they have been shown to be here, then the question needs to be asked : Why is it that most people, specialists as well as laymen, place them at opposite ends of the political spectrum? If they are indeed so similar, why do most people find them so different?

A number of answers may be suggested. The entirely unobjectionable point might be made that the fact that the two writers are in some respects very similar does not nullify the fact that in other respects they are very different; and from this true but unenlightening remark might be drawn the unhelpful conclusion that people since the eighteenth century have simply chosen to note the differences between the writings of the two men rather than the likenesses. But of course this response is not adequate because it misses the point; we want to know *why* the differences are noted and the similarities (by comparison) neglected. People do not 'simply choose' in matters like these; there are reasons why things have fallen out this way and not another.

Not the least important reasons are to be found in the lives, experiences and writing style of the two men, and in the attachment of their names to certain historical events in Europe. It is these matters that we shall consider briefly here. The great differences between the childhood experience and education of Rousseau and

Burke were noted in the first chapter (Part I), and it was pointed out that the contrast between their personal lives could hardly be greater. A look at their professional careers will show that in this domain as well there is scant similarity.

After leaving Geneva as a young man, Rousseau lived under a weakening absolutist government whose centralized structure denied most of the ambitious citizens of the country a chance to obtain practical political education. As a consequence, men who were moved to speculate about politics generally did so without the benefit of concrete political experience.[1] Political thought and political action were very much distinct from one another during most of the eighteenth century in France. Most French-language political writers were in no doubt that the government was on the 'other' side (along with the church); indeed, they felt they were waging a battle against the forces of reaction represented by the civil and ecclesiastical authorities. Apart from a few months' experience as a minor official in the French embassy at Venice,[2] Rousseau's major 'political' activity, in common with so many of his fellow writers, consisted of trying to get his books past the censorship of the civil and ecclesiastical authorities.

Edmund Burke, for his part, lived in a country whose limited parliamentary political system was the admiration of all Europe; English political institutions were the favourite empirical models of the French *philosophes*. Burke's own career symbolizes the fact that, if not easy, the rise from humble beginnings to political prominence in the House of Commons was a broader and better beaten path than the equivalent ascent in France. Burke, in the course of a long parliamentary career,[3] acquired a rich stock of concrete political experience, and it is clear from his writings that his perspective, whether his party was in power or not, was that of the statesman, that of the man who had to consider ruling as well as being ruled. This being so, it is not surprising that there was never a hint of any difficulty in Burke's getting his writings published;[4] his writings naturally displeased political opponents and government officials at times, but there was no question of their being regarded as seditious. Considering its contents, there is no difficulty in appreciating why George III is reported to have said of the *Reflections on the Revolution in France*, that it was a good book, a very good book, and every gentleman ought to read it.

Burke was a practising politician living in England, and England in the eighteenth century had successfully passed through her civil convulsions. Burke had one, or, after the American War of Independence, two revolutions behind him which he accepted; he had a revolutionary settlement (1688) to preserve, and by 1789 a world to lose, and nothing substantial to gain. Rousseau, on the other hand, was a theoretician living under a slowly disintegrating authoritarian regime, and in an intellectual climate infused with the spirit of opposition and discontent. Whatever one may think of his prophetic powers,[5] it is manifest that Rousseau *felt* acutely that the European states were in trouble. But he nevertheless lived in a country which had a revolution *ahead* of it, not behind it. The memory of painful disorders was not present in the minds of French writers as it was in those of most Englishmen. We know that Rousseau saw little that he regarded as admirable in contemporary society (it should be remembered, however, that his discontent was broadly *social,* not merely political), but his moral pessimism engendered a political conservatism. He diagnosed the ills of society in a vivid and disturbing fashion, but he had little faith in the efficacy of any possible solutions, and his practical recommendations were therefore the very model of Burkean caution. Nevertheless, readers were struck by his radical criticism and his theoretical justification of rebellion, and missed the circumspect, empirical side of his thought. By way of contrast, readers noticed Burke's cautious conservatism and neglected his insistence on the right of rebellion and his at times almost zealous spirit of reform.[6]

Also, in accounting for the divergent reputations of the two writers, it must be borne in mind that Rousseau died before and Burke lived through the French Revolution. Burke's last years were blackened and his European reputation made by this event. A comment of Lord Acton points out the difference in the political situations in England and in France during that time, as well as suggesting Burke's state of mind :

Burke forgot that the Revolution of 1688 came after the experiment of 1640. France could not do at once what took us fifty years. Besides, in England the institutions survived, and the Revolution preserved them. In France the Monarchy had destroyed them. Democracy was historic in one country as aristocracy was in the other.[7]

Given the nature of eighteenth-century criticism, it is impossible not to see Burke and Rousseau through the mists of the Revolution.

We know in detail what Burke thought of it. But what would Jean-Jacques Rousseau have made of it? A common assumption is that Rousseau is one of the intellectual fathers of the Revolution, but who is to say what Rousseau would have thought of the things done in his name? On the basis of the evidence presented in this study, it is as plausible to argue that he would have criticized the revolutionaries with the vigour of Burke as to argue that he would have supported them. Indeed, even Burke himself in the *Reflections* gives it as his opinion 'that were Rousseau alive, and in one of his lucid intervals, he would be shocked at the practical phrensy of his scholars...'.[8]

Strictly speaking, of course, speculation about what Rousseau 'would have done' is neither here nor there in the examination of his political thought, but it is made necessary by the need to right the balance, or rather, to free him from the praise or condemnation of later writers contemplating later events. The truth is that the French Revolution is irrelevant to the specific study of Rousseau's work;[9] it becomes a consideration only because of the difficulty in getting a clear view of him, and in dissipating the clouds of extraneous criticism.

Both Rousseau and Burke, approached and interpreted in the light of 1789 and what followed, have become in some degree symbols, and have entered what might be called the 'mythology' of European history. This is no doubt in part because the Revolution is still regarded as a matter of contemporary relevance. People tend to take a more than academic interest in it; they applaud or denigrate it according to whether they hold it responsible for the good or the ill of the modern age. And as a rule the admirers and critics of Burke and Rousseau, though they agree in little else, are of one mind when it comes to locating the position of each in respect of the Revolution. Alfred Cobban writes of Rousseau that 'his name was inevitably associated with the revolution, both with the popular disorders in which it began, and the excess of governmental authority in which it ended. For both these developments in turn he has been made chiefly responsible'.[10] Edmund Burke is viewed by friends and foes alike as the most eloquent spokesman of the counter-revolution, and he predicted and opposed both the phases which Cobban describes above.

These historical contingencies, then, can go some way towards explaining why the two writers have been viewed by many as polar opposites. And when these facts are placed beside the most marked variations in writing style and approach, then the orthodox critical interpretation becomes quite intelligible.

Edmund Burke's writing style[11] is in some ways like the ancient battlements and castles to which he often compared the British constitution. His work is massive, but not the expression of a single grand design, intricate, varied in its component parts; it displays an excellence of composition rather than an excellence of simplicity. Hazlitt, who says that at one time in his life his three favourite writers were Burke, Junius and Rousseau, describes Burke's methods thus :

He says what he wants to say, by any means, nearer or more remote, within his reach. He makes use of the most common or scientific terms, of the longest or shortest sentences, of the plainest and most downright, or of the most figurative modes of speech. . . .[12]

His style, then, is no technical acquirement, but the natural product of his thinking processes and the uniquely appropriate vehicle for the expression of his thoughts. The impression left on the reader is one of complexity, balanced and qualified judgement,[13] and moral earnestness. He describes himself as exhibiting 'a kind of earnest and anxious perseverance of mind'.[14] A phrase from Milton which someone once applied to Burke catches very well the curious effect which his language and personality sometimes had on his contemporaries : 'The elephant to make them sport wreathed his proboscis lithe.'[15] His writing does not charm or captivate, it does not provoke astonishment, but as Burke soberly and sometimes ponderously winds his way into a subject, his language produces a powerful cumulative effect upon the reader. Hazlitt asserts that 'there is no single speech which can convey a satisfactory idea of his powers of mind; . . . the only specimen of Burke is, *all that he wrote*'.[16] One suspects that the reformist spirit of the man and the distinct liberal strain in his thought is for many readers lost in the cautious circumlocutions of his language.

The style of Rousseau, 'ce hardi et éloquent auteur à paradoxes' as Grimm called him,[17] is very different indeed. Where Burke is sober and discursive, Rousseau is bold, sparkling, and concise; where Burke hedges and confines, Rousseau strips and lays bare; where Burke opens a discussion with a calm, understated paragraph laden with conditional sentences,[18] Rousseau begins with a pungent and memorable paradox.[19] Coleridge speculates about why the presence of Dr Johnson should be so vivid in Boswell's *Life* and that of Burke so shadowy. His comments on the stylistic gulf which lies between Burke and Johnson are not entirely inapplicable to the gulf which lies between Burke and Rousseau. 'The fact is,' Coleridge says,

Burke, like all men of genius who love to talk at all, was very discursive and continuous; hence he is not reported; he seldom said the sharp, short things that Johnson almost always did, which produce a more decided effect at the moment and which are so much more easy to carry off.[20]

It was the sharp, short things Rousseau said that had the greatest impact on readers and which proved to be most easy to carry off. Rousseau characteristically began with a statement calculated to shock or startle, and proceeded thereafter to fill in and qualify and explain; but the technique had its disadvantages, for it tends to be the bold beginning rather than the careful explication that is remembered. He complained throughout his life of being misunderstood, but it must be admitted that his method of presentation had a good deal to do with the false impression he wrought in the minds of others.

All these factors, then – the differences in personal life, professional experience, and writing style of Burke and Rousseau, the cultural and political disparity between France and England and between the kind of political activity which was possible in the two countries, the entanglement of the names and reputations of Rousseau and Burke with the events of the French Revolution – all these factors help us to appreciate how the conventional critical antithesis came about. However, this study has suggested the inadequacy of the conventional interpretation of Burke and Rousseau, and has argued that an undue preoccupation with the differences between the two writers has tended to obscure more than it has revealed. A willingness to accept too readily the 'symbolic' or 'mythological' positions of Rousseau and Burke leads one to ignore or minimize the obscurities, ambiguities, and downright similarities which cloud or dissolve the contrast.

II Conclusion

At the outset of this enquiry we provided a brief sketch of three traditions in philosophical thought and indicated the type of political discourse in the seventeenth and eighteenth centuries which would appear to conform to these traditions. It was our contention that the most useful perspective in which to view and compare the social and political reflection of Edmund Burke and Jean-Jacques Rousseau was one which situated their work at the intersection of these three traditions and which identified the tendency or current of their thinking, generally speaking, as flowing away from rationalist and empiricist forms of social and political enquiry and towards idealist forms.

The adoption of this perspective as an explanatory and comparative technique did not, of course, commit us to saying that Rousseau and Burke were philosophical idealists before their time, nor did it require an assumption that the two men had washed all traces of rationalism and empiricism from their thoughts. Quite the reverse; one of the points of locating them at the 'intersection' of these traditions is to underline the fact that no settled, internally consistent social theory has so far been satisfactorily attributed to either writer. Also, to argue that there is a general current or direction evident in their thinking is to imply that an examination of the writings of the two men will disclose a tendency to criticize rather than to elaborate or refine the rationalist and empiricist modes of social analysis popular in their day, and a positive attempt to engage in the development of a method and a doctrine characteristic in certain respects of 'idealist' political theory. But this implication, far from encouraging unrealistic hopes, reinforces the expectation that a study of the writings of Rousseau and Burke will yield evidence of the tensions and ambiguities attendant upon the exploration of unfamiliar intellectual terrain rather than a nicely ordered report of a discovery already made and fully digested.

We have sought coherence in this study, it is true, but it is a coherence issuing out of a set of dissatisfactions shared by Burke and Rousseau, a common recognition of problems, and frequently similar intellectual efforts to meet the difficulties. It has not been, then, a comparative study of two systematic theories, but a comparative examination of the posture of two European intellectuals facing what were in many respects broadly similar issues and concerns, and offering what were very often broadly similar commentaries and prescriptions. Thus the very inconsistencies, false starts, hesitations and partial solutions which characterize the writings of Rousseau and Burke have been advanced on many occasions in this study, as evidence of the continuity of preoccupation which they share.

In the light of these remarks, it should be clear that it would be inappropriate to conclude the study by considering the theories of the two writers in the light of systematic idealist philosophies. In view of the theoretical level at which we have approached Rousseau and Burke, such a procedure would surely be ill-advised, and a likely result of employing at this stage the idealism of Kant or Hegel as a foil for understanding the writings of Burke and Rousseau would be that the latter were interpreted at a higher level of theoretical generality than the evidence warranted, and were applauded or faulted for success or failure in an enterprise which neither of them had undertaken.

Alfred Cobban in *Rousseau and the Modern State* avoids this pitfall neatly and intelligently by comparing Burke and Rousseau within the unpretentious framework of what he calls 'the political theory of romanticism'.[21] In this comparative study we have shared with Cobban an appreciation of both Rousseau and Burke as influential men of letters and as political theorists, but not necessarily as systematic and highly abstract philosophers. A clue directing us to an appropriate procedure when summing up the findings of this enquiry is provided by Michael Oakeshott in a comment which he made in his introduction to *Leviathan* and to which we have referred earlier.[22] He identified three main traditions of political philosophy in terms of what he called their 'master-conceptions'. Roughly speaking, what we have distinguished as the rationalist tradition in political thinking he associates with the master-conceptions of *reason* and *nature*; empiricism is linked to the master-conceptions of *will* and *artifice*; and idealism is recognized by its master-conception of the *rational will*.

While it is clear that this simply stated but penetrating insight could serve as a point of departure for a highly theoretical discussion of the character of European political philosophy, it is equally true that it is possible to employ it in a much less systematic way to structure an approach to particular authors and works. It is, of course, primarily in this latter way that Oakeshott's statements have been useful in this study, not only in helping to identify the three traditions, but also in making it possible to appreciate the kind of intellectual stress that a political thinker would experience who was deeply influenced by both of the older traditions and yet was dissatisfied with each, and who was concerned to subject them to criticism and to replace them if possible with a more comprehensive understanding of politics and man.

In the broadest sense, we have endeavoured in this enquiry to approach Rousseau and Burke in terms of their efforts to examine and reformulate or perhaps transcend certain of the antitheses which provide some of the most basic organizing categories of western social thought; the distinction, for example, between nature and artifice, reason and will, duty and interest, theory and fact, the individual and the community, the private and the public, and so on. Rousseau and Burke used these everyday distinctions, of course, as we all do, but they came to be noticeably more self-conscious about them than were many of their contemporaries and predecessors; each recognized that they were indispensable conceptual tools for classifying and interpreting the things of this world, but both knew that the accuracy with which these concepts represented the world could not be assumed, that in fact the relationship between these organizing concepts and reality was deeply problematical.

If we attempt to sum up generally the social thought of Rousseau and Burke in the light of Oakeshott's 'master-conceptions', we shall find some important differences of emphasis within a broad context of similarity. Both writers lie at the juncture of the three traditions, but the centre of gravity of their thinking is in each case somewhat different. One might characterize Edmund Burke's primary concern as an attempt to criticize and overcome the limitations of the antithesis between nature and art, whereas Rousseau's central preoccupation, at least in his political theory, is with problems issuing out of the two concepts of reason and will. This is not to deny, of course, that both writers address themselves to both problems, but simply to indicate where the predominant weight of concern lies in each case.

Time and again in this enquiry we have noted Edmund Burke's antipathy to what may appropriately be called 'abstraction' in political and social thinking, the tendency Burke discerned in so many of his contemporaries to take the part for the whole. No doubt he would have regarded this inclination as constituting little more than a set of harmless mistakes had it been confined to the classroom, but in his opinion a habit of accepting partial and simplified truths as the whole story was corrupting practical political discourse and action, and it is this which accounts for his unrelenting criticism of the approach.

Much of Burke's unease about the French Enlightenment's mode of political thinking may be accounted for in these terms; his famous metaphor[23] describing the refraction of 'metaphysic' natural rights as they leave the rarefied atmosphere of speculation and enter the denser medium of practical political life is just one of a host of obvious examples from Burke's writings which indicate both his reservations about the most prominent mode of theorizing in the eighteenth century and also the extent to which he himself shared, albeit in equivocal fashion, many of the assumptions of his opponents (for, of course, the Burkean metaphor accepts the existence of natural rights in some form).

Burke's insight into the transformation that overtakes general theoretical principles as they experience concrete embodiment in reality is expressed most fully in what is perhaps his major specific contribution to political theory, that is to say, his conception of tradition. It is here in particular that Burke attempts to establish the content and work out the implications of his perception that so far as human beings are concerned 'nature' implies 'culture' and the making of artifacts. It is not that he gives up the idea of nature as a criterion; it is rather than he gives it up as something which is external to and set over against ordinary men and institutions, and insists that the criterion is in some fashion immanent in the day-to-day affairs of men.

This is a view that has existed in some form since the time of the Greeks, but it took a distinctive shape in Burke, in part because of the presence of the school of natural rights against which it was directed, and in part because of its combination with other Burkean views and doctrines. An appreciation of the importance of this general perspective in Burke's thought makes it possible, not to resolve, but to understand many of the hiatuses and vexing ambiguities present in his writings. We have often discovered in this enquiry that it is not possible to push analysis of Burkean doctrine beyond a certain point, that one must frequently accept incoherence or engage in surmise; but an understanding of the major problems to which Burke was addressing himself helps to make the fragmentary character of portions of his thought intelligible.

The concept of tradition for Burke was an indispensable vehicle for articulating his views on nature, reason, will, politics and human beings, and in what he had to say about each he avoided what he took to be the particular and the abstract, and sought the more inclusive and the more comprehensive. It is surely not unfair to suggest, by way of example, that his position on natural law is unclear because he asserted at least three distinct views on the subject, namely, that there exist universal, eternal moral principles which are the product of divine reason and will, that these moral principles receive concrete expression in the historical process which itself displays a rational character, and that men are free to 'make history' (which includes the freedom to commit evil and to decline into irrationality, for example, during the French Revolution). Burke would presumably assert that all three of these views must be included in any adequate understanding of the matter, but as we have indicated earlier he does not make it clear how this might be done.

Burke's understanding of tradition leads him to invest customary practices and habitual modes of behaviour with a rational status which is the product of no single mind; a tradition of behaviour emerges as the result of a great many people exercising both will and reason over a long period of time. Not only is there in Burke a presumption that ancient customs and assumptions and long-standing institutions will be capable of yielding upon inspection a rational account of themselves, but also there is the belief that an individual who is born into a traditional community and who inherits its way of life may, by unthinkingly ordering his behaviour according to accepted practices, act more rationally than the person who rebels against his community's customs or the unfortunate who has no tradition worth speaking of and who must therefore refer everything to his naked, shivering reason. Burke's conception of tradition, then, while it quite drastically undermines the distinction between what is natural and what is artificial in human affairs, tends also to blur the difference between reason and will and the commonplace distinction between the sphere of the individual and the sphere of the community.

We have suggested that Rousseau's political thinking is addressed primarily to problems issuing out of the concepts of reason and will and their relationship to one another. However, if one considers more generally his social thought, for example, in *Émile* and the

Discours sur l'inégalité, it becomes apparent that the concept of nature and its status as a criterion for social life is of major concern to Rousseau as well, and we shall consider this for a moment.

In the *Discours sur l'inégalité* Rousseau calls into question the common usage of 'nature' to criticize civilization. At the beginning of this work he indicates that it is not the distinction between nature and art itself which is unwarranted, but rather the particular way in which the line is drawn between the two by his contemporaries and predecessors. 'Les Philosophes qui ont examiné les fondemens de la société, ont tous senti la nécessité de remonter jusqu'à l'état de Nature, mais aucun d'eux n'y est arrivé.'[24] However, in combating this specific failing, Rousseau reveals in the course of his treatise a more fundamental scepticism about the utility of the enterprise itself. His particular employment of the state-of-nature model strains the assumptions of that approach to the breaking point and constitutes the logical terminus beyond which the concept of natural man must be twisted beyond recognition or abandoned altogether.

In terms of our interest at the moment, the effect of Rousseau's hypothetical journey back into the origins of man is to reveal the ultimate unreality of the attempt to separate the natural from the artificial. Rousseau undertakes this journey in pursuit of natural man only to find an animal at the source – an animal with certain human potentialities, it is true, but to all outward appearances at any rate, an animal nonetheless. The lesson here is that 'nature', as customarily defined by many of the most prominent seventeenth- and eighteenth-century writers, cannot provide a satisfactory criterion for human life, personal or political. Such a criterion must rather be grounded in man's existence and experience as a social, a civilized, an 'artificial' creature. To say that politics will not finds its answers in 'nature' is in effect to give up the nature-artifice distinction in its traditional form; as Rousseau says in the Geneva manuscript, it is to 'l'art perfectionné' that man must look for 'la réparation des maux que l'art commencé fit à la nature'.[25] This is not, of course, to suggest that Rousseau foregoes all talk of 'nature' and related terms; it is obvious that these words are as much on his lips as on anyone else's, but it can be seen that when he does employ them he is very often attempting to develop new ideas within an old terminological framework.

It is in Rousseau's political theory, and especially in the *Contrat social*, that one can find plentiful evidence of a concern

The social thought of Rousseau and Burke

with problems related to the concepts of reason and will. Rousseau figures prominently in the liberal-democratic tradition, but his position in that tradition is not easy to define – indeed, the very meaning or significance of his work is problematical in a way that the work of many others in the tradition is not, as is indicated by the radically disparate interpretations of his thought that have been offered by scholars since he wrote. What I take to be one important reason why this is so, and one, moreover, which is relevant to the topic we currently have in hand, lies in his uncompromising and persistent effort to unite the two ancient political ideals of *good* government – good according to some objective standard – and *self-*government.

At the start of the *Contrat*, Rousseau states the fundamental problem of politics as he sees it in the form of a lengthy statement which begins : 'Trouver une forme d'association qui défende et protege de toute la force commune la personne et les biens de chaque associé. . .'. So far, Rousseau appears to be outlining a problem which writers such as Hobbes, Locke and Burke would all agree was of central importance : how is it possible to achieve security or peace and at the same time to ensure the protection of personal and property rights?

But Rousseau inserts an additional stipulation, one which neither Hobbes nor Locke nor Burke would include in his statement of the fundamental problem of politics : 'Trouver une forme d'association ... par laquelle chacun s'unissant à tous n'obéisse pourtant qu'à lui-même et reste aussi libre qu'auparavant.'[27] Rousseau is pitching his demands much higher than the others; he seeks not only peace and the protection of rights, but peace, the protection of rights and genuine self-government as well. He wants to guarantee the right of the citizens to *make* political decisions, and at the same time to ensure that the *right* decisions will be made. In this sense, then, Rousseau's objective is to bring together and to harmonize in political life the two faculties of will and reason; it is only in a state where this objective is achieved that legitimate government can exist.

In the *Contrat* Rousseau works out his solution primarily via his notion of the general will, and it will be useful to consider certain aspects of this concept for a moment. He was clearly attempting to express a single political idea with what he calls 'la volonté générale', but he employs the term to describe a number of rather different things. The character of Rousseau's efforts to understand reason and volition and to relate them satisfactorily to one another in political life may be appreciated most readily by clarifying his two major conceptions of the general will.

The first way in which Rousseau understands the general will is as a critical concept in political philosophy; that is to say, it is understood as a criterion and it constitutes in sum a philosophical account of the grounds of the legitimate state. An expression of the general will is law properly speaking, such that it provides a standard for assessing the positive law of actual states. In elaborating his conception of law, Rousseau tries to answer the question : what are the conditions which a political decision must fulfil in order to qualify as an expression of the general will? Although the general will is obviously very different in character, it performs in Rousseau's scheme of things a critical function which is broadly similar to that of natural law in, say, Locke's political theory, where both obedience and resistance to the political powers-that-be are in large measure justified by reference to the state's adherence (or otherwise) to the principles of natural law.

Most students of Rousseau, of course, interpret the general will in this way, as a critical concept; the important thing to bear in mind about this general understanding is the fact that it calls attention to the precise character of an act of the general will, to the form of a political decision. It involves assessing positive law according to a standard, and thus directs concern to what is provided for in the law.

Rousseau's second way of conceiving the general will is to view it as a set of procedures for making political decisions. He attempts to elaborate a set of institutional arrangements – regular public meetings, special formulae for submitting issues to a vote, detailed mechanisms for voting and for calculating the results, rules requiring differential majorities for cases of varying importance and urgency and so forth – a set of arrangements of this kind which if followed will guarantee the expression of the general will. The emphasis here is on the *method* by which decisions are reached rather than on the *quality* of the decisions themselves. The method Rousseau advocates, of course, is direct participation by the entire citizen body.[28]

This understanding of the general will as a set of procedures is commonly regarded as being of secondary importance in

Rousseau's political thought. It is occasionally viewed as little more than an awkward and at times comic attempt on the part of Rousseau to put a criterion or standard into actual practice. But to see it from this limited point of view is to neglect features of fundamental significance in Rousseau's thought. Rousseau clearly assumed that the general will was a single coherent concept, and he must therefore have believed that there was an unbreakable link between the general will in the first sense and the general will in the second, between the general will as a standard of proper decision-making and the general will as a procedure for making political decisions good or bad. But it does not appear that Rousseau was successful in establishing this; indeed, much of the evidence to be found in the *Contrat social* suggests the reverse. There may be an empirical connection between the procedure and the substance of decision-making – popular participation and the various mechanisms described in the *Contrat* may be more likely than other procedures to produce rational and humane government – but Rousseau does not seriously address himself to this issue.

Consider the example of the lawgiver. Rousseau introduces this extraordinary figure into the second section of the *Contrat* – significantly, at a point where he is forced to consider how it might be that a body of ordinary citizens (or, to use his words, a 'blind multitude') could undertake by itself to complete an enterprise as vast and as difficult as a system of legislation. At this point in the treatise, he has given a fairly thorough theoretical account of the general will; he is now faced with the problem of showing how it could be given some practical reality.

Rousseau's introduction and description of the lawgiver leaves the reader in no doubt about the transcendent qualities which are necessary for the task and the enormity of the enterprise that the lawgiver faces. Not only must he possess superhuman intelligence, understanding the passions of men without sharing them and furthering their happiness without reward, he must be able to labour in one age and enjoy the fruits in another. The function of the lawgiver is to create, not simply the state, but the citizens who are to run the state as well. Culturally, his job is to socialize or politicize the members of the community; politically, his task is to discern what the general will requires for the particular association. Rousseau insists, however, that the actions of the lawgiver must be ratified by the whole community and that his proposals cannot become law until they are expressly declared to be so by the general will.

Now, if one employs what I have called the critical understanding of the general will, there would seem to be no reason why democratic decision-making is necessary for the expression of the general will, if a community is lucky enough to have the services of a genuine lawgiver. What counts is that the right decision for the community is made, not the process by which it is reached. If the lawgiver is to perform the functions Rousseau assigns to him, then the necessity of popular participation is not evident. And anyway, the task of the populace in these circumstances bears greater resemblance to an appreciative vote of confidence in a wise leader than it does to any genuinely creative legislative activity.

But if Rousseau wishes to argue that genuine popular legislative activity is indispensable in the formulation of the general will, that is to say, if the procedural requirements are essential, then the position of the lawgiver is undermined, and the chances of his fulfilling his mission drastically reduced. It is not possible at the best of times to be sanguine about the capacity of a blind multitude to recognize and appreciate the wisdom of the lawgiver; still less is it conceivable that such a body could participate actively in the making of policy without doing harm.

Rousseau, who fully recognized the dilemma, was constrained nevertheless to face it because of two incompatible assumptions about human nature which he held simultaneously. The liberal theory of Hobbes, Locke or James Mill assumes a rational adult citizen who knows his own interests and is capable of acting intelligently to further them. Rousseau's political theory, with its insistence on the need for public wisdom *and* individual self-expression in political life, both does and does not. If a state is to function successfully according to democratic principles, one must assume a rational and politically sophisticated citizenry. However, Rousseau, despite or because of his democratic beliefs, criticizes liberal and representative political systems precisely because in them men are kept in political tutelage and irrationality, and one of his most basic theoretical and practical goals is the *making* of citizens and men, the provision of circumstances in which men and communities can realize the best they have in them.

One might state the central paradox here in terms of a vicious circle of the following kind: good, rational citizens are required to run the legitimate state; but the legitimate state is necessary to create good citizens; since both human nature and the state as we find them are corrupt or woefully imperfect, how is either the legitimate state or the good citizen ever going to come into being? It is at this point in the *Contrat* that the paternalistic figure of the lawgiver provides perhaps a happy escape in theory, if not in practice.

To vest political power in the people is to say nothing about how the power will be used. If the citizens are already all that the theorist could wish then this need create no insurmountable problems. However, if one of the major reasons for relocating power in the community as a whole is the stifled potential of the citizens, then the theorist is faced with a conceptual difficulty, and, conceivably, if empirical experiments are undertaken, with considerable practical unpleasantness as well. In this light, one can see why there is not only a radical democrat in Rousseau, but a rank tory as well.

In the matter of reconciling reason and will in politics, then, it is not possible to account Rousseau's efforts a success, although the energetic clarity of his style and the startling originality of his thought helped to initiate a new mode of political reflection. It is tempting to conclude that he set himself an impossible task, and failed brilliantly in its execution. One might say of him what was said of Phaeton : 'He did not succeed in driving the horses of the sun, but he failed in a great endeavour.'

All in all, one is left with a picture of two writers who are in some instances remote from one another in their thought, in many instances only circumstantially different, and in a large number of cases substantially in agreement. This enquiry has uncovered in both Edmund Burke and Jean-Jacques Rousseau a serious dissatisfaction with the prevailing methods and the doctrines of contemporary political debate. It has also brought to light the numerous major and minor points of similarity, some of them quite striking, which can be found in the social and political writings of the two famous eighteenth-century figures. The study has, in sum, attempted to show that Rousseau and Burke are similar in their negations, and similar in their efforts to elaborate what in their view would be a more satisfactory account of political life. One would not wish to assert that Edmund Burke and Jean-Jacques Rousseau are, politically speaking, brothers under the skin, but the contrary view, that they constitute polar opposites in eighteenth-century political opinion, has been shown to be untenable. There is at least as much to unite them as to divide them.

Notes

1 Introduction

1 Gibbon's remark comes from his *Autobiography*, Oxford University Press (London 1959), p. 258. For d'Alembert's comment see Voltaire's *Correspondence*, ed. Theodore Besterman, (Geneva 1953–66), xlv, 8948. Consider also Coleridge's statement about Burke (*Coleridge's Miscellaneous Criticism*, ed. T. M. Raysor, Constable (London 1936), p. 401), and Byron's poetic description of Rousseau, *Childe Harold*, Cantos 77 and 80.

2 From the book review of *Émile* in the *Annual Register*, 1762. Presumably, from the style, an article of Burke's, and taken to be so by most critics. On the general problem of identifying Burke's hand in the *Annual Register*, see the third and fourth essays in Thomas W. Copeland's *Our Eminent Friend Edmund Burke*, Yale University Press (New Haven 1949).

3 *The Heavenly City of the Eighteenth Century Philosophers*, (1932), Yale University Press (London 1965), pp. 29, 31. For an assessment of this influential book, see *Carl Becker's Heavenly City Revisited*, ed. R. O. Rockwood, Archon Books (New York 1968). Robert Derathé provides an instance of this approach within Rousseau scholarship itself: 'Au lieu de prendre cet écrit (*Du Contrat social*) comme un point de départ, comme l'avènement d'une nouvelle époque de la pensée politique, nous le considérons comme l'aboutissement d'un courant d'idées, qui a pris naissance avec la Réforme. . . .' (*Jean-Jacques Rousseau et la science politique de son temps*, Presses Universitaires de France (Paris 1950), p. 62.)

4 Alfred Cobban (*Rousseau and the Modern State*, revised edition, George Allen and Unwin (London 1964), p. 159) makes the closely related point that this dichotomy was fostered because Rousseau's name was identified with the Revolution and Burke's with the counter-Revolution.

5 Joan McDonald examines Rousseau's practical political influence in France in *Rousseau and the French Revolution 1762–1791*, Athlone Press (London 1965).

6 He did not, for example, castigate the American colonists' use of abstract theory some years earlier.

181

[7] *Annual Register*, 1762, p. 227.

[8] Cf. Burke's comment in the *Reflections* 'when kings are hurled from their thrones' Englishmen 'are alarmed into reflection. . . .' (*Works*, II, 353).

[9] John Murray, 3rd edition, (London 1902), vol. 2, p. 187. All quotations from second volume.

[10] Ibid., p. 193.

[11] Ibid., p. 223.

[12] Ibid., p. 191.

[13] Ibid., p. 193.

[14] Ibid., p. 266.

[15] For other examples of writers who have contrasted Burke and Rousseau, see: F. P. Canavan, *The Political Reason of Edmund Burke*, Duke University Press (Durham 1960), pp. 57, 75, 104–6, 126; C. P. Courtney, *Montesquieu and Burke*, Blackwell (Oxford 1963), pp. 15, 41–2, 148; John H. Hallowell, *Main Currents in Modern Political Thought*, Henry Holt and Co. (New York 1957), pp. 166, 186, 189; Jeffrey Hart, 'Burke and Radical Freedom', *The Review of Politics*, vol. 29 (1967), pp. 221–38; Russell Kirk, 'Burke and Natural Rights', *The Review of Politics*, vol. 13 (1951), pp. 441–56, esp. 442, 443, 448; W. E. H. Lecky, *History of England in the Eighteenth Century*, Longmans Green (London, 1887 edition), vol. 5, pp. 347–8, 362–3, 368; Charles Parkin, *The Moral Basis of Burke's Political Thought*, Cambridge University Press (Cambridge 1956), pp. 63, 77, 80, 86, 94–5, 107 and much of ch. vii.

[16] Stephen, *History of English Thought in the Eighteenth Century*, p. 191.

[17] Ibid., pp. 225–6.

[18] However, it is noteworthy that both men were 'outsiders' in the societies in which they chose to make their way; Burke was an Irishman in the English House of Commons, Rousseau, a Genevan among French *littérateurs*.

[19] But passages in Rousseau sometimes suggest a similar view. See, for example, the final sentences of the Preface to the second *Discours*. However, it is possible that these were inserted primarily to please the Genevans. After all, Rousseau believed outward conformity to local religious beliefs to be a sort of political virtue.

[20] See Part IV of this chapter for a consideration of the distinction between practical and theoretical or explanatory writing, and the methodological problems which are involved in comparative study.

[21] Biographers of Burke are accustomed to divide his life into such periods as American affairs, Warren Hastings and India, the French Revolution, and so forth.

[22] It could be argued that one of the reasons for the characteristically abstract quality of French political writing during the eighteenth century was the separation, encouraged and sustained by the public authorities, between letters and learning on the one hand and political activity on

the other. Rousseau (the theorist with no practical political experience) and Burke (the professional politician) could be taken to be symbolic of the differences between France and England in this regard. This will be discussed in more detail in the concluding chapter.

23 His writings attest to his extraordinary breadth of interest: compositions and criticism in music and theatre, an epistolary novel, speculations on the origin of language, a treatise on education with its influential passage on religious belief, a number of personal apologies – an assessment of his general position in eighteenth-century letters would have to take into account all of these.

24 C. B. Macpherson (*The Political Theory of Possessive Individualism*, ch. II, part i) explores this question in connection with Hobbes and the seventeenth century.

25 *Works*, II, 349 (*Reflections*).

26 We shall discuss certain difficulties in Burke's approach in Chapter 3, Part VII below.

27 *Waverley* (Signet ed.), pp. 114–15.

28 The phrase is an allusion to one of Burke's, *Works*, II, 334.

29 *Works*, II, 399.

30 *Oeuvres*, III, 420 (*Contrat*, III, ix). See also the first fragment in the section 'De la population', p. 527.

31 *Works*, II, 399–404. See also *Works*, II, 389 ff. for another instance of Burke's use of statistical methods.

32 See, for example, *Works*, II, 307–8 (which also utilizes the notion of a great chain of being), 331–5, 358–9.

33 The methodological problems to which these differences give rise in a comparative study are considered in Part IV of this chapter.

34 A. B. C. Cobban, *Edmund Burke and the Revolt against the Eighteenth Century*; C. E. Vaughan, *The Romantic Revolt* (Vaughan, like many writers, sees the change from both negative and positive points of view); Basil Willey, *The Eighteenth-Century Background*, ch. III.

35 The phrase constitutes the title of Part III (1760–1830) of Bronowski and Mazlish, *The Western Intellectual Tradition*.

36 A view of many men living at the time; certainly true, regarding the French Revolution, of the revolutionaries themselves, and of many of their opponents, including Burke.

37 Eg., G. H. Sabine, *A History of Political Theory*, ch. XVII.

38 *Rousseau*, Macmillan (London 1896), vol. 2, p. 3. Morley's remark refers specifically to the French Revolution.

39 For examples: see on conservatism, Peter Viereck, *Conservatism*. On nationalism, Elie Kedourie, *Nationalism*; Hans Kohn, *Nationalism*. On romanticism, A. B. C. Cobban, *Rousseau and the Modern State* (revised ed.), ch. VI, part 2 (as well as *Burke and the Revolt*); C. E. Vaughan, *The Romantic Revolt*. On philosophical idealism, see the writings of Cobban,

Vaughan, Michael Oakeshott, and W. H. Greenleaf, all of whom are discussed in the pages that follow.

[40] On the liberal experiment, see H. A. L. Fisher, *History of Europe*, Part III. The phrase on history is R. G. Collingwood's, *The Idea of History*, Part III.

[41] *The Romantic Revolt*, Charles Scribner (New York 1907), p. 3. See also the general discussion of this change in Crane Brinton's Introduction to his *The Political Ideas of the English Romanticists* (1926).

[42] Michael Oakeshott, Introduction to the *Leviathan*, p. xii.

[43] See Oakeshott's remarks on this subject (Ibid., p. xii).

[44] Something more will be said about this mode of philosophical thinking in Part III of this chapter.

[45] See ch. II of his book.

[46] *Great Chain of Being*, Harvard University Press (Cambridge, Mass. 1936), pp. 25–6.

[47] *Great Chain*, p. 25.

[48] Introduction, p. xii.

[49] *Oakeshott's Philosophical Politics*, Longmans (London 1966). I am indebted to this essay for clarifying my thought on this question, as well as for pointing to the way in which Burke and Rousseau might be seen in these terms.

[50] Ibid., p. 37.

[51] Part I, ch. vi.

[52] *Système de la nature*, pseud. M. Mirabaud (Londres 1770), vol. I, Preface.

[53] Preface to *La Politique naturelle*.

[54] The fascination with travel literature during this time suggests a growing interest in the empirical observation of social life.

[55] Identification (and disentanglement) of the two strains is not always easy. On this point, consider the comment of G. H. Sabine: 'In the seventeenth century no sharp line was drawn as would be now, between mathematics and the physical sciences of experiment and observation, probably because the experimental data required in mechanics were not very great, while the mathematical observation was considerable.' (*History of Political Theory*, 3rd ed., p. 363.)

[56] It will be noted that this study interprets Hobbes as an empiricist and Locke as a *political* rationalist, and reads their natural-law theories in a manner consistent with this view. Needless to say, there are strong alternative lines of interpretation in existence, but for the purposes of this study these other approaches need not concern us here.

[57] See, for example, Peter Laslett, Introduction to the *Two Treatises*, ch. IV, part ii.

[58] *Two Treatises* (ed. Laslett), Intro. p. 94.

[59] Ibid., p. 95.

[60] *History of England in the Eighteenth Century*, 1887 edition, Longmans, Green

(London), vol. 5, p. 363. But see p. 362 for a more serious attempt at comparison.

61 'Burke', *British Academy Lecture,* The Annual Lecture on a Master Mind Series, 1943, pp. 34–5. For other brief comparative remarks, see: Kingsley Martin, *French Liberal Thought in the Eighteenth Century,* (1929), Harper and Row (New York 1963), p. 208; R. S. Peters, 'Hegel and Nation-State', *Political Ideas,* (ed. David Thomson), Watts and Co. (London 1966), p. 136; John Plamenatz, *Man and Society,* Longmans, Green (London 1963), vol. 1, pp. 322, 364. Sheldon Wolin makes an implicit comparison between Rousseau and Burke in his discussion of Durkheim's theory of 'collective representations' (*Politics and Vision,* George Allen and Unwin (London 1961), pp. 372–3, note No. 67 of ch. x).

62 *The Political Writings of Jean-Jacques Rousseau,* (1915), Basil Blackwell (Oxford 1962), vol. 1, p. 1.

63 For examples of the numerous places where he compares Rousseau and Burke in this publication, see introduction, vol. 1, pp. 2, 6, 37 (footnote No. 6), 54–6, 77, 82, 103.

64 Manchester University Press (Manchester 1918). Quotation from pp. xxv–xxvi; see also pp. xxxvi, xlix.

65 Blackwell (London 1923), p. 330.

66 Manchester University Press (Manchester 1925), vol. II, p. 57. He goes on briefly to draw some distinctions which he finds between the two men. See also p. 62.

67 *The Meaning of Rousseau,* Oxford University Press (London 1929). Both quotations from footnote on p. 108. See also p. 106.

68 But see Vaughan's self-contradictory remark on this subject in *Political Writings,* vol. 1, p. 6.

69 Although see Vaughan, *Political Writings,* vol. 1, p. 4.

70 *A History of Political Theory,* 3rd ed., Holt Rinehart and Winston (New York 1961), p. 606.

71 Ibid., p. 618. Next quotation same page.

72 Ibid., p. 595. Next quotation same page.

73 *Oakeshott's Philosophical Politics,* Longmans (London 1966). All quotations from p. 39.

74 *Edmund Burke and the Revolt against the Eighteenth Century,* (1929), George Allen and Unwin (London 1960); *Rousseau and the Modern State,* (1934), revised edition, George Allen and Unwin (London 1964).

75 *Rousseau,* p. 159.

76 See pp. 158–64.

77 See *Burke,* pp. 45, 110, 252, passim.

78 Oxford University Press (London 1940). Reprinted, Russell and Russell (New York 1964). Here is a brief résumé of the contents of the book:

Ch. 1 *The Insane Socrates.* A detailed account of Burke's aversion to Rousseau.

Ch. 2 *Whig Trusteeship.* An account of British politics and political thinking during the late seventeenth and the eighteenth centuries, and Burke's view of this period of English history.

Ch. 3 *New Lamps for Old.* A parallel account of events on the continent, particularly in France, during the same period.

Ch. 4 *Rousseau, Man and Thinker.* A biographical sketch.

Ch. 5 *The Disciple of Montesquieu.* A biographical sketch of Burke.

Ch. 6 *The Foundations of the Modern State.* A general comparative chapter.

Ch. 7 *The General Will.* A study of Rousseau's political theory. (Burke's does not enter into it.)

Ch. 8 *The British Constitution.* An examination of Burke's political doctrine, with allusions to Rousseau.

Ch. 9 *The Principles of Government.* An exploration of the similarities in the political thinking of Rousseau and Burke.

Ch. 10 *Statesman and 'Philosophe'.* A brief, comparative summing-up.

Apart from many specific points of disagreement between Osborn's book and this enquiry, there is the fact that she concentrates by far the greater part of her attention on three of Rousseau's most famous works – the *Contrat*, *Émile* and the second *Discours*; in the Index the total number of entries for the three works is fifty-two, and the total number for all other works is twenty-eight. However, we devote a good deal of time to Rousseau's other writings, especially to his lesser-known political works such as the two treatises on Corsica and Poland, the *Lettres de la montagne* and the more important political fragments.

[79] 'Du Côté de chez Vaughan: Rousseau Revisited', *Political Studies*, June, 1964, p. 231.

[80] 'The History of Political Thought: A Methodological Inquiry', *Philosophy, Politics and Society* (2nd series), Blackwell (Oxford 1962).

[81] *Confucian China and its Modern Fate: The Problem of Intellectual Continuity*, Routledge and Kegan Paul (London 1958), vol. 1, Intro. p. xv. Employing Levenson's own terminology, we might say that this quotation denies the alternative notion held by John Plamenatz who, in the Introduction to *Man and Society*, writes: 'Those who say that to understand a theory we must understand the conditions in which it was produced sometimes put their case too strongly. They speak as if, to understand what a man is saying, we must know why he is saying it. But this is not true. We need understand only the sense in which he is using words.' This is perhaps the confrontation of an historical (Levenson) and a philosophical (Plamenatz) way of thinking and the distinctive forms of understanding which they seek.

[82] Ibid., p. xiv.

[83] Ibid., p. xix. For examples of other writers with similar views: R. G.

Collingwood, *An Autobiography*, ch. v, and *The Idea of History*; Susanne K. Langer, *Philosophy in a New Key*, pp. 1–4; C. V. Wedgwood, *The King's Peace*, Introduction, pp. 16–17.

[84] Levenson, p. xvi.

[85] See comment of Jean Starobinski in his Introduction to the second *Discours* (*Oeuvres*, III, p. lxv–lxvi).

[86] Ibid., pp. 185–6.

[87] *Works*, II, 368 (*Reflections*); *Oeuvres*, III, 360 (*Contrat*, I, vi).

[88] J. G. A. Pocock has written an excellent essay on this subject: 'Burke and the Ancient Constitution; A Problem in the History of Ideas', *The Historical Journal*, II, 2, (1960), pp. 125–43.

[89] It would perhaps be possible to argue that the world became a different world after 1789, and so limit the significance of this fact. But the *Reflections* and the later writings do not constitute a radical departure, either in method or in content, from Burke's earlier work, although, to say no more, they are 'heightened' in tone. It is interesting to speculate what Rousseau would have thought of the *Reflections* in the light of what was then going on in France.

[90] Assuming we are correct in recognizing Burke's hand in the relevant articles of the *Annual Register*.

[91] *Rationalism in Politics*, Methuen (London 1962), p. 120.

[92] *Edmund Burke and the Revolt*, p. 45.

[93] A study comparing, say, Burke and Aristotle or Cicero would not benefit from these advantages. If such a study were undertaken, it is more likely that it would turn into a study of the *influence* of either of the second two on Burke, rather than a straightforward comparison. This book restricts itself to the latter.

[94] *Works*, II, 358 (*Reflections*). Next quote from p. 359.

[95] *Works*, I, 86–7. Next quotation from p. 50.

[96] Vaughan, *Political Writings*, vol. II, p. 357. See also pp. 514–15.

[97] Cf. on this issue, E. H. Wright, *The Meaning of Rousseau*, Oxford University Press (Oxford 1929), pp. 15–16.

[98] See de Tocqueville's discussion of eighteenth-century French intellectual life, *L'Ancien régime*, III, ch. 1–3.

[99] *Works*, I, 376.

[100] *Works*, VI, 148.

[101] John Morley, *Rousseau* (1886), Macmillan (London 1896), vol. I, p. 85.

[102] Ibid., p. 85.

2 Notions of Human Nature in Rousseau and Burke

[1] See above, Chapter 1, Part II, for a general account of these important

ways of thinking. For a fuller discussion of empiricism, see Part III of this chapter below.

2 One might say that natural rights in early-modern Europe have in a sense always been political. However, in the sixteenth and early seventeenth centuries they were part of the (political) affirmation of religious rights. With the increasingly clear distinction between the religious and temporal authorities (and between religious and political argument), they gradually became part of the (political) affirmation of political rights. D. G. Ritchie asserts that 'the theory of natural rights is Protestantism transferred to the region of worldly affairs . . .' (*Natural Rights*, (1894), Allen and Unwin (London 1916), p. 13).

3 Margaret MacDonald, in her article 'Natural Rights', makes the same point (*Philosophy, Politics and Society*, first series, p. 47).

4 *De Republica*, III, xxii, 33.

5 *De Legibus*, I, x, 29; xii, 33.

6 *The Eighteenth-Century Background*, (1940), Penguin (London 1965), p. 23. On this point, see also, Leo Strauss, *Natural Right and History*, (1953), University of Chicago Press (Chicago 1965), p. 183.

7 J. J. Burlamaqui, *The Principles of Natural Law*, (1747), (trans. Nugent), (London 1748), p.2.

8 Ibid., p. 6.

9 *Laws of War and Peace* (1625), Prolegomena, 11; Bk. I, ch. I, sect. x. H. A. Rommen entitles the third chapter of his book, *The Natural Law*: 'The Turning Point: Hugo Grotius'. Of Grotius he writes: 'He may be said to have marked the transition from the metaphysical to the rationalist natural law.' (second paragraph, ch. III).

10 A. P. d'Entrèves, *Natural Law*, Hutchinson University Library (London 1964), p. 53.

11 For examples of students of the eighteenth century who consider one or more of these features (rights, rationalism, individualism) to be a major part of the early-modern transformation of natural-law thought, see: A. P. d'Entrèves, *Natural Law*, ch. III (esp. p. 49); Denis Lloyd, *The Idea of Law*, Penguin (London 1964), pp. 81–5; D. G. Ritchie, *Natural Rights*, (1894), Allen and Unwin (London 1916), ch. I; H. A. Rommen, *The Natural Law*, Herder Book Co. (London 1949), ch. IV ('Natural Law in the age of individualism and rationalism'); G. H. Sabine, *A History of Political Theory*, Holt, Rinehart (New York 1961), ch. XXI (esp. pp. 432–3), pp. 544, 547–8; P. J. Stanlis, *Edmund Burke and the Natural Law*, University of Michigan Press (Ann Arbour 1965), pp. 23–4; Leo Strauss, *Natural Right and History*, (1953), University of Chicago Press (Chicago 1965), ch. V (esp. pp. 182–4); Basil Willey, *The Eighteenth-Century Background*, pp. 10, 23; Otto Gierke, *Natural Law and the Theory of Society*, (trans. E. Barker), Cambridge University Press (Cambridge 1934), vol. I ch. ii (esp. pp. 95–105).

[12] Cf. R. G. Collingwood's remark about Enlightenment historians in *The Idea of History*, (1946), Oxford University Press (Oxford 1963), p. 82.

[13] The natural-right view of man as fundamentally unchanging is in this respect similar to the sensationalist and utilitarian doctrine; utilitarians claimed that men invariably act in accordance with certain fundamental principles, and that it is through the manipulation of rewards and punishments that men can be got to live together satisfactorily.

[14] John Locke, *Second Treatise*, no. 124.

[15] A point made by Kingsley Martin, *French Liberal Thought*, p. 117. Following reference from next page.

[16] *Principles of Natural Law* (trans. Nugent), p. 6. See also p. 43. See our quotation of the first passage in this section above.

[17] This is one of the points on which Rousseau joins the natural-right school.

[18] *Second Treatise*, no. 6.

[19] 'The Parallel of Deism and Classicism', *Essays in the History of Ideas*, Johns Hopkins Press (Baltimore 1948), p. 79.

[20] A. O. Lovejoy, in the article quoted above, makes a worthwhile distinction between 'romantic individualism', which looked for the unique and the eccentric, and 'rationalist individualism', which saw each man sharing the common quality of reason. This paragraph owes a good deal to Lovejoy's article. Much of what is said in this paragraph about the 'uniformitarian' conception of man applies to the sensationalist psychologists as well as to the natural-right thinkers, hence the use of the broader term, 'Enlightenment'.

[21] Lovejoy has explained deism as the outcome of the application of Enlightenment rationalism to religious belief.

[22] *Works*, v, 139.

[23] *Works*, iii, 67.

[24] *Works*, vi, 177–8. Following quotation from p. 178.

[25] *Works*, vi, 29. See also vi, 16. This passage may be compared with, of all things, the opening lines of the *Déclaration des droits de l'homme et du citoyen* (1789): 'Les représentans du peuple francais . . . considérant que l'ignorance, l'oubli, ou le mépris des droits de l'homme sont les seules causes des malheurs publics et de la corruption des gouvernemens ont résolu d'exposer . . . les droits naturels, inaliénables et sacrés de l'homme. . . .'

[26] *Works*, v, 473.

[27] *Works*, ii, 176 (*Speech on Mr Fox's East India Bill*).

[28] See discussion below, Chapter 2, Part iv.

[29] *The Problem of Burke's Political Philosophy*, Clarendon Press (Oxford 1967), pp. 77–8. His discussion takes place in a slightly different context.

[30] *Works*, iii, 95.

[31] *Works*, ii, 332. For other examples suggesting Burke's notion that natural rights cannot be carried over into civil society, see *Works*, ii, 331–6; iii, 109; v, 473; vi, 99.

[32] *Works*, II, 30.

[33] See C. E. Vaughan on this point, *Studies in the History of Philosophy*, Manchester University Press (Manchester 1925), vol. II, pp. 41–2.

[34] See, for example, *Works*: IV, 267; VII, the speech on the third day of the Impeachment, and particularly, 16, 21, 42–7 (esp. p. 44), 92–108, 114, 190, 229, 482, 491. In vol. VII, p. 44, Burke makes the revealing remark: 'We know what the empire of opinion is in human nature. I had almost said that the law of opinion was human nature itself. It is, however, the strongest principle in the composition of the frame of the human mind . . .' Many of the passages noted here are occupied with the double task of showing that in the large questions of right and wrong there is a code which is applicable both in India and in England, but that in other respects 'we must govern them [the Indians] upon their own principles and maxims, and not upon ours' (VII, 44).

[35] *Works*, II, 370.

[36] *Works*, II, 366.

[37] *The Romantic Revolt*, Blackwell (London 1923), p. 3.

[38] Another distinguishing characteristic of Burke's doctrine of human nature was his insistence on the importance of the non-intellectual side of mankind. Laws must appeal to human habit and emotion, fully as much as to human reason.

[39] *Works*, VI, 147. There are difficulties with this view, of course, but consideration of them will be postponed for the moment.

[40] *Works*, III, 86, Cf. Burlamaqui's comment in *The Principles of Natural Law* (trans. Nugent), p. 43: 'when we speak of the natural state of man, we are to understand not only that natural and primitive state, in which he is placed, as it were, by the hands of nature herself; but moreover all those into which man enters by his own act and agreement, and that are conformable in the main to his own nature. . . .'

[41] For examples of Stephen's comments on this point, see his *History of English Thought*, 3rd ed., John Murray (London 1902), vol. II, pp. 187, 191, 192.

[42] The precise configuration of natural man is not clear. He appears to have moral capabilities latent in the instinct of 'pitié' (or in the mutual workings of 'amour de soi' and 'pitié'), but 'pitié' is also something he shares ('sometimes') with the animals (see *Oeuvres*, III, 154). In addition, it is said that natural man is subject to the rule of instincts, but that he is able to 'choose' between them, which seems to imply a rational capacity. It would appear that Rousseau was trying to have it both ways. These points are discussed in more detail later in this section and in Part IV below.

[43] See, for example, *Contrat*, I, vii (*Oeuvres*, III, 364–5), from which the quotations immediately below come.

[44] Though in circular fashion Rousseau also felt that society is the product of man.

[45] Even in an early work like the second *Discours*, we find Rousseau stressing the physical superiority of the natural man, but not his moral or intellectual capacities. In natural man, Rousseau says, 'je vois un animal moins fort que les uns, moins agile que les autres, mais à tout prendre, organizé le plus avantageusement de tous . . .' (*Oeuvres*, III, 134–5). The savage is a magnificent animal, and in his strength and bodily vigour much superior to social man, but he is not a match for social man when it comes to intelligence or ethical discernment. As Rousseau points out (pp. 135–6), set 'l'homme civilisé', with all his equipment and paraphernalia against 'l'homme Sauvage' and the savage would no doubt lose the match, but set them against one another naked, and the opposite result would occur. What Rousseau is suggesting here is that each is sovereign in his own domain – the savage man, in a situation where physical strength and agility is vital, the social man, where knowledge of human artifacts is the crucial thing.

[46] *Contrat*, I, viii (*Oeuvres*, III, 364).

[47] *Political Writings* (ed. Vaughan), II, 145.

[48] Provisionally, we might state our belief that it is impossible to find a satisfactory position for Rousseau in either the classical or the early-modern (natural-right) variant of the natural-law tradition.

[49] In a passage owing something to the sensationalist doctrines of Locke and Condillac, Rousseau argues that every animal has ideas 'puis qu'il a des sens', and the capacity of combining them together in some measure. Rousseau therefore claims that the difference in rationality, between man and beast, conceived in these terms, is one of degree rather than kind, and says: 'Ce n'est donc pas l'entendement qui fait parmi les animaux la distinction spécifique de l'homme que sa qualité d'agent libre.' (*Oeuvres*, III, 141.) But one would have thought that free agency would entail a rational capacity of quite a different sort from that possessed by a creature ruled by instinct.

[50] Writers who place him at the head of the romantic movement are usually implying this.

[51] *Oeuvres*, III, 15.

[52] *Oeuvres*, III, 42.

[53] *Émile*, IV, 348. But see p. 48: 'La raison seule nous apprend à connaître le bien et le mal. La conscience qui nous fait aimer l'un et haïr l'autre, quoique indépendente de la raison, ne peut donc se développer sans elle. Avant l'âge de raison, nous faisons le bien et le mal sans le connaître; et il n'y a point de moralité dans nos actions. . . .'

[54] It may be argued that Rousseau holds a theory of natural rights, but that he is grounding it on man's instinctive or intuitive 'knowledge' of good and evil rather than on his reason, on 'conscience' or 'pitié' rather than

on reason. But even if this is thought to be true, Rousseau's theory is still readily distinguishable from the rationalist theory of rights we have described.

⁵⁵ *Studies in the History of Political Philosophy*, Manchester University Press (Manchester 1925), vol. II, p. 51.

⁵⁶ *French Liberal Thought*, pp. 7–8. Cf. Shirley Letwin, *The Pursuit of Certainty*, Cambridge University Press (Cambridge 1965), p. 141, and Peter Gay, *The Party of Humanity*, Alfred Knopf (New York 1964), pp. 198–202. While Martin's belief that both trends 'wanted the same things', and that they 'were equally confident that the recognition of their principles would render man happy and virtuous' seems fair, his contention that the two 'make the same fundamental assumptions about the nature of man and society' is in my opinion highly dubious.

⁵⁷ See, on this issue, J. Brownowski and Bruce Mazlish, *The Western Intellectual Tradition*, ch. 10.

⁵⁸ *De l'Esprit*, Durand Libraire (Paris 1758).

⁵⁹ See Kingsley Martin's *French Liberal Thought*, pp. 13–15, on these points.

⁶⁰ William Letwin, *The Origin of Scientific Economics*.

⁶¹ The search for such a technique owed much, of course, to Francis Bacon. See, on this point, Professor Oakeshott's *Rationalism in Politics*, Methuen (London 1962), pp. 14–16.

⁶² Intro. to *Leviathan*, p. li.

⁶³ Rousseau is a particularly interesting case in point. He rarely mentioned Hobbes favourably, but it could be argued that there was no one to whom he owed more.

⁶⁴ From the 'Extrait raisonné' of his *Traité des sensations*.

⁶⁵ His Introduction to *Two Treatises*, II, 3. See also Alfred Cobban's essay on this subject in *In Search of Humanity*, George Braziller (New York 1960), ch. 7. It should be noted that Burke's only work of philosophical speculation, *A Philosophical Inquiry into the Origin of our Ideas of the Sublime and Beautiful*, published when Burke was in his late twenties, is in the empiricist tradition; if his epistemological views here are incompatible with the natural-law views in his social and political thought, then an inconsistency such as we have suggested may be ascribed to Locke may also be ascribed to Burke.

⁶⁶ Bk. II, ch. i, 1.

⁶⁷ Bk. II, ch. i, 2.

⁶⁸ G. H. Sabine, *A History of Political Theory*, both quotations p. 546. On this same issue, see: Carl Becker, *The Heavenly City*, Yale University Press paperback (New Haven 1965), pp. 60–5; Paul Hazard, *European Thought in the Eighteenth Century*, (1946), Penguin (London 1965), p. 321; Kingsley Martin, *French Liberal Thought*, pp. 93, 122–3; A. N. Whitehead, *Adventures of Ideas*, (1933), New American Library (New York 1958), pp. 26, 36. Whitehead writes of eighteenth-century French thought:

'It was derived from the English thought of the seventeenth century, Francis Bacon, Isaac Newton, and John Locke. Also it gained inspiration from the English revolutions of the same epoch.' (p. 26).

[69] Letter XIII.

[70] Letter XII. Alfred Cobban notes the role of Huguenot exiles in conveying a favourable picture of the English political system to France, giving as an example Rapin-Thoyras, whose *Histoire de l'Angleterre* (1723–5) and earlier *Dissertation sur les Whigs et Tories* (1717) were widely read (*In Search of Humanity*, p. 103).

[71] Baron von Holbach (pseud. M. Mirabaud), *Système de la nature ou des loix du monde physique et du monde moral*, (Londres 1770), vol. I, pp. 1–2. (Accents missing in text here and elsewhere.)

[72] Consider Hobbes's remark, *Leviathan* (Oakeshott ed.), p. 174. See also p. 109. John Plamenatz states that 'natural rights, in the traditional sense, are as unnecessary to Hobbes's political philosophy as to that of any of the utilitarians' (*The English Utilitarians*, Blackwell, Oxford 1958, p. 13).

[73] From *De l'Esprit*, abstract of the first discourse. Passage quoted below.

[74] *Système de la nature*, p. 170.

[75] Rousseau's 'l'homme Sauvage' might at first appear to be a cipher, too, but in fact as we have pointed out he is a creature with two innate *principes*; 'amour de soi' and 'pitié', which constitute the primitive source of morality.

[76] *Système de la nature*, p. 2.

[77] *Système de la nature*, p. 157.

[78] This change is perhaps seen most clearly in what came to be known as utilitarian thought.

[79] *Man and Society*, (1963), Longmans Green (London 1967), vol. I, pp. 366–7.

[80] *Works*, II, 370.

[81] A remark which John Chapman makes about Rousseau, but which applies to Burke as well. (*Rousseau: Totalitarian or Liberal?*, Columbia University Press (New York 1956,) p. 122.

[82] *The English Utilitarians*, 2nd ed., Blackwell (Oxford 1958), p. 11.

[83] See Bentham's remark in *A Fragment on Government*, (Wilfrid Harrison ed.), p. 125. See also A. D. Lindsay's comments in *The Modern Democratic State*, Oxford University Press, pp. 141–2.

[84] *Rousseau and the French Revolution*, Athlone Press (London 1965), p. 26. Cf. Plamenatz's remark about the utilitarians; the only purpose of education for them 'is to make men more efficient producers of happiness' (*English Utilitarians*, p. 12). There is perhaps an apparent conflict here between Rousseau's educational and political theory; the human personality is to be *developed* in *Émile*, but it is to be *remoulded* in the *Contrat*, but in each case the idea of *self-improvement* is central.

[85] Consider Burke's reported distinction between mere 'school acquirement', which 'may be bought by any rich Vulgar parents', and education, which 'should be considered as improvement to the heart as well as mind', and which can only be got from guardians who have a 'thorough and refined sense of True Virtue' ('Extracts from Mr Burke's Table-Talk', Mrs Frances Anne Crewe, *Burke Newsletter*, vol. v., no. 2 [Winter 1963–4], pp. 277–92, Entry 15, 'Education'). Full quotation given below, Chapter 3, Part v.

[86] Burke, *Works*, ii, 334.

[87] With regard to the utilitarians, it has been pointed out that utilitarianism and egoism are incompatible doctrines, although both views were in fact held by such men as Bentham and James Mill. (John Plamenatz, *The English Utilitarians*, 2nd ed., p. 9). See also A. D. Lindsay, *The Modern Democratic State*, ch. v, sect. 3.

[88] *Edmund Burke and the Revolt Against the Eighteenth Century*, George Allen and Unwin (London 1929), p. 252.

[89] Chapter 2, Part ii.

[90] There is a helpful if rather unsympathetic discussion of this interpretation in Peter Stanlis, *Edmund Burke and the Natural Law*, ch. iii, part i ('Burke's Supposed Utilitarianism').

[91] The quotations are from Sir Leslie Stephen's *History of English Thought in the Eighteenth Century*, 3rd edition, vol. ii, 225–6. Stephen goes one better and suggests that these 'transient deviations' are only superficial, and are in fact basically consistent with the utilitarian system. Reference has already been made to this passage; see above, Chapter 1, Part i.

[92] Cobban discusses Rousseauist interpretation in *Rousseau and the Modern State*, revised edition, Preface and ch. 1 ('The Interpretation of Rousseau'). See also the excellent essay on the same subject by Peter Gay in *The Party of Humanity*, ch. 8.

[93] Peter J. Stanlis, *Edmund Burke and the Natural Law*. (Reference is here made to the 1965 paperback edition.) B. T. Wilkins, *The Problem of Burke's Political Philosophy*, Clarendon Press (Oxford 1967). A few articles and brief remarks noting Burke's use of the law of nature had preceded Stanlis's account, for example: R. J. S. Hoffman, *Burke's Politics* (1949), Preface; Russell Kirk, 'Burke and Natural Rights', *Review of Politics*, (October 1951), pp. 441–56; Leo Strauss, *Natural Right and History* (1953), ch. vi, section B; Charles Parkin, *The Moral Basis of Burke's Political Thought* (1956). Since the appearance of Stanlis's book in 1958 there have been a number of studies which (like Parkin's in 1956) assume, but do not set out to show in detail that Burke is a part of the classical natural-law tradition: see, for example, F. P. Canavan, *The Political Reason of Edmund Burke*, Duke University Press (Durham 1960); G. W. Chapman, *Edmund Burke: The Practical Imagination*, Harvard University Press (Cambridge, Mass. 1967), esp. pp. 7, 155–6, 273–4.

⁹⁴ Presses Universitaires de France, Paris (hereafter cited in this section as *La Science politique*). See also Franz Haymann, 'La loi naturelle dans la philosophie politique de J.-J. Rousseau', *Annales J. J. Rousseau*, vol. xxx, pp. 65–110.

⁹⁵ *Rousseau and the Modern State*, revised edition, Preface. See also his article, 'New Light on the Political Thought of Rousseau', *Political Science Quarterly*, vol. LXVI (1951), pp. 272–84.

⁹⁶ See, for example, *Rousseau and the Modern State*, 2nd ed., pp. 65, 69, 76, 169.

⁹⁷ *La Science politique*, 'Avertissement', p. 1. He repeats the statement on p. 51.

⁹⁸ Ibid., p. 343 both quotations. See in general pp. 341–4, 236–7.

⁹⁹ Ibid., p. 168. Pages 151–71 contain the heart of his argument on this subject.

¹⁰⁰ Ibid., p. 166.

¹⁰¹ Ibid., p. 166.

¹⁰² Ibid., pp. 166–7.

¹⁰³ Ibid., p. 163.

¹⁰⁴ Derathé, referring to the state of nature, does speak of 'cette morale naturelle faite de bonté ou de pitié', but he does on the whole, I think, consider that moral behaviour entails a rational capacity, and hence in Rousseau's case a social condition; it is this mode of behaviour that he terms 'une morale rationelle ou morale de la loi' (p. 167 both quotations). At any rate, I fail to see how a creature who needs no guide but instinct can be understood to make moral judgements.

¹⁰⁵ Ibid., p. 168.

¹⁰⁶ Ibid., p. 159 (his italics). See also p. 160. The author seems to have some hesitations about this, as well he might (see p. 159 n. 1, p. 160 n. 4, p. 165). For if the primitive 'droit naturel' is associated with the instincts of men and animals, as he says it is, then it is difficult to see in what sense it is a *moral* principle, and in what sense it can provide a moral sanction for the contract which creates society. Derathé indicates very clearly his awareness of the problem when he writes (on p. 165) that 'loin d'avoir abandonné l'idée de loi naturelle, Rousseau ne l'a écartée de l'état de nature que pour le réintroduire dans l'état civil. Mais il n'en reste pas moins vrai que la loi naturelle ne saurait servir de fondement au pacte social, si elle lui est postérieure'. Derathé finds himself in this dilemma because he accepts Vaughan's contention that the concept of a social contract necessarily implies the idea of a morally obligatory natural law (see pp. 159–60). But with the existence of social-contract writers whose theories of natural law are as radically disparate as are those of Hobbes and Locke, this is at least a debatable claim.

¹⁰⁷ Ibid., p. 168. First quote p. 166.

108 Rousseau's *Oeuvres*, III, 142–3. They are quoted in *La Science politique* on p. 162.

109 *Oeuvres*, III, 142–3.

110 *Oeuvres*, III, 141: 'Tout animal a des idées puis qu'il a des sens, il combine même ses idées jusqu'à un certain point, et l'homme ne diffère à cet égard de la Bête que du plus ou moins. . . .'

111 *Oeuvres*, III, 141.

112 *Oeuvres*, III, 141–2.

113 *Oeuvres*, III, 142: 'c'est surtout dans la conscience de cette liberté que se montre la spiritualité de son ame.' Of this passage Voltaire remarked: 'voilà une assez mauvaise métaphisique.' (Quoted in editors' note, *Oeuvres*, III, 1316 [note 1 to page 142].)

114 Rousseau mentions another quality which decisively separates men from beasts: 'la faculté de se perfectionner' (p. 142). But – since his description of this quality leaves one in no doubt that it is not a characteristic which insures the *necessary improvement* of mankind, but rather one which simply makes change *possible*, for better or for worse (see, e.g., *Oeuvres*, III, 142) – 'perfectibilité' can be considered, from our present point of view, simply as an elaboration of his notion of free agency.

115 *Oeuvres*, III, 708. See also the fragment (*Oeuvres*, I, 1129) in which he says that the proof that he has less logic than wit can be seen in the fact that it is always the transitions that cost him the biggest effort. (This passage was brought to my attention by Mr William Pickles.)

116 *La Science politique*, p. 52.

117 Ibid., p. 70.

118 Ibid., p. 51. But it must be noted that these also formed important parts of the vocabulary and speculative equipment of many famous political writers outside the *jurisconsulte* school.

119 By Peter Stanlis in his preface to *Burke and the Natural Law*.

120 Cf. on this point Wilkins, *Burke's Political Philosophy*, p. 10 ff.

121 *Edmund Burke and the Natural Law*, Preface, p. ix.

122 Ibid., p. ix.

123 Ibid., p. xi.

124 Quoted in *Edmund Burke and the Natural Law*, pp. 16–17. The passage is from the preface to Strauss's *The Political Philosophy of Hobbes*. See also Strauss's *Natural Right and History*, University of Chicago Press (Chicago 1953), p. 182.

125 See, for example, Ch. VI, sect. ii ('Natural Law and Christian Revelation: Burke's Conception of Man's Moral and Spiritual Nature'), pp. 176–94.

126 *Burke's Political Philosophy*, Preface.

127 Ibid., p. 82.

128 Ibid., p. 17.

129 See, for example, ibid., p. 18. He notes the similar opinion of a reviewer

of Stanlis's book (J. L. Montrose, 'Review-Essay', *Natural Law Forum*, VI (1961), pp. 204, 216–17).

130 Ibid., p. 19; see also pp. 20–3, 248. But if Stanlis has erred in drawing the line too deeply between traditional natural law and modern natural rights, it is possible to suspect that Wilkins has gone awry in the other direction: are the continuities in natural-law thought between Aquinas and Locke more striking than the discontinuities?

131 See, for example, ibid., p. 70, where Wilkins writes that, despite significant differences, 'Burke's philosophy seems consonant with, and, in some respects, perhaps ultimately derived from Thomism'. See also pp. 30, 32–5, 42, 226, 247–8. For references to some of the differences between Thomist and Burkean natural law see: pp. 56–60, 63, 67, 70.

132 No evidence exists proving Burke's first-hand knowledge of Aquinas (see on this point Wilkins, ibid., pp. 32–5). For a general summary of Burke's reading, see Stanlis, *Burke and the Natural Law*, ch. III, sect. ii ('Burke's Knowledge of the Natural Law Tradition'), pp. 34–40. Francis P. Canavan ('Burke's College Study of Philosophy', *Notes and Queries*, N.S., IV, 12 December 1957, pp. 538–43) discusses the question of the books with which Burke was likely to have been acquainted while at university. This article is also published as an appendix to Canavan's book, *The Political Reason of Edmund Burke* (1960).

133 Both Stanlis and Wilkins, for example, refer extensively to the *Tracts on the Popery Laws* which was written in the 1760s but never completed, and which was not published during Burke's lifetime. The lengthy speeches Burke gave in the course of the Hastings impeachment constitute another important source for the study of Burke's natural-law beliefs, although they have not in the past been regarded as centrally important sources in the study of Burke's general social theory.

134 For these and other examples, see: *Works*, I, 300; II, 14, 28, 52, 167, 365, 369, 370, 372; III, 79; V, 245, 278; VI, 24, 32, 236; VII, 99–102, 232, 233.

135 The phrase is Wilkins's, *Burke's Political Philosophy*, p. 11.

136 A typical example is found in his *Tracts on the Popery Laws*, where he describes equity and utility, the two foundations of law, as being 'grounded upon our common nature', as being 'connected ... with, and derived directly from, our rational nature'. He prefaces this remark with the statement that a positive law prejudicial to the whole community would be null and void, 'because it would be made against the principle of a superior law, which it is not in the power of any community, or of the whole race of man, to alter – I mean the will of Him who gave us our nature, and in giving impressed an invariable law upon it.' (*Works*, VI, 21–2.)

137 *Burke's Political Philosophy*, p. 14. But see Burke's comment (*Works*, II, 167) to the effect that God himself may not be competent to alter the framework of right and wrong.

[138] His *Philosophical Inquiry* qualifies as systematic theory, but it pertains to one aspect of human nature, not to human nature itself. Cf. Wilkins, *Burke's Political Philosophy*, pp. 91–3.

[139] *The Political Reason of Edmund Burke*, p. 17.

[140] Letter of 20 February 1790 (*Correspondence*, I, 571). In *An Appeal from the New to the Old Whigs* Burke defends himself at length against the charge of inconsistency (*Works*, III, 24 ff). On p. 24 he says of himself: '... if he could venture to value himself upon anything, it is on the virtue of consistency that he would value himself most. Strip him of this, and you leave him naked indeed.'

[141] *Burke*, Macmillan (London 1887), p. 169. Wilkins has a chapter discussing the difficulties involved in the claim of Burke's consistency (*Burke's Political Philosophy*, ch. IV, pp. 72–89). Robert M. Hutchins maintains that Burke did in fact substantially alter his opinions about natural law as he grew older ('The Theory of the State: Edmund Burke', *Review of Politics*, V (April 1943), p. 146 ff).

[142] *Émile*, IV, 279.

[143] Part IV of the following chapter focuses upon society rather than upon human nature in an attempt to reveal the two writers' views regarding the part played by the historical process in the composition of nations and states.

[144] See, for example, *Works*, II, 348–9.

[145] He speaks, for example, in his essay on the laws of England of the instructiveness of observing the 'first principles of Right springing up, involved in superstition, and polluted with violence' (*Works*, VI, 413). Elsewhere he talks of violent governments mellowed by time into legality (*Works*, II, 435; see also ibid., III, 9, and the undated letter to Captain Mercer, *Correspondence*, I, 577).

[146] See, for example, his *An Abridgment of English History*, and his *Fragment towards an History of the Laws of England* (*Works*, VI).

[147] For a discussion of this characteristically Burkean approach, using selections from the *Reflections* as examples, see J. G. A. Pocock, 'Burke and the Ancient Constitution – a Problem in the History of Ideas', *The Historical Journal*, III, 2 (1960), esp. pp. 127–8. But note Coleridge's comment about Burke: 'No one has read history as philosophically as he seems to have done' (*Coleridge's Miscellaneous Criticism*, ed. T. M. Raysor, Constable [London 1936], 418).

[148] *Contrat social* (Geneva ms.), I, v (*Oeuvres*, III, 297). This famous statement does not, of course, always accurately reflect Rousseau's approach.

[149] *Works*, II, 364.

[150] *Works*, II, 365–6. Following quotation from p. 366.

[151] *Works*, II, 370.

[152] *Works*, III, 86. This breaking down of the antithesis between nature and convention is a characteristic feature of his thought. See, for example:

Works, I, 124, where he says, 'very justly is use called a secon
and *Works*, IV, 276, where, with reference to the Indians, he s⊦
'*their* natural laws' (my italics). In understanding human natu.
developmental terms, and in seeing the state as a necessary instrumȩ
in this development, Burke is close to the thought of Rousseau.

[153] *Works*, v, 278.

[154] See *Works*, III, 86.

[155] Cf. Francis P. Canavan, *The Political Reason of Edmund Burke*, pp. 60–1, 177; and Charles Parkin, *The Moral Basis of Burke's Political Thought*, p. 22.

[156] Introduction to his translation of Otto Gierke's *Natural Law and the Theory of Society*, Cambridge University Press (Cambridge 1934), pp. xxxiv–xxxv.

[157] *Works*, II, 368.

[158] In *An Abridgment to English History* Burke, in considering the over-running by barbarians of the western part of the Roman Empire, suggests that 'we are in a manner compelled to acknowledge the hand of God in those immense revolutions by which at certain periods he so signally asserts his supreme dominion' (*Works*, VI, 236). A little later in the same work, referring to the introduction of Christianity into Britain, Burke writes: 'It is by no means impossible, that, for an end as worthy, Providence on some occasions might directly have interposed.' (p. 241.)

[159] For a discussion of Burke's conception of history and of the particular matter of concern here, see J. C. Weston, 'Edmund Burke's View of History', *Review of Politics*, XXII, 2 (April 1961), pp. 203–29, esp. pp. 214–16. See also: B. T. Wilkins, *The Problem of Burke's Political Philosophy*, pp. 93–4; F. P. Canavan, *The Political Reason of Edmund Burke*, pp. 180–7; A. B. C. Cobban, *Edmund Burke and the Revolt Against the Eighteenth Century*, pp. 89, 94.

[160] *Oeuvres*, III, 380 (*Contrat social*, II, vi).

[161] *Works*, II, 138. See also Burke's letter to Messrs Harford, Cowles and Co., May 12, 1778.

[162] *Works*, II, 359. For other places where Burke discusses prejudice and superstition, see: *Works*, II, 362, 429–30; VI, 52.

[163] *Works*, II, 167. Cf. Grotius's statement in *De Iure Belli ac Pacis*, I, i, x (A. C. Campbell trans., *The Rights of War and Peace*, Pontefract 1814, p. 19): 'Now the Law of Nature is so unalterable, that it cannot be changed even by God himself. For although the power of God is infinite, yet there are some things to which it does not extend, because things so expressed would have no true meaning, but imply a contradiction.'

[164] *Works*, II, 165.

[165] *Works*, II, 454. Burke sees Agricola as an example of a wise ruler in that he adjusts his policies to the people. (*Works*, VI, 214–15). Cf. the task of Rousseau's Legislator in *Contrat*, II, 7.

[166] *Works*, VI, 148. See also ibid., III, 109.

[167] Wilkins, *Burke's Political Philosophy*, p. 90. Wilkins argues that a willingness to consider human nature in general is one of the marks of a natural-law writer; but it would seem that this mark applies to other theorists (such as utilitarians) as well.

[168] See, on this general issue, *Works*, VII, 93–4, 99–102, 118–19, 248, 504. Cf. Rousseau, *Émile*, IV, 351.

[169] *Works*, VII, 44.

[170] *Works*, VII, 93. For instances of Burke's concern with the unique character of the Indian way of life, see: IV, 323; VII, 16, 43–4, 46–7, 190–1.

[171] *Oeuvres*, III, 425 (*Contrat*, III, xii).

[172] *Oeuvres*, III, 364 (*Contrat*, I, viii). The chapter in which he makes this remark ('De l'état civil') constitutes a brief sketch of the enormous change which he feels comes over man upon entering civil society. Natural and civil man respectively are described in the Geneva manuscript as follows: 'stupides hommes des prémiers tems', 'hommes éclairés des tems postérieurs' (*Oeuvres*, III, 283).

[173] *Oeuvres*, III, 381.

[174] *Oeuvres*, III, 313 (my italics). See also p. 653.

[175] Burke's *Philosophical Inquiry* on the sublime and the beautiful is systematic, but it deals specifically with aesthetics.

[176] Rousseau is quite explicit that Émile is to be formed to live in a social order. See, for example, the passage beginning: 'Émile n'est pas fait pour rester toujours solitaire; membre de la société, il en doit remplir les devoirs' (*Émile*, IV, 407; see also p. 240).

[177] See *Oeuvres*, III, 123 (Preface to the second *Discours*).

[178] *Émile*, I, 24–5.

[179] See, for example, *Émile*, I, 12; II, 84. James Boswell reports an exchange between himself and Rousseau thus: 'I said "Vous ne parlez point des devoirs d'un enfant envers ses Parens. Vous ne dites rien du Père de votre Émile." [Rousseau]: "O! Il n'en avoit point. Il n'existoit pas." ' (*Private Papers of James Boswell*, 'Boswell with Rousseau and Voltaire', privately printed by Ralph Isham, 1928, vol. IV (1764), p. 98). And Grimm gives the following account of an admirer's visit with Rousseau: 'M. Angar a été lui rendre visite, et lui a dit: Vous voyez, Monsieur, un homme qui a élevé son fils suivant les principes qu'il a eu le bonheur de puiser dans votre Émile. Jean-Jacques a répondu à M. Angar: Tant pis, monsieur, pour vous et votre fils; tant pis.' (Grimm and Diderot, *Correspondance littéraire, philosophique et critique addressée à un souverain d'Allemagne depuis 1753 jusqu'en 1769*, Longchamps-Buissons [Paris 1813], vol. V, p. 99 [Décembre 1765].)

[180] 'Lettres sur les Ecrits et le Caractère de Jean-Jacques Rousseau', *Oeuvres Complètes*, Treattel et Wurtz, (Paris 1820), Vol. I, p. 24.

[181] *Émile*, I, 7.

182 *Émile*, I, 7–8.

183 'La nature veut que les enfants soient enfants avant que d'être hommes. Si nous voulons pervertir cet ordre, nous produirons des fruits précoces, qui n'auront ni maturité ni saveur, et ne tarderont pas à se corrompre.' (*Émile*, II, 78; see also pp. 40–1, 60–3, 76–84.)

184 *Émile*, II, 78.

185 See *Émile*, II, 62–3, 83–4. To comprehend the principle of development, however, Rousseau does not consider it necessary to know the ultimate end of that development: 'On connaît donc, ou l'on peut connaître le premier point d'où part chacun de nous pour arriver au degré commun de l'entendement; mais qui est-ce qui connaît l'autre extrémité? Chacun avance plus ou moins selon son génie, son goût, ses besoins, ses talents, son zèle, et les occasions qu'il a de s'y livrer. . . . Nous ignorons ce que notre nature nous permet d'être; nul de nous n'a mesuré la distance qui peut se trouver entre un homme et un autre homme.' (*Émile*, I, 41.)

186 *Émile*, III, 239–40.

187 *The Meaning of Rousseau*, Oxford University Press (London 1929), p. 164.

188 In the next few pages we shall discuss (among other things) what Rousseau took being 'properly constituted' to involve. This explicitly developmental notion of human nature is more characteristic of *Émile* than of, say the *Contrat*, where emphasis is laid on a thorough transformation of human character.

189 *Oeuvres*, III, 133.

190 *Oeuvres*, III, 122. On page 132 Rousseau asks: 'De quoi s'agit-il donc précisément dans ce Discours? De marquer dans le progrés des choses, le moment où le Droit succedant à la Violence, la Nature fut soumise à la Loi; d'expliquer par quel enchaînement de prodiges le fort put se resoudre à servir le foible, et le Peuple à acheter un repos en idée, au prix d'une félicité réelle.' Here we have the characteristic Rousseauist notion that a society based on law replaces a natural order based on strength and violence, but that, unhappily, the laws of society have not in practice been properly constituted. Cf. *Oeuvres*, III, 187.

191 In n. 1, p. 123 of the *Oeuvres* (note on p. 1294), the editors suggest that Rousseau uses the phrase 'constitution humaine' when he is speaking of what is subject to change in man, and 'nature Humaine' when he is referring to what is immutable, but this is not convincing.

192 See, for example, *Oeuvres*, III, 122–3.

193 See, for example, the 'Dédicace' to Geneva at the beginning of the *Discours sur l'inégalité*. Geneva did not always live up to his expectations. See also *Lettre à d'Alembert* (ed. Fuchs), 80–2.

194 The golden age in the second *Discours* was simple, but, it should be noted, unequivocally social; it was not the first stage of almost complete independence. We have already noted above Rousseau's sympathetic description in the opening pages of the second *Discours* of natural man's

physical, but not mental, superiority. His dislike of cities is a thread which runs through all his work (see, for example, note IX to the second *Discours*, [*Oeuvres*, III, 202–8, esp. 203–4]; *Émile*, I, 37), but an equally constant feature of his thought was the insistence that man *cannot* return to a primitive pre-social condition. Rousseau, at the last moment, even sent his publisher an addition to the anti-social note referred to above, which scorns the notion that it is necessary or possible 'retourner vivre dans les forêts avec les Ours' (p. 207). See as well, *Dialogues*, III, 275–6.

[195] This is not to deny that there may at times be a doctrinal inconsistency as well; but of itself it is not enough to account for such widespread misunderstanding.

[196] Professor A. O. Lovejoy claims that Rousseau enumerates four such stages ('The Supposed Primitivism of Rousseau's Discourse on Inequality', *Essays in the History of Ideas*, Johns Hopkins Press (Baltimore 1949), pp. 14–37); I myself am inclined to think that there are one or even two more, but the exact number is not at this point important.

[197] *Oeuvres*, III, 167.

[198] *Oeuvres*, III, 191–2. For other places in the second *Discours* where the idea of a 'lente succession des choses' appears, see: *Oeuvres*, III, 127, 134, 146, 160, 162, 164, 187. We should point out one significant event in Rousseau's presentation which does not fit easily into his notion of gradual change – the conspiracy of the rich to enslave the poor by an agreement instituting a civil order biased in favour of the former. It is not clear why Rousseau employs this apparently clumsy device. If he were to regard this pact as creating a legitimate order, it would make some sense as describing the grounds of political obligation, but clearly the agreement in the second *Discours* cannot in Rousseau's eyes create a legitimate social order, for it is designed to benefit one class of citizens at the expense of the other.

[199] *Oeuvres*, III, 192.

[200] He is well aware that his is a more radical attempt than that of many of his predecessors; see, for example, *Oeuvres*, III, 124–5, 132. Following quotation p. 125.

[201] At any rate there are these two basic principles in the *Discours*; but Rousseau sometimes appears to believe that pity or compassion is a derivative of 'amour de soi' – hence not essential in the same sense. For example, in *Émile* (II, 81) Rousseau states that 'la seule passion naturelle à l'homme est l'amour de soi-même'. See also p. 247.

[202] *Oeuvres*, III, 142.

[203] Harald Höffding, *Jean-Jacques Rousseau and his Philosophy*, trans. Richards and Saidla, Yale University Press (New Haven 1930), p. 116. Cf. the remarks of M. Jean Starobinski (*Oeuvres*, III, lviii). Höffding maintains, however, that in the second *Discours* Rousseau felt that 'the necessary progress of things led to tyranny' (p. 92), and that it was not until his

later works that he arrived at the view that this degeneration was not necessary, but merely possible (and, in fact, actual). But it appears to me that this latter view can be found in the second *Discours*, and even in the first *Discours* as well. A contrary theme in Rousseau's thought (in the political realm) can be found in the *Contrat*, III, x (*Oeuvres*, III, 421-3), where Rousseau speaks of the eventual, inevitable suppression of the sovereign by the executive.

204 This issue is discussed in more detail in the section immediately following.

205 *Oeuvres*, III, 193. This thought crops up frequently in Rousseau's writings. Cf. *Émile* (I, 9): 'L'homme naturel est tout pour lui; il est l'unité numérique, l'entier absolu, qui n'a de rapport qu'à lui-même ou à son semblable. L'homme civil n'est qu'une unité fractionnaire qui tient au dénominateur, et dont la valeur est dans son rapport avec l'entier, qui est le corps social.' See also pp. 63-4.

206 See, on this point, *Oeuvres*, III, 157, 170. A passage on p. 170 states that as soon as men began to value one another 'tout tort volontaire devint un outrage, parce qu'avec le mal qui résultoit de l'injure, l'offensé y voyoit le mépris de sa personne souvent plus insuportable que le mal même'.

207 It consists of the passion to place oneself above others, both in one's own opinion and in the opinion of the others; as such, it can never be finally satisfied. The envious fellow a rung or two lower on the ladder struggles to get above his superiors, and those higher up attempt to maintain their position or rise higher.

208 *Autobiography of Edward Gibbon*, ed. Sheffield, Oxford University Press (London 1959), p. 218.

209 *Émile*, II, 69. See also II, p. 63.

210 See *Émile*, III, 239-40.

211 *Oeuvres*, III, 288.

212 The discussion of liberty in this study concerns man's relationship to his *social*, not his *natural* environment. Hence 'independence' will not be construed as, say, 'freedom from natural necessity', but as a condition of freedom from one's fellows. In *Émile* Rousseau speaks of dependence on things and dependence on men: 'La dépendance des choses, n'ayant aucune moralité, ne nuit point à la liberté, et n'engendre point de vices.' (*Émile*, II, 70.) The terms 'freedom' and 'liberty' will be used interchangeably.

213 No attempt is made to provide philosophically satisfactory definitions of the two notions; they are *tools*, rather than *subjects* of analysis. In the words of Rousseau, 'le sens philosophique du mot "liberté" n'est pas de mon sujet.' (*Oeuvres*, III, 365 [*Contrat*, I, viii]). Political liberty, the liberty of citizens, will be examined below (Chapter 3, Part VI).

214 *Oeuvres*, III, 283 (Geneva ms.).

215 *Oeuvres*, III, 283 (Geneva ms.). One must obviously be cautious in using

the Geneva manuscript, which Rousseau never published, as evidence of his settled opinions. However, so long as one is citing views which Rousseau has repeated elsewhere in published works, one is on safe ground.

[216] *Oeuvres*, III, 364–5. Rousseau, however, at least in the passage quoted, seems unlike Hobbes to limit natural right to what can be successfully got; Hobbes's uncovenanted man had an unlimited right, but limited power.

[217] See, as an example,'. . . la première loi de la nature est le soin de se conserver' (*Émile*, III, 223).

[218] *Oeuvres*, III, 842.

[219] See Chapter 2, Part IV.

[220] *Oeuvres*, III, 841.

[221] See the discussion below, Chapter 3, Part VI.

[222] *Oeuvres*, III, 510. Cf. *Émile*, 69, 182. In the paragraph following the quotation, Rousseau continues: 'Rendez les h[ommes] consequens à eux-mêmes étant ce qu'ils veulent paroitre et paroissant ce qu'ils sont. Vous aurez mis la loi sociale au fond des coeurs, hommes civils par leur nature et Citoyens par leurs inclinations, ils seront uns, ils seront bons, ils seront heureux, et leur félicité sera celle de la République; car n'étant rien que par elle ils ne seront rien que pour elle, elle aura tout ce qu'ils ont et sera tout ce qu'ils sont.'

[223] These, it will be seen, are closely related to the issues to be discussed below in Chapter 3, Part VI, dealing with political liberty. What is meant by the phrase 'lower nature' will be seen in a few pages below.

[224] A point which Burke also makes: 'It is better to cherish virtue and humanity, by leaving much to free will, even with some loss to the object, than to attempt to make men mere machines and instruments of a political benevolence. The world on the whole will gain by a liberty, without which virtue cannot exist.' (*Works*, II, 375.)

[225] *Oeuvres*, III, 356 (*Contrat*, I, iv). Cf. his remark in the second *Discours*: 'Ce n'est donc pas tant l'entendement qui fait parmi les animaux la distinction spécifique de l'homme que sa qualité d'agent libre.' (p. 141.)

[226] *Oeuvres*, III, 171.

[227] *Oeuvres*, III, 171.

[228] *Oeuvres*, III, 174–5. See also pp. 169–70, 188–9.

[229] See the discussion of this point above in the previous section.

[230] But one's scope for moral action was of course drastically limited as well.

[231] Rousseau himself clung to the monotonous trade of music-copying long after he was in a position to stop. Indeed, he refused a pension, or rather refused to allow himself to be offered a pension by Louis XV because to him it smacked of subjection. Burke took strong exception to this (*Works*, II, 537). Also, Rousseau devoted almost a dozen pages to considering the importance of a trade for Émile (*Émile*, III, 224–34). He argues that, because

of the uncertainty of life, a man should have some 'métier' for security, whatever his station in life.

232 See, for example, his description of the Swiss village in *Lettre à d'Alembert* (pp. 80–3); consider also his description of the golden age in the second *Discours* (*Oeuvres*, III, 167–71).

233 *Émile*, III, 182.

234 Not, of course, in every case the *conscious* limitation of desire; but a peasant way of life cannot be sustained by city folk living in the country.

235 *Émile*, II, 63–4.

236 *Confessions*, Book IX. Cf. *Émile*, IV, 279.

237 The political dimension is discussed in the following chapter (part vi).

238 *Freedom: A New Analysis*, (1953), Longmans (London 1967), part i, p. 22.

239 'Two concepts of Liberty', in *Four Essays on Liberty*, Oxford University Press (Oxford 1969).

240 *Émile*, IV, 339–40.

241 *Oeuvres*, III, 365 (*Contrat*, I, viii).

242 *Émile*, V, 568.

243 *Émile*, IV, 404.

244 This platonic phrase does not seem inappropriate to describe this aspect of Rousseau's thought (nor, as we shall see, to describe a similar aspect of Burke's).

245 See below Chapter III, Part VI.

246 See, on this point, *Works*, V, 216. Burke does, however, occasionally engage in this sort of speculation; see, for example, *Works*, I, 500; II, 332. But note that it is a contrast (as with Hobbes and Locke) between a condition without any settled pattern of coercive authority, and one with such a pattern. Unlike Rousseau, Burke considers both the natural and the civil state to be social.

247 See above, for example: Chapter 1, Part V; Chapter 2, Part II. See below, Chapter 3, Part V.

248 *Works*, II, 282. Following quotation same page.

249 Adaptation of a sentence in *Works*, II, 335. On this general issue see II, 29–31, 282–3, 331–6.

250 *Works*, II, 30. See also V, 424.

251 *Corr.*, I, 558 (October 1789). This long and important letter was part of the correspondence out of which the *Reflections* issued.

252 This assertion fits in with the natural-law reading of Burke, for it seems clear that for Burke a man must always act within a divinely imposed order; hence, actual independence, as we have described it, is impossible, although licence is not.

253 *Works*, V, 117. See also I, 441; II, 163, 308, 515; *Corr.*, I, 558. Professor Cobban discusses this aspect of Burke's conception in the section 'Order and Liberty', *Edmund Burke*, Allen and Unwin (London 1929), pp. 53–8.

254 *Works*, VII, 101.

²⁵⁵ *Works*, VII, 99.

²⁵⁶ *Works*, VI, 150.

²⁵⁷ See, for example, *Works*, II, 283. Consider, in this light, Rousseau's comment: 'Eh! dans la misere des choses humaines quel bien vaut la peine d'être acheté du sang de nos freres? La liberté même est trop chere à ce prix.' (*Oeuvres*, III, 836.)

²⁵⁸ *Works*, II, 282.

²⁵⁹ *Works*, II, 514–5. Cf. Rousseau's comment in the work on Poland: 'Je ris de ces peuples avilis qui, se laissant ameuter par des ligueurs, osent parler de liberté sans même en avoir l'idée, et, le coeur plein de tous les vices des esclaves, s'imaginent que pour être libres il suffit d'être des mutins.' (*Oeuvres*, III, 974.)

²⁶⁰ *Works*, II, 555.

²⁶¹ Letter to M. Dupont, 1789 (*Corr.*, I, 557–8). We shall return to this letter in the section below on political liberty (Chapter 3, Part VI).

²⁶² Although consider Burke's notion of 'virtuous liberty' in the quotation a few pages back.

²⁶³ A very important issue which has hovered on the fringes of the discussion in this section is the role of 'will' in the creation of moral rules. We have argued here that both writers insist on the close link between liberty and law. The function of will in the formulation of law or moral rules is crucial, and we shall discuss it in Parts VI and VII of the following chapter.

3   The State and the Citizen in Rousseau and Burke

¹ Note the tentative air of the titles of two relevant works: *An Abridgment of English History* (1757), *Hints for an Essay on the Drama* (probably prior to 1765). His *Philosophical Inquiry* (1757) is, of course, much more thorough and systematic.

² Letter to Richard Shackleton, March 21, 1746–7, when Burke was under twenty (*Corr.*, I, 12).

³ Letter to Shackleton, August 31, 1757 (*Corr.*, I, 13).

⁴ Cf. Locke, *Second Treatise*, no. 225; Burke, *Works*, II, 304 (*Reflections*); III, 16 (*An Appeal from the New to the Old Whigs*).

⁵ R. R. Fennessy gives an account of Paine's political thought and his famous row with Burke in *Burke, Paine and the Rights of Man*, Martinus Nijhoff (The Hague 1963). In Fennessy's words: 'The ragged soldiers of Washington's army understood as little of Locke and Rousseau as they did of the distinction between internal and external taxation. But they had no difficulty in understanding Paine when he told them: "To know whether it be the interest of the continent to be independent, we need only ask this easy, simple question: Is it the interest of a man to be a boy all his life?" ' (p. 34).

[6] Quoted in Fennessy, p. 27.

[7] Ultimately, this appears to be the position of Burke as well. See below, Part VII.

[8] *The Rights of Man*, Doubleday and Company (New York 1961), pp. 305–6. Published in this edition together with Burke's *Reflections* to which it was a reply. All subsequent quotations are from this edition.

[9] *Rights of Man*, p. 278.

[10] *Works*, II, 304. There is a lack of clarity about Burke's thought in this matter, however, and, given his natural-law beliefs, it could be argued that in broad outline his views on rebellion are closer to those of his opponents than might be thought. He is just a great deal more cautious and pessimistic than they are.

[11] *Works*, II, 359.

[12] *Rights of Man*, p. 278.

[13] Ibid., p. 282.

[14] See especially Chapter 2, Part II.

[15] All quotations in this paragraph from the first four pages of Burke's *Speech on the Reform of the Representation in the House of Commons*, May 7, 1782 (*Works*, VI, pp. 144–7). For lengthy discussions of Burke and the natural-right school, see: Peter J. Stanlis, *Edmund Burke and the Natural Law*, chapter 4; and Russell Kirk, 'Burke and Natural Rights', *Review of Politics*, October, 1951, pp. 441–56. Both writers are to some extent thrown off course, I think, because of their misunderstanding of Rousseau's political thought. See also B. T. Wilkins, *The Problem of Burke's Political Philosophy*, 1967, part III.

[16] Cf. Rousseau's remarks in the *Contrat*, I, v, where he is considering the differences between a despotism and a properly constituted state: 'Il y aura toujours une grande différence entre soumettre une multitude, et régir une société. Que des hommes épars soient successivement asservis a un seul . . . je ne vois là qu'un maître et des esclaves, je n'y vois point un peuple et son chef; c'est si l'on veut une aggrégation, mais non pas une association; il n'y a la ni bien public ni corps politique.'

[17] Note here H. A. Rommen's comment that the eighteenth-century rationalists 'knew, in effect, only the harsh antithesis of individual and state' (*The Natural Law*, London, 1949, p. 82).

[18] *The State and the Citizen*, Hutchinson Ltd. (Grey Arrow), (London 1958), p. 33.

[19] Chapter 2, Part II. See also Chapter 2, Part VI.

[20] *Oeuvres*, III, 248. 'Rétablit' (rather than 'établit') gives Rousseau a footing in both camps, however. But the general flow of his thought was away from natural right. There is not very much natural-right talk in the *Contrat*.

[21] *Oeuvres*, III, 259.

[22] There are times when Rousseau appears to be saying that, where atti-

tudes have been properly formed, the individual is sometimes (as in the case of the lawgiver) in a position to discern what is the good of all. But the lawgiver's proposals must always be submitted to the people and ratified by them.

23 See above, Chapter 2, Part II.

24 G. Beaulavon, *Contrat social*, ed. 1903 (2nd ed. 1914), p. 17. Cited in Cobban, *Rousseau and the Modern State*, p. 37.

25 *Rousseau and the Modern State*, p. 162.

26 *Oeuvres*, III, 114. For other instances of his non-revolutionary disposition, see: pp. 95, 635, 637–9, 822, 881, 901, 1036–7; Preface to *Narcisse*.

27 See Chapter 2, Parts II and IV.

28 From almost all that follows in this section, one would have to except David Hume, reminding us once again that the discussion of these rationalist and empirilist traditions is suggestive rather than definitive.

29 In the Epistle Dedicatory to the *Elements of Philosophy*.

30 See the chapter on him in William Letwin's *The Origin of Scientific Economics*.

31 Quoted in Miss Shirley Letwin's *The Pursuit of Certainty*, Cambridge University Press (Cambridge 1965), pp. 166–7. With regard to this conception of politics as simple, consider also the prevalence of projects for setting things right in the eighteenth century, such as the Abbé de Saint-Pierre's *Projet de paix perpétuelle*.

32 One can see here how the two approaches come together at certain points, especially in their practical objectives.

33 It has been suggested (I think rightly) that, although Burke had a deep religious belief in the providential working out of God's will in the world, and thought he could see the hand of God in the European past, he nevertheless had little faith (especially in his old age) in the continued benevolent influence of the divine will in the future of Europe. Centuries of change had produced the perfection which was eighteenth-century Europe; Burke hoped that basically it would stay that way. See, for example, Philip Magnus, *Edmund Burke*, John Murray (London 1939), p. 62; and J. C. Weston, 'Burke's View of History', *Review of Politics*, XXIII (April 1961), p. 220.

34 *Oeuvres*, III, 637. See also pp. 114, 618, 635, 639, 811, 953–4, 1041.

35 This and the following quotation from *Edmund Burke and the Revolt against the Eighteenth Century*, p. 88. There may well be objections to painting Burke's attitude to social life in this language, but nevertheless it is at least plausible when applied to him, utterly inappropriate when applied to an empiricist. John Plamenatz suggests that Hume's political advice is very similar to Burke's, but adds: 'Yet how different the spirit and style of the giver! Hume is quite without reverence or admiration; he sees nothing majestic or divine about the State; it is merely a contrivance in the public interest.' (*Man and Society*, vol. I, p. 316.) Elsewhere he

writes: 'Loyalty to the community differs in kind from personal affection, and is not less necessary to happiness. This side of life, which meant so much to Rousseau and Hegel (and also to Burke), was taken almost no notice of by the utilitarians.' (*The English Utilitarians*, 2nd ed., p. 176.)

[36] J. G. A. Pocock, 'Burke and the Ancient Constitution', *The Historical Journal*, III, 2 (1960), p. 125. This article is concerned with the way in which the presence of Burke's doctrine of traditionalism in his thought should be historically explained (p. 125), and Pocock opens with a summary of the conventional wisdom regarding Burke, beginning: 'Burke held . . . that a nation's institutions were the fruit of its experience, that they had taken shape slowly as a result, and were in themselves the record, of a thousand adjustments to the needs of circumstance, each one of which, if it had been found by trial and error to answer recurrent needs, had been preserved in the usages and established rules of the nation concerned.' (p. 125.)

[37] *Works*, V, 253–4. There are affinities between this view and Michael Oakeshott's classification in his lectures at the London School of Economics of modern states as 'telocratic' and 'nomocratic' political communities. Burke's conception of European states is nomocratic. A more frequently quoted passage from Burke goes as follows: '. . . a nation is not an idea only of local extent, and individual momentary aggregation; but it is an idea of continuity, which extends in time as well as in numbers and in space. And this is a choice not of one day, or one set of people, not a tumultuary and giddy choice; it is a deliberate election of ages and of generations; it is a constitution made by what is ten thousand times better than choice, it is made by the peculiar circumstances, occasions, tempers, dispositions, and moral, civil, and social habitudes of the people, which disclose themselves only in a long space of time. It is a vestment, which accommodates itself to the body.' (*Works*, VI, 146–7.) Grouped very generally by topic, here are some other places where features of Burke's traditionalist doctrine may be found. On the particular character of a people and its manners, see ibid.: I, 258; II, 334–5, 467; III, 80, 82, 85, 109; V, 69, 153–4, 208, 268, 424. On political methods, and a statesman's or government's proper attitude and function, see: I, 307; II, 29, 428, 454–5; V, 209; VI, 73, 114, 116, 123–4. On the question of reform see: II, 65, 81–3, 426–8, 439–40, 516–17; III, 283; V, 77–8, 120–2; VI, 2–3, 19, 132, 148–9. On the necessity of different forms of governments to suit nations of different temperaments, see: II, 396; III, 36–7.

[38] See discussion of this issue in Chapter 2, Part V above. Burke does at times speak of 'prescription, which, through long usage, mellows into legality governments that were violent in their commencement' (*Works*, II, 435), and it is certainly possible to construe this and other passages

along historicist lines (for other examples, see *Works*, III, 9; VI, 413). But
Burke makes the connection between history and natural law explicit in a
letter to one Captain Mercer, an Irishman who made a large fortune in
India (*Corr.*, I, 577–8 undated): 'It is possible that many of the estates
about you were obtained by arms; a thing almost as bad as superstitu-
tion, and not much short of ignorance; – but it is old violence; and that
which may be wrong in the beginning, is consecrated by time and
becomes lawful. This may be superstition in me, and ignorance; but I
had rather remain in ignorance and superstition, than be enlightened
and purified out of the first principles of law and natural justice . . .
God is the distributor of his own blessings. I will not impiously attempt
to usurp his throne, but will keep . . . the order of property which I find
established in my country.' Right is *revealed*, not *made*, in the course of
time (or if it is made, it is made in conjunction with God's will). See also
Works, VI, 79–80. There are unresolved problems in Burke's holding of
these two views simultaneously, as we shall see below.

³⁹ *Works*, VI, 22. See in general pp. 18–23.

⁴⁰ *Works*, VI, 21. See also ibid.: I, 310–11; II, 325; III, 492–3. Cf. Rousseau's
very different remark: 'un peuple est toujours le maitre de changer ses
loix, mêmes les meilleures; car s'il lui plait de se faire mal à lui-même,
qui est-ce qui a droit de l'en empêcher?' (*Oeuvres* III, 394 [*Contrat*, II, xii].)
What Rousseau is suggesting is that, given the nature of sovereignty, no
subordinate person has the right to challenge or disobey laws legiti-
mately arrived at, nor are there any formal limitations restricting what
the sovereign may decide to do; this could not be, without the sovereign
ceasing to be sovereign. He goes to considerable lengths in his procedural
requirements for just law, however, to ensure that the laws will not only
be just, but also in the interest of the citizens. Cf. a rather similar section
of Burke in which he states in part: 'It would be dreadful indeed, if there
was any power in the nation capable of resisting its unanimous desire,
or even the desire of any very great and decided majority of the people.'
(*Works*, VI, 3.)

⁴¹ *Works*, III, 30.

⁴² *Works*, II, 304. Following quotation from *Works*, III, 16. See also ibid.: II,
236, 290–1 passim; V, 473; VI, 99. Burke also believed that there were
occasions when it was a moral duty, not simply a matter of national
self-interest, to wage war. At the end of his life, he was, in effect, urging
a *crusade* against revolutionary France.

⁴³ See above, Chapter 1, Part 1. From Stephen's *History of English Thought
in the Eighteenth Century*, 3rd ed., John Murray (London 1902) II, 191.

⁴⁴ *The Political Writings of Jean-Jacques Rousseau*, vol. I, 44.

⁴⁵ Grimm and Diderot, *Correspondence littéraire philosophique et critique*,
Longchamps-Buisson (Paris 1813), vol. I, 395–6 (entry for July 1755).

⁴⁶ 'Lettres sur les écrits et le caractère de J. J. Rousseau', *Oeuvres complètes*,

Treattel et Wurtz (Paris 1820), vol. I, 66–7. Cf. the last sentence in this quotation with Burke, *Works*, III, 110; VI, 148. In the first passage Burke claims that his is a theory, 'not to furnish principles for making a new constitution, but for illustrating the principles of a constitution already made. It is a theory drawn from the *fact* of our government'.

[47] Vaughan, *Political Writings*, I, 45.

[48] Consider, for example, John Morley's remark: Rousseau 'mistakes the multiplication of propositions for the discovery of fresh truth. Many pages of the *Social Contract* are mere logical deductions from verbal definitions: the slightest attempt to confront them with actual fact would have shown them to be not only valueless, but wholly meaningless, in connection with real human nature and the visible working of human affairs.' (*Rousseau*, Macmillan, London 1896, [1886], II, 138.)

[49] *Oeuvres*, III, 353 (opening sentence of *Contrat*).

[50] Cf. Maurice Cranston's brief discussion in his introduction to his translation of the *Contrat* (Penguin, 1968), p. 26–8.

[51] See, for example, Bk. II, ch. viii, ix and x, all on 'le peuple'. In the Geneva manuscript, at the start of the passage which was eventually to be broken up into these three chapters, Rousseau writes: 'Quoique je traitte ici du droit et non des convenances, je ne puis m'empêcher de jetter en passant quelques coups d'oeil sur celles qui sont indispensables dans toute bonne institution.' (*Oeuvres*, III, 318.)

[52] See, for example, Bk. III, ch. iii, viii and ix. Note that there can be an infinite variety of governments ('le Gouvernement est réellement susceptible d'autant de formes diverses que l'Etat a de Citoyens' [Bk. III, ch. iii]), but only one legitimate form of sovereignty; the former is a matter of convenience (in the sense of what is suitable in the circumstances), the latter a matter of right.

[53] There is a certain inconsistency, perhaps, in adducing as evidence of Rousseau's historical bent, his discussions of a lawgiver or legislator who in large part seems to stand outside history. In one respect, the lawgiver constitutes Rousseau's not altogether satisfactory attempt to get over a theoretical difficulty (how to understand a blind multitude transforming itself into a political society of citizens). The legislator is also an expression of Rousseau's admiration for the great lawgivers of antiquity whose feats were described in Plutarch's *Lives* and elsewhere. However, it is not unfair to see in the legislator an agent, as it were, of the historical process. He assists the coming into being of a people, with a due deference to the character that people has aready assumed. His task is described in the following passage: 'Il faut lui [the general will] faire voir les objets tels qu'ils sont, quelquefois tels qu'ils doivent lui paraoitre, lui montrer le bon chemin qu'elle cherche, la garantir de la séduction des volontés particulieres, rapprocher à ses yeux les lieux et les tems, balancer

l'attrait des avantages présens et sensibles, par le danger des maux éloignés et cachés,' (*Oeuvres*, III, 380.) If in his semi-divine nature the legislator seems to transcend history, his work nevertheless has unequivocally to do with time, with the product of the past and the likely exigencies of the future.

[54] Cf. his remark: 'Je regarde les nations modernes: j'y vois force faiseurs de loix et pas un legislateur,' (*Oeuvres*, III, 956.)

[55] *Oeuvres*, III, 394.

[56] *Oeuvres*, III, 251–2. On p. 250 Rousseau writes: 'C'en sera même assez pour que l'état ne soit pas mal gouverné, si le legislateur a pourvû comme il le devoit à tout ce qu'exigeoient les lieux, le climat, le sol, les moeurs, le voisinage, et tous les rapports particuliers du peuple qu'il avoit à instituer.'

[57] *Oeuvres*, III, 956–7. All quotations in this paragraph from pp. 956–9.

[58] Note the passage in the *Contrat*, III, xi (*Oeuvres*, III, 424–5) where Rousseau extolls the superior merits of old law.

[59] *Oeuvres*, III, 381 (*Contrat*, II, vii). See also p. 459. According to the Pléiade editors, the quotation is from Montesquieu's *Considérations sur les causes de la grandeur des Romains et de leur décadence*, an addition to the first chapter of the 1748 edition.

[60] *Oeuvres*, III, 381. Next quotation from following page. A belief that the founding of a state was miraculous is, of course, thoroughly inconsistent with a doctrine of political traditionalism. But, since Rousseau discusses the political functions of legislators and refers to actual historical figures as models, it does not seem unfair to interpret Rousseau's assertion that the lawgiver must be divine or semi-divine as a means of emphasizing the extreme difficulty of the task, rather than its human impossibility.

[61] Introduction to the Everyman edition of the *Social Contract and Discourses*, xxiv.

[62] *Works*, VI, 215. Cf. Rousseau's discussion of Lycurgus's 'joug de fer' (*Oeuvres*, III, 957). The emphasis of both Rousseau and Burke in these passages is upon reconciling men to government by adapting their manners, or in Rousseau's words: 'Former le gouvernement pour la nation est sans doute une chose utile, j'en connois cependant une plus utile encore, c'est de former la nation pour le gouvernement.' (*Oeuvres*, III, editor's note 2 to p. 901 [p. 1726]. The passage in the Rousseau text to which this note is attached repeats the same thought.)

[63] *Oeuvres*, III, 950.

[64] *Oeuvres*, III, 902. Nevertheless, even here Rousseau puts this sobering thought at the beginning of his study: 'Toutes choses ont leurs abus souvent nécessaires et ceux des établissemens politiques sont si voisins de leur institution que ce n'est presque pas la peine de la fair pour la voir si

vite degenerer.' (p. 901.) Burke's frequent remarks about practical affairs being a mixture of good and evil come to mind here.

⁶⁵ *Oeuvres*, III, 947. In this respect he separates himself from the *Contrat* legislator (Bk. II, ch. vii) who employs techniques of deception and persuasion to further his work.

⁶⁶ The words are Jean Fabre's in the Introduction to the *Considérations sur le gouvernement de Pologne* (*Oeuvres*, III, ccxl).

⁶⁷ *Oeuvres*, III, 953. In fact, however, he has more institutional proposals for Poland than for Corsica.

⁶⁸ *Oeuvres*, III, 953. In his *Ecrits sur l'Abbé de Saint-Pierre* (*Oeuvres*, III, 618) Rousseau writes of the ruler of a large empire: 'Forcé d'abandonner à d'autres ce qu'on appelle le détail et que j'appellerois, mois, le essentiel du Gouvernement, il se reserve les grandes affaires, le verbiage des Ambassadeurs, les tracasseries de ses favoris. . . .' See also p. 250.

⁶⁹ See, for example, *Oeuvres*, III, 960.

⁷⁰ Rousseau writes that it is necessary 'établir tellement la République dans les coeurs des Polonois, qu'elle y subsiste malgré tous les efforts de ses oppresseurs.' (*Oeuvres*, III, 959. See also p. 955). If this is not too far-fetched, one might suggest that by detaching to some extent the concept of 'patrie' from the soil (thus making it something much nearer to 'nation'), Rousseau is exposing a certain affinity to Burke when the latter speaks of France during the Revolution being outside herself, of the moral and political country being located outside the geographical frontiers of France. For examples of Burke's use of this notion, see: *Works*, III, 414–5, 418, 422, passim; IV, 220, 260, 363–4.

⁷¹ Rousseau applauds the work of Moses largely because he created an exclusive Jewish identity which would not mix with other peoples' (*Oeuvres*, III, 956–7. See also pp. 958, 960).

⁷² Rousseau writes: 'Ce sont les institutions nationales qui forment le génie, le caractère, les gouts, et les moeurs d'un peuple, qui le font être lui et non pas un autre.' (*Oeuvres*, III, 960.) On p. 966 Rousseau states that 'à vingt ans un Polonois ne doit pas être un autre homme; il doit être un Polonois', and on p. 962 he says it is a good thing that the Poles still have 'un habillement particulier'. For Rousseau's discussion of patriotism in the *Considérations*, see especially the first three sections: 'Etat de la question', 'Esprit des anciennes institutions', 'Application' (*Oeuvres*, III, 953–66).

⁷³ *Oeuvres*, III, 56–7 (first *Discours*). For other instances (outside the *Considérations*) of his approach to reform and his emphasis on the importance of time and circumstance, see: *Oeuvres*, III, 95, 112–14, 250, 324–5, 381, 384–6, 387, 389, 392–3, 414–19, 424–5, 618, 637–9, 655, 811, 822, 901, 913, 933.

⁷⁴ *Oeuvres*, III, 954. Cf. p. 971: 'Ah je ne saurois trop le redire; pensez-y

bien avant de toucher à vos loix, et surtout à celles qui vous firent ce que vous étes.'

75 *Oeuvres*, III, 955.

76 *Oeuvres*, III, 1041.

77 *Oeuvres*, III, 1028 (But for a different approach, see p. 975). Cf. Burke, *Works*, II, 439–40: 'Time is required to produce that union of minds which alone can produce all the good we aim at. Our patience will achieve more than our force. . . . By a slow but well-sustained progress, the effect of each step is watched; the good or ill success of the first gives light to us in the second; and so, from light to light, we are conducted with safety through the whole series.' See also Burke, *Works*, II, 65.

78 *Oeuvres*, III, 1037.

79 See, for example, *Oeuvres*, III, 965 (on luxury), 974 (on the Polish serfs), 994 (on hereditary nobility), 1009 (on a money economy). On the first subject, Rousseau writes: 'Oter tout à fait le luxe où regne l'inégalité me paroit, je l'avoue, une entreprise bien difficile. Mais n'y auroit-il pas moyen de changer les objets de ce luxe et d'en rendre l'exemple moins pernicieux?'

80 *Works*, I, 258.

81 *Works*, II, 467. This is a phrase Burke employs in his attack on the revolutionaries' 'rationalization' of the administrative subdivisions of France. His point is that Frenchmen have a partiality and affection for the traditionally defined regions which they cannot feel for 'a description of square measurement'.

82 See, for example, *Works*, II, 352, 358–9, 362–3.

83 *Works*, II, 359. Cf. Rousseau's avowed intention in the *Contrat* to bring justice and interest together, and note the following fragment: 'La loi n'agit qu'en dehors et ne règle que les actions; les moeurs seules pénétrent intérieurement et dirigent les volontés.' (*Oeuvres*, III, 555.)

84 *Works*, II, 314.

85 The discussion takes place in *Oeuvres*, III, 400–1 (*Contrat*, III, ii). It would seem that what Rousseau means by a *natural* order of priority is in this case the order that would prevail among civilized men in the absence of some cultural or political conditions which would affect a reversal.

86 John Chapman (*Rousseau-Totalitarian or Liberal*, [1956], AMS Press New York 1968) devotes a chapter to discussing what he calls 'the intensification of social sentiment' in Rousseau's political theory. In particular, he examines the tension between Rousseau's moral and political theory and argues that there is an incompatability between one form of social sentiment (humanitarianism) and another (patriotism).

87 See, for example: John H. Hallowell, *Main Currents in Modern Political Thought*, Holt (New York 1957), p. 166; Gustave Lanson, *Histoire de la litterature francaise*, 12th ed. (1912), p. 774; Jacques Maritain, *Three Reformers*, (1928), Sheed and Ward (London 1944), p. 96; John

Morley, *Rousseau*, (1886), Macmillan (London 1896), vol. I, p. 85.

88 See for example, *Oeuvres*, III, 9 (first *Discours*): 'Où il n'y a nul effet, il n'y a point de cause à chercher: mais ici l'effet est certain, la dépravation réelle, et nos ames se sont corrumpuës a mesure que nos Sciences et nos Arts se sont avancés à la perfection.' According to these pages, the virtue of a people varies inversely with the 'contagion des vaines connoissances' from which the community is suffering (p. 11). Rousseau even disingenuously pictures Socrates, 'le plus Sage des hommes au Jugement des Dieux', 'faisant l'Eloge de l'ignorance!' (p. 13). See also pp. 14–15, 17. However, the effect of the first *Discours* as a whole is rather different from the impression left by abstracted segments of it; this is discussed below.

89 See his comment at the opening of the first *Discours*: 'Ce n'est point la Science que je maltraite ... c'est la Vertu que je défends. ...' (*Oeuvres*, III, 5.)

90 Consider, for example, the following: 'Si elle [Nature] nous a destinés à être sains, j'ose presque assurer, que l'état de réflexion est un état contre Nature, et que l'homme qui médite est un animal dépravé.' (*Oeuvres*, III, 138.) This passage has been subject to serious misunderstanding and distortion. G. D. H. Cole, for example, in his translation of the second *Discours* deletes the qualifying word 'presque'. The clue to the meaning of this passage is, I believe, found a few pages later when Rousseau writes: 'Je n'ai considéré jusqu'ici que l'Homme *Physique*. ...' (p. 141, my italics.) The thinking man is depraved or vitiated *physically*, as an animal.

91 Note his remark in one of his replies to critics: 'J'ai dejà dit cent fois qu'il est bon qu'il y ait des Philosophes, pourvû que le Peuple ne se mêle pas de l'être.' (*Oeuvres*, III, 78).

92 *Oeuvres*, III, 29.

93 *Oeuvres*, III, 29.

94 A phrase which Burke used in connection with the question of who should judge when civil rebellion was justified and necessary – 'it is not to be agitated by common minds.' (*Works*, II, 304.) Cf. Rousseau's phrase 'des hommes vulgaires' (*Oeuvres*, III, 72).

95 *Oeuvres*, III, 29. For a further exposition of Rousseau's general opinions in this matter, see his replies to various critics of the discourse. (Ibid., 31–107. See especially pp. 31, 36, 72–3, 78, 95.) Cf. the following passages from Burke. Of the British constitution he writes: 'We ought to understand it according to our measure; and to venerate where we are not able presently to comprehend.' (*Works*, III, 114.) In the *Reflections* he asserts: 'The occupation of a hairdresser, or of a working tallow-chandler, cannot be a matter of honour to any person – to say nothing of a number of other more servile employments. Such descriptions of

men ought not to suffer oppression from the state; but the state suffers oppression, if such as they, either individually or collectively, are permitted to rule.' (*Works*, II, 322.)

⁹⁶ C. W. Hendel claims (*Jean-Jacques Rousseau: Moralist*, Oxford University Press (London 1934), vol. I, 18) that Rousseau began by accepting the Socratic injunction, but moved away from it: 'From the belief that knowledge is virtue, he [Rousseau] had advanced to the perception that knowledge is not good unless it is possessed by one who already has the makings of character.' But the reduction of the ethical role of knowledge is a feature of his entire career; the first *Discours* is in line with this attitude, as the remainder of the paragraph in the text shows.

⁹⁷ See, for example, *Émile*, 81, 348–9, 352, 354–5. But see also p. 48.

⁹⁸ *Oeuvres*, III, 15. In a defence of the first discourse, Rousseau writes that 'le beau tems, le tems de la vertu de chaque Peuple, a été celui de son ignorance . . . à mesure qu'il est devenu sçavant, Artiste, et Philosophe, il a perdu ses moeurs et sa probité. . . .' (p. 76. See also p. 228.)

⁹⁹ *Oeuvres*, III, 14.

¹⁰⁰ *Oeuvres*, III, 30. See also p. 42.

¹⁰¹ 'La première éducation doit donc être purement négative. Elle consiste, non point à enseigner la vertu ni la vérité, mais à garantir le coeur du vice et l'esprit de l'erreur.' (*Émile*, II, 83.)

¹⁰² *Oeuvres*, III, 177–8.

¹⁰³ *Oeuvres*, III, 286–7. Following quotation from same passage.

¹⁰⁴ *Oeuvres*, III, 380.

¹⁰⁵ *Oeuvres*, III, 380.

¹⁰⁶ *Oeuvres*, III, 380 (last few sentences of the chapter).

¹⁰⁷ *Oeuvres*, III, 383 (both phrases).

¹⁰⁸ *Oeuvres*, III, 251.

¹⁰⁹ *Oeuvres*, III, 186.

¹¹⁰ For example, in the 'Dédicace' to the second *Discours* Rousseau note the following truths: 'que c'est surtout la grande antiquité des Loix qu les rend saintes et vénérables, que le Peuple méprise bientôt celles qu'i voit changer tous les jours, et qu'en s'accoutumant à négliger les anciens usages sous prétexte de faire mieux, on introduit souvent de grands maux pour en corriger de moindres.' (*Oeuvres*, III, 114. Cf. p. 425. There are also numerous passages in the *Pologne*.)

¹¹¹ *Oeuvres*, III, 243.

¹¹² Cf. Burke's remark, *Works*, VI, 52, about the impossibility of *creating* a prejudice.

¹¹³ See, on this issue, *Oeuvres*, III, 459, 960.

¹¹⁴ *Oeuvres*, III, 424–5; also pp. 958, 971 (but see p. 316). Cf. the quoted passage on prejudice taken from the *Reflections*: '. . . instead of casting away all our old prejudices, we cherish them to a very considerable degree, and, to take more shame to ourselves, we cherish them because

they are prejudices; and the longer they have lasted, and the more generally they have prevailed, the more we cherish them.' (*Works*, II, 359.)

115 *Oeuvres*, III, 556. It should be noted, however, that the legitimizing acquiescence is always *current*. See, for example, *Oeuvres*, III, 385.

116 See the Geneva ms. (*Oeuvres*, III, 303.) It is important to note, however, that stress is laid primarily on 'une longue *violence*' (my italics). But this is still to imply that 'la prescription seule', time *in itself*, is not sufficient to legitimize a political order.

117 Chapter 3, Part VII, discusses this issue.

118 A phrase which Rousseau applies to laws in general. *Oeuvres*, III, 243: 'les abus sont inévitables et leurs suites funestes dans toute société, où l'intérêt public et les lois n'ont aucune force naturelle. . . .'

119 *Oeuvres*, III, 113. Previous quotation from previous page. There is an echo in the following statements of Burke: 'There is a sacred veil to be drawn over the beginnings of all governments. . . . Time, in the origin of most governments, has thrown this mysterious veil over them.' (*Works*, VII, 60.) See also Burke's claim that Parliament during the 1688 Revolution threw 'a politic, well-wrought veil' over circumstances which tended to weaken the rights which were to be perpetuated. (*Works*, II, 293. See also VI, 75.)

120 Burke, *Works*, II, 435.

121 *Oeuvres*, III, 554. But see editor's note no. 1 to p. 554 (p. 1538).

122 *The Romantic Revolt*, Blackwell and Sons (London 1923), p. 134. Peter Stanlis describes this as 'one of the most ambiguous and challenging statements ever written about Burke.' (First sentence of Ch. VI, *Edmund Burke and the Natural Law*.)

123 *Works*, II, 359.

124 *Works*, II, 120. This phrase, which denotes the type of reasoning which we are discussing here, and the misuse which Burke is so often attacking in his writings, appears in Burke's speech on economic reform: 'This plan, I really flatter myself, is laid, not in official formality, nor in airy speculation, but in real life, and in human nature, in what "comes home (as Bacon says) to the business and bosoms of men".'

125 *Works*, VI, 148. See also VI, 113–14.

126 The two phrases are from *Works*, II, p. 7 and p. 58 respectively.

127 *Works*, I, 50.

128 *Works*, I, 86–7. Cf. Rousseau (*Oeuvres*, III, 380): 'De lui-même le peuple veut toujours le bien . . . le jugement qui la [the general will] guide n'est pas toujours éclairé.'

129 *Works*, II, 358. See also pp. 382–4.

130 See, for example, *Works*, III, 81. See also III, 99.

131 *Works*, VI, 148.

132 There are certain obvious affinities between Burke's thought and that

of Professor Michael Oakeshott. Consider, for example, their respective views of tradition and the relationship between theory and practice.

133 *Works,* VI, 148.

134 *Works,* III, 15. See also II, 353; VII, 204.

135 See, for example, *Works,* II, 33–6, 334–5, 440; VI, 114.

136 *Works,* II, 350.

137 *Works,* II, 334.

138 *Works,* II, 440.

139 *Works,* I, 464–5. He frequently makes this point in his American speeches.

140 *Works,* I, 474.

141 These include religious dissent, the institution of slavery, the litigious system of education, and the colonies' remoteness from the mother country (*Works,* I, 467–9).

142 *Works,* II, 307–8.

143 Burke uses this phrase to describe jurisprudence which combines 'the principles of original justice with the infinite variety of human concerns . . .' (*Works,* II, 367).

144 See *Works,* III, 113; VI, 147.

145 Consider what Burke is reported to have said about education: '[it] should be considered as improvement to the heart as well as the mind. It is too often in this Age mentioned merely as school acquirement, the last may be bought by any rich Vulgar parents; but the first can only be imbibed from domestic Guardians who have, themselves, a thorough and refined sense of True Virtue.' (Frances Anne Crewe, 'Extracts from Mr Burke's Table Talk', *Burke Newsletter,* vol. v, no. 2 [Winter 1963–4], 282.)

146 *Works,* I, 280. Cf. Rousseau's remark in the Considérations: 'Il n'y aura jamais de bonne et solide constitution que celle où la loi régnera sur les coeurs des citoyens. Tant que la force législative n'ira pas jusques là, les loix seront toujours éludées.' (*Oeuvres,* III, 955. See also p. 495.)

147 Burke's assault occupies a half-dozen pages. (*Works,* II, 535–41. All quotations in these first three paragraphs are from this passage.) Vanity, according to Burke, constitutes what might be called the vicious organizing principle of Rousseau's life and thought; however, compare, on the question of vanity, Rousseau's recurrent diatribes against 'amour-propre', the social passion which drives men to seek prominence, to run after positions in which they seem better than their fellows. Burke decries Rousseau as 'a lover of his kind, but a hater of his kindred': 'Benevolence to the whole species, and want of feeling for every individual with whom the professors come in contact, form the character of the new philosophy'; but Rousseau himself scorns what he calls 'ces prétendus Cosmopolites, qui justifiant leur amour pour la patrie per leur amour pour le genre humain, se vantent d'aimer tout le monde pour avoir droit de n'aime. personne'. (*Oeuvres,* III, 287; see his similar point in *Émile,* I, 9).

Finally, Burke claims that the Parisian philosophers, following Rousseau, are doing away with the vitally important 'ligaments' of society, such as family ties and a whole range of un-rationalized affections; but Rousseau was as aware as Burke of the importance of such things in maintaining a stable political order (see above, Chapter 3, Parts IV and V).

148 *Works*, V, 122. See also *Works*, I, 447; II, 325, 333, 555; III, 76, 78; VI, 21; VII, 92–102 (on arbitrary power); and *Corr.*, I, 558; II, 437.

149 *Corr.*, I, 558.

150 *Works*, II, 333. The first sentence in this quotation is very much in keeping with Rousseau's thought. Elsewhere Burke writes: 'Society cannot exist unless a controlling power upon will and appetite be placed somewhere, and the less of it there is within, the more there must be without.' (*Works*, II, 555; see also II, 308; IV, 20.) But to assume from this interpretation that Burke must therefore have relied heavily on 'reason' is inadequate; indeed, as we have observed, one of his most persistent complaints against the rights-of-man theorists was their excessive rationalism. In the section immediately following and in the final chapter, we shall examine how Burke tries to surmount this problem of 'reason' and 'will' by employing the notion of a 'superior wisdom' or a 'reasonable will'.

151 See the chapters discussing the general will in the *Contrat*, especially Bk. II. ch. iii.

152 '... l'essence du corps politique est dans l'accord de l'obéissance et de la liberté, et ... ces mots de "sujet" et de "souverain" sont des corrélations identiques dont l'idée se réunit sous le seul mot de Citoyen.' (*Oeuvres*, III, 427 [*Contrat*, III, xiii].) Cf. Burke, *Works*, II, 515.

153 *Oeuvres*, III, 362 (*Contrat*, I, vi).

154 Rousseau argues that in a slave-holding community both the master and the slave are unfree, for the master needs the slave. (See, for example, *Oeuvres*, III, 174–5, 351.)

155 *Oeuvres*, III, 379 (*Contrat*, II, vi). See also, *Oeuvres*, III, 492. In the *Lettres de la montagne* he describes what is to be found in his *Contrat social* ('ce Livre si décrié, mais si nécessaire'): 'Vous y verrez partout la Loi mise au dessus des hommes; vous y verrez par tout la liberté réclamée, mais toujours sous l'autorité des loix, sans lesquelles la liberté ne peut exister, et sous lesquelles on est toujours libre, de quelque façon qu'on soit gouverné.' (*Oeuvres*, III, 811.)

156 'Par de nouvelles associations, corrigeons, s'il se peut, le défaut de l'association générale. ... Montrons lui ['notre violent interlocuteur'] dans l'art perfectionné la réparation des maux que l'art commencé fit à la nature.' (*Oeuvres*, III, 288 [Geneva ms.]; see also p. 248.)

157 *Works*, II, 517.

158 'The distinguishing part of our constitution is its liberty. To preserve that

liberty inviolate, seems the particular duty and proper trust of a member of the House of Commons.' (*Works*, I, 441.)

[159] He is, of course, to this extent different from Rousseau, whose major discussion of liberty (despite a disclaimer in the *Contrat*, I, viii) is highly theoretical.

[160] Burke even speaks of the English subject's spirit of 'liberal obedience' as the bond which unites and invigorates the whole (*Works*, I, 509).

[161] *Works*, II, 515. Cf. *Works*, II, 438–40.

[162] *Works*, II, 304–9. In the Dupont letter Burke radically expands the notion of inheritance: 'You hope, sir, that I think the French deserving of liberty. I certainly do. I certainly think that all men who desire it, deserve it. It is not the reward of our merit, or the acquisition of our industry. It is our inheritance. It is the birthright of our species.' (*Corr.*, I, 557). Burke is here again blurring the art-nature antithesis in the notion of an inheritance of the entire human species.

[163] *Works*, II, 308.

[164] *Works*, II, 30. On this general point, see *Works*, I, 464–70 (esp. 464); II, 29–31, 333–5; and *Corr.*, I, 561.

[165] *Corr.*, I, 561.

[166] *Works*, II, 30. See also on this point, *Works*, I, 464–70 (esp. 469).

[167] *Works*, II, 283. A good part of Burke's above-mentioned letter to M. Dupont is nothing more than a catalogue of the signs by which one may recognize a free and a despotic form of government.

[168] *Works*, I, 441.

[169] *Corr.*, I, 558. It is perhaps not too farfetched to see in Burke's castigation of 'partial freedom' as a state of unfreedom (*Works*, II, 7–8, 163–4; VI, 63, 103) a parallel to Rousseau's insistence upon the impersonal, generality of law. Partial freedom, a situation in which civil benefits are allocated selectively, Burke calls 'privilege and prerogative, and not liberty' (VI, 63), 'a most invidious form of slavery' (II, 8). Rousseau felt similarly about 'partial law', law which did not issue from and apply to all the citizens.

[170] *Oeuvres*, III, 841.

[171] For Rousseau's famous statement of the paradox, see the *Contrat*, I, vii.

[172] See the *Contrat*, IV, ii, for Rousseau's attempt to deal with this issue.

[173] Maurice Cranston discusses the importance of this distinction, calling one 'rational freedom' and the other 'enforceable rational freedom'. See *Freedom*, (1953), Longmans (London 1967), esp. ch. 3.

[174] 'Ce qui ne signifie autre chose sinon qu'on le forcera d'être libre,' *Annales de la philosophie politique*, 5 (1965), p. 151.

[175] *Émile*, IV, 404. See above Chapter 2, Part VI.

[176] For Burke's views on representation, see *Works*, II, 329; III, 298–344 (esp. 333–6); VI, 144–58.

[177] This contention, which is undoubtedly based on his experience as a

legislator, issues from his belief that government is a matter of collective wisdom, not will, and that therefore an MP is elected to exercise his judgement rather than merely to reflect or transmit his constituents' ill-informed preferences.

178 *Works*, I, 447–8.

179 *Works*, V, 227.

180 *Oeuvres*, III, 430 (*Contrat*, III, xv). However, the nature of Rousseau's distinction between law-making (by all the citizens) and rule-making (by representatives) must always be borne in mind. One could perhaps argue that the purpose of Rousseauist law-making is to get the kind of consensus on basic matters that in England had been produced by history. (It remains true, however, that the British Parliament was then and is now the body with authority to make all major decisions, however, fundamental.) More experience of the practice of government might have taught Rousseau that the area he was leaving to representatives was enormous, and that the boundary between legislation and administration is in practice non-existent. (I am indebted to William Pickles for raising the point.)

181 *Works*, II, 555. For other places in Burke's writings where this theme emerges, or appears to emerge, see *Works*, III, 76–80; V, 424; VI, 151.

182 *Works*, II, 332–3. Parts of this important passage have already been discussed in this section. All quotations in this paragraph are from the two pages noted.

183 *Leviathan*, Pt. II, ch. 21.

184 *Second Treatise*, ch. VI, no. 57.

185 *Oeuvres*, III, 248.

186 For primitive communities, see Mill's discussion of slavery in *Representative Government*, ch. II (pp. 198–9 in the Everyman edition). For contemporary England, see his discussion of plural voting for the mentally superior in *Representative Government*, ch. VIII (pp. 285–90).

187 *Works*, V, 523.

188 By this phrase we mean to describe the view that a government can be legitimized by virtue of its longevity alone. On this, see Burke, *Works*, II, 26, 293, 367–70, 435; VI, 75–6, 146, 413; VII, 60. In *Works*, VI, 146, Burke asserts that the British constitution is 'a prescriptive constitution; it is a constitution whose sole authority is that it has existed time out of mind.' And in *Works*, II, 435, he describes the 'time of prescription' as that which 'thro' long usage, mellows into legality governments that were violent in their commencement'.

189 In the opening chapters (i–iv) of the *Contrat* Rousseau makes the general point that force cannot be understood to create right. In the Geneva ms. he applies this principle specifically to the 'prescriptive' thesis: 'Que par le laps de temps une violente usurpation devienne enfin un pouvoir legitime; que la prescription seule puisse changer un Usurpateur en

magistrat suprême et un troupeau d'esclaves en corps de nation, c'est ce que beaucoup de savans hommes ont osé soutenir et à quoi il ne manque d'autre autorité que celle de la raison. Bien loin qu'une longue violence puisse à force de tems se transformer en un gouvernement juste, il est incontestable au contraire. . . .' (*Oeuvres*, III, 303.)

190 For all *practical* purposes, the question, 'Why should I obey the government?' may be adequately answered, 'Because it has existed time out of mind'; that is, it may succeed in stopping further inquiries, but it is not, Burke realizes, a theoretically satisfactory response. This is consistent with his remark: 'It is always to be lamented when men are driven to search into the foundations of the commonwealth.' (*Works*, VI, 132; see also *Works*, II, 26.)

191 See on this, *Works*, VI, 146.

192 'Speech on the Fourth Day of the Impeachment of Warren Hastings, Esq.', (*Works*, VII, 56–126 [Especially 92–103].) The speech was delivered on 16 February 1788.

193 *Works*, VII, 101.

194 *Works*, VII, 100. Quotations following are from the same page. Cf. Rousseau, *Oeuvres*, III, 303–5 (Geneva ms.), 354–8 (*Contrat*, I, iii, iv).

195 *Works*, VII, 99.

196 *Works*, II, 360.

197 On this see, *Works*, III, 82, 87. Cf. Rousseau, *Oeuvres*, III, 359.

198 *Works*, VI, 147.

199 *Works*, II, 300. Cf. Rousseau's contemptuous dismissal of this doctrine in *Contrat*, I, ii, last paragraph.

200 In his *Appeal from the New to the Old Whigs* (*Works*, III, 24).

201 In *Works*, III, 79, Burke writes of the duties of parenthood: 'But out of physical causes, unknown to us, perhaps unknowable, arise moral duties, which, as we are able perfectly to comprehend, we are bound indispensably to perform.'

202 But see a passage where he contradicts this, *Works*, III, 82: 'But the idea of a people is the idea of a corporation. It is wholly artificial. . . .'

203 *Works*, II, 368.

204 *Works*, II, 300.

205 There is warrant for this analogy in Burke's writings. Consider the following comment from his early work, *An Abridgment of English History* (Works, VI, 416): 'But the truth is, the present system of our laws, like our language and our learning, is a very mixed and heterogeneous mass; in some respects our own; in more borrowed from the policy of foreign nations, and compounded, altered, and variously modified, according to the various necessities, which the manners, the religion, and the commerce of the people have at different times imposed.' But cf. here Rousseau's objections to piecemeal legislation (*Oeuvres*, III, 975).

206 See the passage in *Works*, III, 78–9.

207 *Works*, II, 307.

208 For instances of places where Burke discusses this issue, see *Works*, II, 17, 236, 304; III, 16; V, 473; VIII, 524. See also *Corr.*, I, 563 (Letter to M. Dupont, October, 1789).

209 *Works*, II, 236.

210 *Works*, II, 304 (both quotations).

211 *Works*, II, 422. See also his letter to his son, Richard Burke, on Irish affairs (1795/6?) in which he makes a similar claim (*Works*, VI, 79–80).

212 *Works*, VI, 147. Elsewhere (V, 278) Burke makes the same point more concisely: 'Never was there a jar or discord between genuine sentiment and sound policy. Never, no never, did Nature say one thing and Wisdom say another.' As it stands, this amounts to little more than an article of faith; it certainly does not constitute the ground of a theoretical system. Cf. the superficially similar remark of Rousseau (*Oeuvres*, III, 475).

213 See on this point, *Works*, II, 435.

214 *Tract on the Popery Laws* (*Works*, VI, 20).

215 *Works*, VI, 3.

216 *Oeuvres*, III, 297.

217 *Oeuvres*, III, 297 (Geneva ms.). We shall see in what sense Rousseau meant this below, end of section.

218 *Works*, III, 85 (see in general 82–6). Burke occasionally uses the phrase, 'general will', which Rousseau made so famous (see also III, 83; and VI, 3, where he speaks of 'the general wish'). Indeed, it does not seem an inappropriate expression to describe Burke's recurrent notion of the 'deliberate sense of the kingdom' (VI, 3), 'the deliberate election of ages and generations' (VI, 147), and 'the real sense of the people' (VI, 3, 4; see also V, 294–5; II, 66).

219 Although even, in this regard, when Rousseau begins to fudge his principle with the notion of 'tacit consent' (see, eg. *Oeuvres*, III, 250–1 [*Économie politique*]; *Oeuvres*, III, 368–9 [*Contrat social*, II, i]), and Burke takes it upon himself to insist that the 'absolutely essential' remote and efficient cause of law is the consent of the people (*Works*, VI, 20–2), it is not impossible to make a case for bringing them closer together again.

220 See *Oeuvres*, III, 176–8.

221 *Oeuvres*, III, 178.

222 *Man and Society*, vol. I, 371.

223 Rousseau tried to get round the impracticabilities of this rigorous theory of political obligation by greatly restricting the legislative function and calling most of what we would describe as law 'decrees', by claiming that a legitimate state could only be small in population, even by allowing at times tacit consent, and so forth. But, this idea of democratic participation in law-making, this notion of political self-rule, is one of the things for which he is most justly remembered.

[224] *Oeuvres*, III, 305.

[225] *Oeuvres*, III, 113.

[226] 'In some significant sense' because Rousseau is not always clear what legislative participation entails.

[227] *Oeuvres*, III, 427.

[228] See, for example, *Oeuvres*, III, 362–4 (*Contrat*, I, vii).

[229] *Oeuvres*, III, 373, 379.

[230] Burke's *Works*, VI, 4.

[231] 'Subordinate' might be a better word than 'minor', in the case of Burke. His traditionalist thought was vitally important, but we have argued that in the matter of obligation tradition was subsidiary to natural law.

[232] *Oeuvres*, III, 425 (*Contrat*, III, xii). Rousseau cannot understand how the Poles have maintained themselves as a distinct national unit for so long: 'En lisant l'histoire du gouvernement de Pologne, on a peine à comprendre comment un Etat si bizarrement constitué a pu subsister si longtems.' (*Oeuvres*, III, 953.) Later on he writes: 'Il est étonnant, il est prodigieux que la vaste étendue de la Pologne n'ait pas déja cent fois opéré la conversion du gouvernement en despotisme, abâtardi les ames des Polonois, et corrompu la masse de la nation.'

4   Summary

[1] Consider Burke's comment, *Works*, II, 314.

[2] Rousseau was employed in effect as the secretary to the French ambassador, 'le comte de Montaigu', from September, 1743, to the beginning of August, 1744.

[3] Active editorship of the *Annual Register*, probably from 1758 to 1773, must also have served as an invaluable aid in obtaining detailed information about current affairs.

[4] A more liberal publishing policy existed in England, too, of course.

[5] See, for example, *Oeuvres*, III, 386 (*Contrat*, II, viii). His persistent pessimism is matched by Burke's when the latter is overcome by depression late in his life by the course of the French Revolution.

[6] See, for example, his *Speech on the Economical Reform* (1780). In it he writes: 'When the reason of old establishments is gone, it is absurd to preserve nothing but the burthen of them. It is superstitiously to embalm a carcass not worth an ounce of the gums that are used to preserve it.' (*Works*, II, 83.)

[7] George Fasnacht, *Lord Acton on Nationality and Socialism*, Oxford University Press, (London, 1949), p. 32. The quotation is in an Appendix entitled 'Acton's manuscripts on Burke'.

[8] *Works*, II, 441–2.

[9] Though not, of course, to the study of Rousseauist criticism, nor to the exploration of Rousseau's influence.

10 *Rousseau and the Modern State,* revised ed., p. 20. However, Cobban points out that in this respect antipathy to Rousseau is by far the most common attitude. 'The one point on which most political opinions have concurred is hostility to Jean-Jacques.' (p. 20.)

11 On his style see: James T. Boulton, *The Language of Politics in the Age of Wilkes and Burke,* Routledge and Kegan Paul (London 1963); John J. Fitzgerald, 'The Logical style of Burke's *Thoughts on the causes of the present discontents*', *Burke Newsletter,* vii, 1 (Autumn 1965), 465–78; William Hazlitt, 'Edmund Burke', *Selected Essays,* Nonesuch Press (London 1930), pp. 693–710; Somerset Maugham 'After Reading Burke,' *Cornhill,* no. 985 (Winter 1950–51), pp. 28–49.

12 Quoted in Maugham, 'After reading Burke', p. 29.

13 The degree to which his judgement about the French Revolution is balanced, however, is open to debate.

14 *Works,* II, 122.

15 Quoted in Hazlitt, *Selected Essays,* p. 694. (Hazlitt misquotes Milton, *Paradise Lost,* IV, 343.)

16 Ibid., p. 693.

17 *Correspondance Littéraire, philosophique et critique,* vol. III, p. 140 (entry for July 1762).

18 John Fitzgerald analyses the opening paragraph of Burke's *Thoughts on the Causes of the Present Discontents* (1770) which begins: 'It is an undertaking of some delicacy to examine into the cause of public disorders. If a man happens not to succeed in such an enquiry, he will be thought weak and visionary; if he touches the true grievance, there is a danger that he may come near to persons of weight and consequence, who will rather be exasperated at the discovery of their errors, than thankful for the occasion of correcting them.' (*Works,* I, 306.)

19 Consider, for example, the first sentence, part ii, of the second *Discours*: 'Le premier qui ayant enclos un terrain, s'avisa de dire, *ceci est à moi,* et trouva des gens assés simples pour le croire, fut le vrai fondateur de la société civile.' And the first sentence of the *Contrat,* I, i: 'L'homme est né libre et par-tout il est dans le fers.' And the first sentence of *Émile*: 'Tout est bien sortant des mains de l'Auteur des choses, tout dégénère entre les mains de l'homme.' And the first two sentences of the *Reveries*: 'Me voici donc seul sur la terre, n'ayant plus de frère, de prochain, d'ami, de société que moi-même. Le plus sociable et le plus aimant des humains en a été proscrit par un accord unanime.'

20 *Coleridge's Miscellaneous Criticism* (ed. T. M. Raysor), Constable and Co. (London 1936), p. 423. Thomas W. Copeland also writes on this subject from a rather different perspective: 'Boswell's portrait of Burke', in *Our Eminent Friend Edmund Burke,* Yale University Press (New Haven 1949), pp. 11–35.

21 *Rousseau and the Modern State,* revised ed., 158–64.

[22] Introduction to *Leviathan*, p. xii.

[23] *Works*, II, 334.

[24] *Oeuvres*, III, 132.

[25] *Oeuvres*, III, 288.

[26] *Oeuvres*, III, 360.

[27] *Oeuvres*, III, 360.

[28] There is a third way in which Rousseau understands the general will, but it is not relevant to our immediate concern. He sometimes asserts that possession of a general will is a defining characteristic of any association, whether it be a state, a bridge-club or knitting society, or a band of thieves. In this sense, having a general will is simply one of the features that distinguishes an association with some corporate identity from a mere aggregation of individuals.

Bibliography

Works by Burke

The Correspondence of Edmund Burke (general ed. T. W. Copeland). University of Chicago Press (Chicago) and Cambridge University Press (Cambridge 1958–69), 9 vols.

A Note-book of Edmund Burke (ed. H. V. F. Somerset). Cambridge University Press (Cambridge 1957).

Speeches of The Right Honourable Edmund Burke. Longmans, Hurst, Rees (London 1816), 4 vols.

The Works and Correspondence of The Right Honourable Edmund Burke. Frances and John Rivington (London 1852), 8 vols.

The Works of Edmund Burke. George Bell and Sons (Bohn's Standard Library) (London 1900), 8 vols.

Works by Rousseau

Du contrat social (ed. C. E. Vaughan). Manchester University Press (Manchester 1918).

Correspondance complète de Jean-Jacques Rousseau (ed. R. A. Leigh). Publications de l'Institut et Musée Voltaire (Geneva), 16 vols so far.

Correspondance générale de J.-J. Rousseau (ed. T. Dufour). Librairie Armand Colin (Paris 1924–34), 20 vols.

Émile ou de l'éducation (ed. François et Pierre Richard). Garnier Frères (Paris 1964).

Lettre à Mr d'Alembert sur les spectacles (ed. M. Fuchs). Librairie Giard (Lille 1948).

Ouvres complètes de Jean-Jacques Rousseau (general ed. Bernard Gagnebin and Marcel Raymond). Gallimard (Bibliothèque de la Pléiade) (Dijon 1959–73), 4 vols so far.

Bibliography

The Political Writings of Jean-Jacques Rousseau (ed. C. E. Vaughan). Basil Blackwell (Oxford 1962).

Les Rêveries du promeneur solitaire (ed. Henri Roddier). Garnier Frères (Paris 1960).

Rousseau juge de Jean-Jacques: dialogues (ed. Michel Foucault). Librairie Armand Colin (Bibliothèque de Cluny) (Paris 1962).

Other Works Cited

Annual Register. 1758–73, 1785–9.

Beaulavon, G. Introduction to *Du contrat social*, F. Reider et Cie (Paris 1903).

Becker, Carl. *The Heavenly City of the Eighteenth Century Philosophers*, Yale University Press (London 1965).

Bentham, Jeremy. *A Fragment on Government* (ed. Wilfrid Harrison), Basil Blackwell (Oxford 1948).

Berlin, Sir Isaiah. *Four Essays on Liberty*, Oxford University Press (Oxford 1969).

Boswell, James. 'Boswell with Rousseau and Voltaire', *Private Papers of James Boswell*. Privately printed by Ralph Isham, 1928, vol. 4 (for the year 1764).

Boulton, James T. *The Language of Politics in the Age of Wilkes and Burke*, Routledge and Kegan Paul (London 1963).

Brinton, Crane. *The Political Ideas of the English Romanticists*, Russell and Russell (New York 1962).

Bronowski, J. and Bruce Mazlish. *The Western Intellectual Tradition*, Penguin (London 1963).

Burlamaqui, J. J. *The Principles of Natural Law* (trans. Mr Nugent), (London 1748).

Burns, J. H. 'Du Côté de chez Vaughan: Rousseau Revisited', *Political Studies*, 12 (June 1964), 229–34.

Byron, George Gordon, Lord. *Childe Harold's Pilgrimage*.

Canavan, Francis P. 'Burke's College Study of Philosophy', *Notes and Queries*. N.S., IV, 12 (Dec., 1957), 538–43.

———. 'Edmund Burke's conception of the role of reason in politics', *Journal of Politics*, vol. 21 (1959), 60–79.

———. *The Political Reason of Edmund Burke*, Duke University Press (Durham 1960).

Chapman, G. W. *Edmund Burke: The Practical Imagination*, Harvard University Press (Cambridge Mass. 1967).

Chapman, John. *Rousseau: Totalitarian or Liberal?*, Columbia University Press (New York 1956).

Cicero. *De Republica.*

———. *De Legibus.*

Cobban, Alfred B. C. *Edmund Burke and the Revolt against the Eighteenth Century*, George Allen and Unwin (London 1929).

———. *In Search of Humanity*, George Braziller (New York 1960).

———. 'New Light on the Political Thought of Rousseau'. *Political Science Quarterly*, vol. LXVI (1951), 272–84.

———. *Rousseau and the Modern State*, revised edition, George Allen and Unwin (London 1964).

Cole, G. D. H. Introduction to *The Social Contract and the Discourses*, Dent (Everyman) (London 1963).

Coleridge, Samuel Taylor. *Coleridge's Miscellaneous Criticism.* (ed. T. M. Raysor), Constable and Co. (London 1936).

Collingwood, R. G. *An Autobiography*, Oxford University Press (Oxford 1939).

———. *The Idea of History.* Oxford University Press paperback (Oxford 1963).

Condillac, Abbé de. 'Traité des animaux', in vol. III of *Oeuvres de Condillac*, Houel (Paris 1798).

———. 'Traité des sensations', in vol. III of *Oeuvres de Condillac*, Houel (Paris 1798).

Copeland, Thomas W. *Our Eminent Friend Edmund Burke*, Yale University Press (New Haven 1949).

Courtney, C. P. *Montesquieu and Burke*, Blackwell (Oxford 1963).

Cranston, Maurice. *Freedom*, Longmans (London 1967).

———. Introduction to *The Social Contract*, Penguin (London 1968).

Crewe, Frances Anne. 'Extracts from Mr Burke's Tabletalk', *Burke Newsletter*, vol. V, no. 2 (Winter, 1963–4), 277–92.

Derathé, Robert. *Jean-Jacques Rousseau et la science politique de son temps*, Presses Universitaires de France (Paris 1950).

de Tocqueville, Alexis C. *L'Ancien régime et la révolution*, (Paris 1856).

d'Entrève, A. P. *Natural Law*, Hutchinson University Library (London 1964).

Fasnacht, George E. *Lord Acton on Nationality and Socialism*, with an appendix on Burke based on the Acton mss., Oxford University Press (London 1949).

Fennessey, R. R. *Burke, Paine and the Rights of Man*, Martinus Nijhoff (The Hague 1963).

Fisher, H. A. L. *History of Europe*, one volume edition, Edward Arnold and Company (London 1941).

Fitzgerald, John J. 'The Logical style of Burke's *Thoughts on the Cause of the Present Discontents*', *Burke Newsletter*, VII, 1 (Autumn, 1965), 465–78.

Gay, Peter. *The Party of Humanity*, Albert Knopf (New York 1964).

Gibbon, Edward. *Autobiography* (Sheffield ed.), Oxford University Press (London 1959).

Gierke, Otto. *Natural Law and the Theory of Society* (trans. E. Barker), Cambridge University Press (Cambridge 1934).

Greenleaf, W. H. *Oakeshott's Philosophical Politics*, Longmans Green (London 1966).

Grimm, Baron de and Denis Diderot. *Correspondance littéraire, philosophique et critique* (Addressée à un souverain d'Allemagne, depuis 1753 jusqu'en 1769), Longchamps-Buisson (Paris 1813), 17 vols.

Grotius, Hugo. *The Rights of War and Peace* (trans. A. C. Campbell), (Pontefract 1814).

Hallowell, John H. *Main Currents in Modern Political Thought*, Henry Holt and Company (New York 1957).

Hart, Jeffrey. 'Burke and Radical Freedom', *The Review of Politics*, vol. 29 (1967), 221–38.

Haymann, Franz. 'La Loi naturelle dans la philosophie politique de J.-J. Rousseau', *Annales J.-J. Rousseau*, vol. XXX, 65–110.

Hazard, Paul. *European Thought in the Eighteenth Century*, Penguin (London 1965).

Hazlitt, William. 'Edmund Burke', in *Selected Essays*, Nonesuch Press (London 1930), 693–710.

Hegel, G. W. F. *Philosophy of Right* (trans. Knox), Clarendon Press (Oxford 1953).

Helvétius, Claude Adrien. *De l'Esprit*, Durand Libraire (Paris 1758).

———. *La Politique naturelle ou discours sur les vrais principes du gouvernement*, (Londres 1773).

Hendel, C. W. *Jean-Jacques Rousseau: Moralist*, Oxford University Press (London 1934), 2 vols.

Hobbes, Thomas. *Elements of Philosophy*, in *The English Works of Thomas Hobbes* (ed. Molesworth), vol. 1, Burt Franklin (New York).

———. *Leviathan* (ed. Michael Oakeshott), Basil Blackwell (Oxford 1965).

Höffding, Harald. *Jean-Jacques Rousseau and his Philosophy* (trans. Richards and Saidla), Yale University Press (New York 1930).

Hoffman, R. J. S. (ed.). *Burke's Politics*, (New York 1949).

Holbach, Paul Heinrich Dietrich (Baron von). *La Politique naturelle*, (Londres 1773).

———, Pseud. M. Mirabaud, *Système de la nature ou des loix du monde physique et du monde moral*, (London 1770).

Hutchins, Robert H. 'The Theory of the State: Edmund Burke', *Review of Politics*, Vol. v (April, 1943), 139–55.

Kedourie, Elie. *Nationalism*, Hutchinson University Library (London 1961).

Kirk, Russell, 'Burke and Natural Rights', *The Review of Politics*, Vol. 13 (October, 1951), 441–56.

Langer, Susanne K. *Philosophy in a New Key*, Oxford University Press: (London 1951).

Lanson, Gustave. *Histoire de la littérature française*, 12th ed., Librairie Hachette (Paris 1912).

Laslett, Peter. Introduction to the *Two Treatises of Government*, New American Library (Mentor ed.), (New York 1965).

Lecky, W. E. H. *A History of England in the Eighteenth Century*, Longmans Green (London 1887), vol. 5.

Letwin, Shirley. *The Pursuit of Certainty*, Cambridge University Press (Cambridge 1965).

Letwin, William. *The Origin of Scientific Economics*, Methuen (London 1963).

Levenson, J. H. *Confucian China and its Modern Fate: The Problem of Intellectual Continuity*, Routledge and Kegan Paul (London 1958), 3 vols.

Lindsay, A. D. *The Modern Democratic State*, Oxford University Press (Oxford 1943).

Lloyd, Denis. *The Idea of Law*, Penguin (London 1964).

Locke, John. *An Essay Concerning Human Understanding*, New ed., George Routledge and Sons (London n.d.).

———. *Two Treatises of Government*, New American Library (Mentor ed.), (New York 1965).

Lovejoy, Arthur O. *Essays in the History of Ideas*, Johns Hopkins Press (Baltimore 1948).

———. *The Great Chain of Being*, Harvard University Press (Cambridge, Mass. 1936).

McDonald, Joan. *Rousseau and the French Revolution 1762–1791*, Athlone Press (London 1965).

MacDonald, Margaret, 'Natural Rights', in *Philosophy, Politics and Society* (1st series), Basil Blackwell (Oxford 1956).

MacPherson, C. B. *Political theory of Possessive Individualism*, Clarendon Press (Oxford 1962).

Mabbott, J. D. *The State and the Citizen*, Hutchinson Ltd (Grey Arrow), (London 1958).

Magnus, Philip. *Edmund Burke*, John Murray (London 1939).

Maritain, Jacques. *Three Reformers*, Sheed and Ward (London 1944).

Martin, Kingsley. *French Liberal Thought in the Eighteenth Century*, Harper and Row (Torchbook), (New York 1962).

Maugham, Somerset. 'After reading Burke', *The Cornhill Magazine*, no. 985 (Winter, 1950–51), 28–49.

Mill, John Stuart. *Utilitarianism, Liberty, Representative Government*, J. M. Dent and Sons (Everyman), (London 1960).

Montrose, J. L. 'Review-Essay', *Natural Law Reform*, VI (1961), 201–25.

Morley, John. *Rousseau*, Macmillan (London 1896), 2 vols.

Oakeshott, Michael. *Rationalism in Politics*, Methuen (London 1962).

———. Introduction to the *Leviathan* by Thomas Hobbes, Basil Blackwell (Oxford 1965).

Osborn, Annie M. *Rousseau and Burke: a Study of the Idea of Liberty in Eighteenth-century Thought*, Oxford University Press (London 1940; reprinted Russell and Russell, New York 1964).

Paine, Thomas. *The Rights of Man*, Doubleday Dolphin, published in this edition with Burke's *Reflections* to which it is a reply, (New York 1961).

Parkin, Charles. *The Moral Basis of Burke's Political Thought*, Cambridge University Press (Cambridge 1956).

Peters, R. S. 'Hegel and the Nation State', in *Political Ideas* (ed. David Thomson), Watts and Co. (London 1966).

Plamenatz, John. *The English Utilitarians*, Blackwell (Oxford 1958).

———. 'Ce Qui signifie autre chose sinon qu'on le forcera d'être libre', *Annales de la philosophie politique*, 5 (1965), 137–53.

———. *Man and Society*, Longmans Green (London 1963).

Pocock, J. G. A. 'Burke and the Ancient Constitution: A Problem in the History of Ideas', *Historical Journal*, II, 2, (1960), 125–43.

———. 'The History of Political Thought: A Methodological

Inquiry', in *Philosophy, Politics and Society* (2nd Series), Blackwell (Oxford 1962).

Ritchie, D. G. *Natural Rights*, George Allen and Unwin (London 1916).

Rockwood, R. O. (ed.). *Carl Becker's Heavenly City Revisited*, Archon Books (Hamden, Conn. 1968).

Rommen, H. A. *The Natural Law*, Herder Book Company (London 1949).

Sabine, G. H. *A History of Political Theory*, 3rd ed., Holt Rinehart and Winston (New York, 1961).

Scott, Sir Walter. *Waverley* (Signet ed.).

Staël, Mme. de. 'Lettres sur les écrits et le caractère de J.-J. Rousseau', *Oeuvres complètes*, Treattel et Würtz (Paris 1820), vol. 1.

Stanlis, P. J. *Edmund Burke and the Natural Law*, University of Michigan Press (Ann Arbor 1958).

Stephen, Sir Leslie. *History of English Thought in the Eighteenth Century*, John Murray (London 1902), 2 vols.

Strauss, Leo. *Natural Right and History*, University of Chicago Press (Chicago 1965).

———. *The Political Philosophy of Hobbes*, (1936), University of Chicago Press (Chicago 1966).

Vaughan, C. E. (ed.) Introduction to *Du Contrat social* by Jean-Jacques Rousseau, Manchester University Press (Manchester 1918).

———. Introduction to *The Political Writings of Jean Jacques Rousseau*, (1915), Blackwell (Oxford 1962).

———. *The Romantic Revolt*, Charles Scribner's Sons (New York 1923).

———. *Studies in the History of Philosophy*, Manchester University Press (Manchester 1925), 2 vols.

Viereck, Peter. *Conservatism*, van Nostrand (Princeton (N.J.), 1956).

Voltaire, François-Marie Arouët de. *Lettres philosophiques*, Basil Blackwell, (Blackwell's French texts), (Oxford).

———. *Voltaire's Correspondence* (ed. Theodore Besterman), (Geneva 1953–66).

Watkins, Frederick. Introduction to *Rousseau: Political Writings*, Thomas Nelson and Sons (London 1953).

Wedgwood, C. V. *The King's Peace 1637–1641*, Collins (Fontana Library), (London 1966).

————. *The King's War 1641–1647*, Collins, (Fontana Library), (London 1966).

Weston, John C. Jr. 'Edmund Burke's view of history', *The Review of Politics*, xxiii, 2 (April, 1961), 203–229.

Whitehead, Alfred North. *Adventures of Ideas*, New American Library (Mentor ed.), (New York 1958).

Wilkins, Burleigh T. *The Problem of Burke's Political Philosophy*, Clarendon Press (Oxford 1967).

Willey, Basil. *The Eighteenth-Century Background*, Penguin (London 1965).

Wolin, Sheldon. *Politics and Vision*, George Allen and Unwin (London 1961).

Wright, E. H. *The Meaning of Rousseau*, Oxford University Press (London 1929).

Young, G. M. 'Burke', *British Academy Lecture*, The Annual Lecture on a Master Mind Series, Henrietta Hertz Trust (London 1943), 19–36.

Index

Index

Index

Osborn, Annie M., 30

Paine, Thomas, 10, 36, 109–10, 111
pantheism, 8
Pascal, Blaise, 60
paternalism, 150–1, 178
patriotism, 125, 127, 130
'perfectibility', Rousseau's notion,
    92–3
Peters, Rev. Hugh, 14
Petty, Sir William, 15, 61
philosophes, 2, 10, 38, 51, 52, 70, 116,
    148, 162
philosophical idealism, 16, 20
Philosophical Inquiry (Burke), 10, 37–8
Philosophie des Rechts (Hegel), 20
philosopy, philosophical traditions,
    15–22, 168–70; and political
    reflections, 22–5
physics, 62
physiocrats, 29
pity, Rousseau's notion, 59, 92
Plamenatz, John, 67–8, 147, 158
Plato, 17–21, 33, 56, 100
Pocock, J. G. A., 31, 32
Poland *see Considérations sur le
    gouvernement de Pologne*
Politica (Althusius), 71
political liberty, 141–51; *see also*
    moral freedom
political obligation (right), 120–1,
    135, 136, 151–61
political theories, orthodox critics'
    approach, 1–8; Burke's views,
    4–5, 9–10, 13–14; and Rousseau's,
    10–11; philosophical background
    to, 15–25; comparative critics'
    approach, 25–30; and methodo-
    logical issues, 30–6; the state and
    the citizen, 107–61: school of
    natural rights, 109–15;
    empiricism, 115–17; tradition-
    alism, 117–27; role of 'public
    spirit', 127–30; limitations of

reason in political activities,
    127–41; and liberty, 141–51; and
    political obligation, 151–61;
    disparity between France and
    England, 163–4; reconciliation of
    will and reason sought by
    Rousseau, 172–8; *see also* human
    nature
'political theory of romanticism',
    Cobban's concept, 29, 169
*The Political Writings of Jean-Jacques
    Rousseau* (ed. Vaughan), 26
'positive liberty' theory, 101
practical *v.* explanatory writing,
    30–2
prejudice ('just prejudice'), Burke's
    concept, 29, 80, 85, 128–9, 135,
    156, 160
prescription, Burke's theory of, 80,
    85, 151, 152, 153, 156, 160, 161
Price, Dr Richard, 13–14, 36
*The Problem of Burke's Political
    Philosophy* (Wilkins), 77
Profession de foi du vicaire Savoyard
    (Rousseau), 60, 101
Projet de Constitution pour la Corse
    (Rousseau), 7, 11, 35, 124
'public spirit', definition of, 127–8;
    Burke's view, 128–9; and
    Rousseau's, 129–30, 134, 136
Pufendorf, Samuel, baron de, 10, 71

'rational freedom' theory, 101,
    146–7
rationalism, 5, 54; philosophical
    tradition, 17–21, 168–70; and
    political counterpart, 22–5;
    Burke's approach to, 36–9, 54–6,
    79, 111, 112, 136–41; and
    Rousseau's, 36–9, 60, 72–5,
    130–6; natural-right school's
    view, 44–5, 49, 50–1, 61, 113; and
    empiricists, 61–3; limitations in
    political life of, 127–41; *see also*

240

Index